BUDDHISM AND ETHICS

BUDDHISM AND ETHICS

M Srivastava

MD PUBLICATIONS PVT LTD
NEW DELHI
www.mdppl.com

Published by :

MD Publications Pvt Ltd
"MD House", 11, Darya Ganj,
New Delhi - 110 002
Phone : +91-11- 45355555
E-mail : contact@mdppl.com
Website: www.mdppl.com

ISBN : 978-81-7533-349-9

Published and Printed by Mr. Pranav Gupta on behalf of **MD Publications Pvt Ltd** at Repro India Limited.

PREFACE

It is well-known that Buddhism is the most ethical of "religions". An important part of the Noble Eightfold Path relates to the development of ethical conduct; for many a layperson Buddhist practice consists mainly in the "keeping of the precepts"; many Bhikkhus see in the Vinaya rules the essence of the religious life; and even many of the pâramitâs expected of those aspiring to Buddhahood are ethical in nature. Yet to present the teaching of the Buddha as being solely and exclusively concerned with ethics could serve as detraction from the real objective of the Buddha-Dhamma, which is to serve as a path or vehicle leading to Enlightenment. While conforming to the norms of Buddhist ethics is essential for this purpose this alone will not guarantee the elimination of ignorance (avijjâ), which is the real meaning of Enlightenment. The tendency of some exponents of the Dhamma to represent Buddhism as just another ethical system is misleading, especially when put before a newcomer to the Dhamma who may not be able to distinguish between Buddhist ethics and the precepts of other ethical teachers, and may conclude that Buddhism has nothing new to offer.

Buddhist ethics are not arbitrary standards invented by man for his own utilitarian purpose. Nor are they arbitrarily imposed from without. Man-made laws and social customs do not form the basis of Buddhist ethics. For example, the styles of dress that are suitable for one climate, period or civilization may be considered indecent in another; but this is entirely a matter of social custom and does not in any way involve ethical considerations. Yet the artificialities of social conventions are continually confused with ethical principles that are valid and unchanging.

Buddhist ethics finds its foundation not on the changing social customs but rather on the unchanging laws of nature. Buddhist ethical values are intrinsically a part of nature, and the unchanging law of cause and effect (kamma). The simple fact that Buddhist ethics are rooted in natural law makes its principles both useful and acceptable to the modern world. The fact that the Buddhist ethical code was formulated over 2,500 years ago does not detract from its timeless character.

The theory of Buddhist ethics finds its practical expression in the various precepts. These precepts or disciplines are nothing but general guides to show the direction in which the Buddhist ought to turn to on his way to final salvation. Although many of these precepts are expressed in a negative form, we must not think that Buddhist morality consists of abstaining from evil without the complement of doing good. Buddhist ethics also recognizes the objectivity of moral value. In other words, the karmic consequences of actions occur in accordance with natural karmic law, regardless of the attitude of the individual or regardless of social attitudes toward the act.

I am very grateful to Mr. Pranav Gupta, Director of MD Publications Pvt Ltd, New Delhi, for his kind cooperation and support for this book.

M Srivastava

CONTENTS

1

Origin and Source of Knowledge

THE ENLIGHTENMENT OF THE BUDDHAH

One happy Vesak night, as he was seated under the famous Pipala tree at Buddha Gaya, with mind tranquilized and purified, in the first watch he developed that supernormal knowledge which enables him to remember his past lives Pubbenivasanussati Nana - Reminiscence of Past Births. In the middle watch he developed vision dealing with the death and rebirth of beings Catupapata Nana - Perception of the Disappearing and Reappearing of Beings. In the last watch of the night he developed the supernormal knowledge with regard to the destruction of passions - Asavakkhaya Nana, and comprehending things they truly are, attained Perfect Enlightenment - Samma Sambodhi. In his 35th year of age he attained Buddhahood, that supreme state of Perfection, He devoted the remainder of that precious life to serve humanity both by example and precept, dominated by no personal motive.

The Buddha was a human being. As a man He was born, as a man He lived, and as a man His life came to an end. Though human, He became an extraordinary man - Acchariya Manussa. The Buddha laid stress on this fact and left no room for anyone to fall into the error of thinking that He was an immortal being. There is no deification in the case of the Buddha. Nor does the Buddha claim to be an incarnation of

Vishnu, nor does He call himself a "Saviour" who freely saves others by His personal salvation. The Buddha exhorts His disciples to depend on themselves for their salvation, for both defilement and purity depend on oneself. "You yourselves should make the exertion. The Tathagatas are only teachers," says the Buddha. The Buddhas pointed out the path, and it is left for us to follow that path to save ourselves. "To depend on others for salvation is negative, but to depend on one is positive."

Dependence on others means a surrender of one's effort. Furthermore, the Buddha does not claim a monopoly of Buddhahood, which as matter of fact is not the prerogative of any specially graced, chosen person. He reached the highest possible state of perfection any person could aspire to; and without the closed fist of a teacher, He revealed the only straight path that leads thereto. According to the teachings of the Buddha anybody may be aspire to that supreme state of perfection if he makes the necessary aspiring determination and necessary exertion. As a man He attained Buddhahood and proclaimed to the world the latent possibilities and the creative power of man. Instead of placing an unseen almighty God over man, and making him subservient to such belief, He raised the worth of mankind.

It was He who taught that man could obtain his Deliverance from sorrow by his own exertion, without depending on a God and mediating priests, or on sacrifices and prayers. It was He who taught the ego-centric world the noble ideal of selfless service. It was He who revolted against the degrading caste system and taught the equality of mankind. He declared that the gates of success and prosperity were open to all, in every condition of life, high and low, saint and sinner, who would care to turn over a new leaf and aspire to Perfection. Irrespective of caste, colour or rank, he established for both deserving men and women a celibate order which was "democratic in constitution and communistic in distribution". He gave complete freedom of thought and wanted us to open our eyes to see things as they truly are. He comforted the bereaved by His consoling words. He ministered to the sick that were deserted.

He helped the poor who were neglected. He ennobled the lives of sinners and purified the corrupted lives of criminals. He encouraged the feeble, united the divided, enlightened the ignorant, clarified the mystic, guided the deluded, elevated the base, and dignified the noble. Rich and poor, saint and sinner, loved Him alike. Despotic and righteous kings, glorious princes and nobles, generous and miserly millionaires, haughty and humble scholars, destitute paupers, downtrodden scavengers, wicked murderers, despised courtesans - all benefited by His words of wisdom and compassion. His noble example was a source of inspiration to all. His Message of Peace was hailed by all with indescribable joy, and was of eternal benefit to everyone who had the fortune to come under its benign influence.

LIFE OF GOTAMA BUDDHA

BIRTH

On the full moon day of May, in the year 623 B.C., a noble prince destined to be the greatest religious teacher of the world was born in the Lumbini Park at Kapilavatthu, on the Indian borders of present Nepal. His father was King Suddhodana of the aristocratic Sakya clan and his mother was Queen Maha Maya. The beloved queen died seven days after his birth. Her younger sister, Maha Pajapati Gotami, who was also married to the King, adopted the child while entrusting her own son, Nanda, to the care of the nurses. Great were the rejoicings of the people over the birth of this illustrious prince. An ascetic of high spiritual attainments, named Asita (also known as Kaladevala), was particularly pleased to hear this happy news. Being a tutor of the King, he visited the palace to see the Royal baby.

The King, who felt honoured by his unexpected visit, carried the child up to him in order to make the child pay him due reverence. To the surprise of all, the child's legs turned and rested on the matted locks of the ascetic. Instantly, the ascetic rose from his seat and, foreseeing with his supernormal vision the child's future greatness, saluted him with clasped hands. The Royal father did likewise. The great ascetic smiled at first and then was sad. Questioned regarding his mingled feelings, he answered that he smiled because the prince would eventually become a Buddha, an Enlightened One, and he was sad because he would not be able to benefit from the superior wisdom of the Enlightened One owing to his prior death and rebirth in a Formless Plane (Arupaloka).

NAMING CEREMONY

On the fifth day after the prince's birth he was named Siddhartha which means "wish fulfilled". His family name was Gotama. In accordance with the ancient Indian custom, many learned Brahmins were invited to the palace for the naming ceremony. Amongst them there were eight distinguished men. Examining the characteristic marks of the child, seven of them raised two fingers each, indicative of two alternative possibilities, that he would either become a Universal Monarch or a Buddha. But the youngest, Kondanna, who excelled others in wisdom, noticing the hair on the forehead turned to the right, raised only one finger and convincingly declared that the prince would definitely retire from the world and become a Buddha.

PLOUGHING FESTIVAL

A very remarkable incident took place in his childhood. It was an unprecedented spiritual experience which, later, during his search after truth, served as a key to his Enlightenment. To promote agriculture, the King arranged for a ploughing festival. It was indeed a festive occasion for all. Both nobles and commoners participated in the ceremony in their best attires. On the appointed day, the King, accompanied by his courtiers, went to the field, taking with him the young prince and his nurses. Placing the child on a screened and canopied couch under the cool shade of a solitary rose-apple tree to be watched by the nurses, the King participated in the ploughing festival.

When the festival was at its height of gaiety, the nurses too stole away from the prince's presence to catch a glimpse of the wonderful spectacle. In striking contrast to the mirth and merriment of the festival, it was all calm and quiet under the rose-apple tree. All the conditions conducive to quiet meditation were there. The pensive child, young in years but old in wisdom, sat cross-legged and seized the opportunity to commence that all-important practice of intent concentration on the breath - on exhalations and inhalations. Then and there, this gained him the one-pointedness of mind known as Samadhi. He thus developed the First Jhana (Ecstasy). The child's nurses, who had abandoned their precious charge to enjoy themselves at the festival, suddenly realized their duty. They hastened to the child and were amazed to see him sitting cross-legged plunged in deep meditation. The King hearing of it, hurried to the spot and, seeing the child in meditative posture, saluted him, saying- "This, dear child, is my second obeisance".

EDUCATION

As a Royal child, Prince Siddhartha must have received a royal education, although no details are given about it. As a scion of the warrior race he also received special training in the art of warfare.

MARRIED LIFE

At the early age of sixteen, he married his beautiful cousin of equal age, Princess Yasodhara. For nearly thirteen years, after his happy marriage, he led a luxurious life, blissfully ignorant of the vicissitudes of life outside the palace gates. Of his luxurious life as prince, he states:

"I was delicate, excessively delicate. In my father's dwelling three lotus-ponds were made purposely for me. Blue lotuses bloomed in one, red in another, and white in another. I used no sandal-wood that was not of Kasi. My turban, tunic, dress and cloak, were all from Kasi."

"Night and day a white parasol was held over me so that I might not be touched by heat or cold, dust, leaves or dew."

"There were three palaces built for me - one for the cold season, one for the hot season, and one for the rainy season. During the four rainy months, I lived in the palace for the rainy season without ever coming down from it, entertained all the while by female musicians. Just as, in the houses of others, food from the husks of rice together with sour gruel is given to the slaves and workmen, even so, in my father's dwelling food with rice and meat was given to the slaves and workmen."

With the march of time, truth gradually dawned upon him. His contemplative nature and boundless compassion did not permit him to spend his time in the mere enjoyment of the fleeting pleasures of the Royal palace. He knew no personal grief but he felt a deep pity for suffering humanity. Amidst comfort and prosperity, he realized the universality of sorrow.

RENUNCIATION

Prince Siddhartha reflected thus:

"Why do I, being subject to birth, decay, disease, death, sorrow and impurities, thus search after things of like nature? How, if I, who am subject to things of such nature, realize their disadvantages and seek after the unattained unsurpassed, perfect security which is Nibbana!" "Cramped and confined is household life, a den of dust, but the life of the homeless one is as the open air of heaven! Hard is it for him who bides at home to live out as it should be lived the Holy Life in all its perfection, in all its purity."

One glorious day as he went out of the palace to the pleasure park to see the world outside, he came in direct contact with the stark realities of life. Within the narrow confines of the palace he saw only the rosy side of life, but the dark side, the common lot of mankind, was purposely veiled from him. What was previously conceived only mentally, he now saw in vivid reality for the first time? On his way to the park his observant eyes met the strange sights of a decrepit old man, a diseased person, a corpse and a dignified hermit. The first three sights convincingly proved to him, the inexorable nature of life, and the universal ailment of humanity. The fourth signified the means to overcome the ills of life and to attain calm and peace. These four unexpected sights served to increase the urge in him to loathe and renounce the world.

Realizing the worthlessness of sensual pleasures, so highly prized by the worldling, and appreciating the value of renunciation in which the wise seek delight, he decided to leave the world in search of Truth and Eternal Peace. When this final decision was taken after much deliberation, the news of the birth of a son was conveyed to him while he was about to leave the park. Contrary to expectations, he was not overjoyed, but regarded his first and only offspring as an impediment. An ordinary father would have welcomed the joyful tidings, but Prince Siddhartha, the extraordinary father as he was, exclaimed - "An impediment (rahu) has been born; a fetter has arisen". The infant son was accordingly named Rahula by his grandfather.

The palace was no longer a congenial place to the contemplative Prince Siddhartha. Neither his charming young wife nor his lovable infant son could deter him from altering the decision he had taken to renounce the world. He was destined to play an infinitely more important and beneficial role than a dutiful husband and father, or even as a king of kings. The allurements of the palace were no more cherished objects of delight to him. Time was ripe to depart. He ordered his favourite charioteer Channa to saddle the horse Kanthaka, and went to the suite of apartments occupied by the princess. Opening the door of the chamber, he stood on the threshold and cast his dispassionate glance on the wife and child who were fast asleep.

Great was his compassion for the two dear ones at this parting moment. Greater was his compassion for suffering humanity. He was not worried about the future worldly happiness and comfort of the mother and child as they had everything in abundance and were well protected. It was not that he loved them the less, but that he loved humanity more. Leaving all behind, he stole away with a light heart from the palace at midnight, and rode into the dark, attended only by his loyal charioteer. Alone and penniless he set out in search of Truth and Peace. Thus did he renounce the world?

It was not the renunciation of an old man who has had his fill of worldly life. It was not the renunciation of a poor man who had nothing to leave behind. It was the renunciation of a prince in the full bloom of youth and in the plenitude of wealth and prosperity - a renunciation unparalleled in history. It was in his twenty-ninth year that Prince Siddhartha made this historic journey. He journeyed far and, crossing the river Anoma, rested on its banks. Here he shaved his hair and beard and handing over his garments and ornaments to Channa with instructions to return to the palace, assumed the simple yellow garb of an ascetic and led a life of voluntary poverty.

The ascetic Siddhartha, who once lived in the lap of luxury, now became a penniless wanderer, living on what little the charitably-minded gave of their own accord. He had no permanent abode. A shady tree or a lonely cave sheltered him by day or night. Bare-footed and bare-headed, he walked in the scorching sun and in the piercing cold. With no possessions to call his own, but a bowl to collect his food and robes just sufficient to cover the body, he concentrated all his energies on the quest of Truth.

SEARCH FOR TRUTH

Thus as a wanderer, a seeker after what is good, searching for the unsurpassed Peace, he approached Alara Kalama, a distinguished ascetic, and said: "I desire, friend Kalama to lead the Holy Life in this Dispensation of yours." Thereupon Alara Kalama told him: "You may stay with me, O Venerable One. Of such sort is this teaching that an intelligent man before long may realize by his own intuitive wisdom his master's doctrine, and abide in the attainment thereof." Before long, he learnt his doctrine, but it brought him no realization of the highest Truth.

Then there came to him the thought: When Alara Kalama declared: "Having myself realized by intuitive knowledge the doctrine, I - 'abide in the attainment thereof -, it could not have been a mere profession of faith; surely Alara Kalama lives having understood and perceived this doctrine." So he went to him and said "How far, friend Kalama, does this doctrine extend which you yourself have with intuitive wisdom realized and attained?" Upon this Alara Kalama made known to him the Realm of Nothingness (Akincannayatana), an advanced stage of Concentration.

Then it occurred to him: "Not only in Alara Kalama is to be found faith, energy, mindfulness, concentration, and wisdom. I too possess these virtues. How now if I strive to realize that doctrine whereof Alara Kalama says that he himself has realized and abides in the attainment thereof!" So, before long, he realized by his own intuitive wisdom that doctrine and attained to that state, but it brought him no realization of the highest Truth. Then he approached Alara Kalama and said; "Is this full extent, friend Kalama, of this doctrine of which you say that you yourself have realized by your wisdom and abide in the attainment thereof?

"But I also, friend, have realized thus far in this doctrine, and abide in the attainment thereof." The unenvious teacher was delighted to hear of the success of his distinguished pupil. He honoured him by placing him on a perfect level with himself and admiringly said:

"Happy, friend, are we, extremely happy; in that we look upon such a venerable fellow-ascetic like you! That same doctrine which I have realized by my wisdom and proclaim, having attained thereunto, you have realized by your wisdom and abide in the attainment thereof... Thus the doctrine which I know, you know too;..... As I am, so are you; as you are, so am I. Come, friend, let both of us lead the company of ascetics."

The ascetic Gotama was not satisfied with a discipline and a doctrine which only led to a high degree of mental concentration, but did not lead to "disgust, detachment, cessation (of suffering), tranquility; intuition, enlightenment, and Nibbana." Nor was he anxious to lead a company of ascetics even with the co-operation of another generous teacher of equal spiritual attainment, without first perfecting himself.

It was, he felt, a case of the blind leading the blind. Dissatisfied with his teaching, he politely took his leave from him. In those happy days when there were no political disturbances, the intellectuals of India were preoccupied with the study and exposition of some religious system or other.

All facilities were provided for those more spiritually inclined to lead holy lives in solitude in accordance with their temperaments, hence most of these teachers had large followings of disciples. It was not difficult for the ascetic Gotama to find another religious teacher who was more competent than the former. On this occasion he approached one Uddacha Ramaputta and expressed his desire to lead the Holy Life in his Dispensation. He was readily admitted as a pupil.

Before long the intelligent ascetic Gotama, mastered his doctrine and attained the final stage of mental concentration, the neither Realm of Neither Perception nor Non-Perception (N'eva Sanna N'asannayatana), revealed by his teacher. This was the highest stage in worldly concentration when consciousness becomes so subtle and refined that it cannot be said that a consciousness either exists or not. Ancient Indian sages could not proceed further in spiritual development.

The noble teacher was delighted to hear of the success of his illustrious royal pupil. Unlike his former teacher the present one honoured him by inviting him to take full charge of all the disciples as their teacher. He said: "Happy friend, are we; yea, extremely happy, in that we see such a venerable fellow-ascetic as you. The doctrine which Rama knew, you know; the doctrine which you know, Rama knew. As was Rama so are you; as you are, so was Rama. Come, friend, henceforth you shall lead this company of ascetics."

Still he felt that his quest of the highest Truth was not achieved. He had gained complete mastery of his mind, but his ultimate goal was far ahead. He was seeking for the Highest, the Nibbana, the complete cessation of suffering, the total eradication of all forms of craving. "Dissatisfied with this doctrine too, he departed thence, content therewith no longer." He realized that his spiritual aspirations were far higher than those under whom he chose to learn. He realized that there was none capable enough to teach him what he yearned for - the highest Truth. He also realized that the highest Truth is to be found within oneself and ceased to seek external aid.

STRUGGLE

Disappointed but not discouraged, the ascetic Gotama, seeker of the incomparable Peace, the highest Truth, wandered through the district of Magadha. He eventually arrived at Uruvela, the market town of Senani. There he spied a lovely spot of ground, a charming forest grove, a flowing river with pleasant sandy fords, and hard by was a village where he could obtain his food. Then he thought thus:

"Lovely, indeed, O Venerable One, is this spot of ground, charming is the forest grove, pleasant is the flowing river with sandy fords, and hard by is the village where I could obtain food. Suitable indeed is this place for spiritual exertion for those noble scions who desire to strive."

The place was congenial for his meditation. The atmosphere was peaceful. The surroundings were pleasant. The scenery was charming. Alone, he resolved to settle down there to achieve his desired object. Hearing of his renunciation, Kondanna, the youngest Brahmin predicted his future, and four sons of the other sages - Bhaddiya, Vappa, Mahanama, and Assaji - also renounced the world and joined his company. In ancient India, great importance was attached to rites, ceremonies, penances and sacrifices.

It was popularly believed that no Deliverance could be gained unless one leads a life of strict asceticism. Accordingly, for six long years the ascetic Gotama made a super-human struggle to practice all forms of the severest austerity. His delicate body was reduced to almost a skeleton. The more he tormented his body the farther his goal receded from him.

How strenuously he struggled, the various methods he employed, and how he eventually succeeded was graphically described in his own words in various Suttas.

"Then the following thought occurred to me:

"How if I were to clench my teeth, press my tongue against the palate, and with (moral) thoughts hold down, subdue and destroy my (immoral) thoughts!"So I clenched my teeth, pressed my tongue against the palate and strove to hold down, subdue, and destroy my (immoral) thoughts with (moral) thoughts. As I struggled thus, perspiration streamed forth from my armpits. "Like unto a strong man who might seize a weaker man by head or shoulders and hold him down, force him down, and bring into subjection, even so did I struggle. "Strenuous and indomitable was my energy. My mindfulness was established and unperturbed. My body was, however, fatigued and was not calmed as a result of that painful endeavour - being overpowered by exertion. Even though such painful sensations arose in me, they did not at all affect my mind.

"Then I thought thus: How if I were to cultivate the non-breathing ecstasy!"Accordingly, I checked inhalation and exhalation from my mouth and nostrils. As I checked inhalation and exhalation from mouth and nostrils, the air issuing from my ears created an exceedingly great noise. Just as a blacksmith's bellows being blown make an exceedingly great noise, even so was the noise created by the air issuing from my ears when I stopped breathing. "Nevertheless, my energy was strenuous and indomitable. Established and unperturbed was my mindfulness. Yet my body was fatigued and was not calmed as a result of that painful endeavour - being overpowered by exertion. Even though such painful sensations arose in me, they did not at all affect my mind.

"Then I thought to myself: How if I were to cultivate that non-breathing exercise!"Accordingly, I checked inhalation and exhalation from mouth, nostrils, and ears. And as I stopped breathing from mouth, nostrils and ears, the (imprisoned) airs beat upon my skull with great violence. Just as if a strong man were to bore one's skull with a sharp drill, even so did the airs beat my skull with great violence as I stopped breathing? Even, though such painful sensations arose in me, they did not at all affect my mind. Then I thought to myself: How if I were to cultivate that non-breathing ecstasy again! "Accordingly, I checked inhalation and exhalation from mouth, nostrils, and ears. And as I stopped breathing thus, terrible pams arose in my head. As would be the pains if a strong man were to bind one's head tightly with a hard leathern thong, even so were the terrible pains that arose in my head.

"Nevertheless, my energy was strenuous. Such painful sensations did not affect my mind. "Then I thought to myself: How if I were to cultivate that non-breathing ecstasy again!" Accordingly, I stopped breathing from mouth, nostrils, and ears. As I checked breathing thus, plentiful airs pierced my belly. Just as if a skilful butcher or a butcher's apprentice were to rip up the belly with a sharp butcher's knife, even so plentiful airs pierced my belly. "Nevertheless, my energy was strenuous. Such painful sensations did not affect my mind. "Again I thought to myself: How if I were to cultivate that non-breathing ecstasy again! "Accordingly, I checked inhalation and exhalation from mouth, nostrils, and ears. As I suppressed my breathing thus, a tremendous burning pervaded my body.

Just as if two strong men were each to seize a weaker man by his arms and scorch and thoroughly burn him in a pit of glowing charcoal, even so did a severe burning pervade my body? "Nevertheless, my energy was strenuous. Such painful sensations did not affect my mind. "Thereupon the deities who saw me thus said: 'The ascetic Gotama is dead.' Some remarked: 'The ascetic Gotama is not dead yet, but is dying.' While some others said: 'The ascetic Gotama is neither dead nor is dying but an Arahant is the ascetic Gotama. Such is the way in which an Arahant abides."

CHANGE OF METHOD: ABSTINENCE FROM FOOD

Then I thought to myself: How if I were to practice complete abstinence from food! "Then deities approached me and said: 'Do not, good sir, practice total abstinence from food. If you do practice it, we will pour celestial essence through your body's pores; with that you will be sustained." "And I thought: 'If I claim to be practicing starvation and if these deities pour celestial essence, through my body's pores and I am sustained thereby, it would be a fraud on my part'. So I refused them, saying 'There is no need'. "Then the following thought occurred to me: How if I take food little by little, a small quantity of the juice of green gram, or vetch, or lentils, or peas!

"As I took such small quantity of solid and liquid food, my body became extremely emaciated. Just as are the joints of knot-grasses or bulrushes, even so did the major and minor parts of my body owe to lack of food? Just as is the camel's hoof, even so were my hips for want of food. Just as is a string of beads, even so did my backbone stand out and bend in, for lack of food. Just as the rafters of a dilapidated hall fall this way and that, even so appeared my ribs through lack of sustenance. Just as in a deep well may be seen stars sunk deep in the water, even so did my eye-balls appear deep sunk in their sockets, being devoid of food. Just as a bitter pumpkin, when cut while raw, will by wind and sun get shrivelled and withered, even so did the skin of my head get shrivelled and withered, due to lack of sustenance.

"And I, intending to touch my belly's skin, would instead seize my backbone. When I intended to touch my backbone, I would seize my belly's skin. So was I that, owing to lack of sufficient food, my belly's skin clung to the backbone, and I, on going to pass excreta or urine, would in that very spot stumble and fall down, for want of food. And I stroked my limbs in order to revive my body. Lo, as I did so, the rotten roots of my body's hairs fell from my body owing to lack of sustenance. The people who saw me said: The ascetic Gotama is black' Some said, 'The ascetic Gotama is not black but blue.' Some others said: 'The ascetic Gotama is neither black nor blue but tawny.' To such an extent was the pure colour of my skin impaired owing to lack of food.

"Then the following thought occurred to me: Whatsoever ascetics or brahmins of the past have experienced acute, painful, sharp and piercing sensations, they must have experienced them to such a high degree as this and not beyond. Whatsoever ascetics and Brahmins of the future will experience acute, painful, and sharp and piercing sensations they too will experience them to such a high degree and not beyond. Yet by all these bitter and difficult austerities I shall not attain to excellence, worthy of supreme knowledge and insight, transcending those of human states. Might there be another path for Enlightenment!"

TEMPTATION OF MARA THE EVIL ONE

His prolonged painful austerities proved utterly futile. They only resulted in the exhaustion of his valuable energy. Though physically a superman his delicately nurtured body could not possibly stand the great strain. His graceful form completely faded almost beyond recognition. His golden coloured skin turned pale, his blood dried up, his sinews and muscles shrivelled up, and his eyes were sunk and blurred. To all appearance he was a living skeleton. He was almost on the verge of death.

At this critical stage, while he was still intent on the Highest (Padhana), abiding on the banks of the Neranjara River, striving and contemplating in order to attain to that state of Perfect Security, came Namuci, uttering kind words thus:

"You are lean and deformed. Near to you is death.

"A thousand parts (of you belong) to death; to life (there remains) but one. Live, O good sir! Life is better. Living, you could perform merit. "By leading a life of celibacy and making fire sacrifices, much merit could be acquired. What will you do with this striving? Hard is the path of striving, difficult and not easily accomplished."

Mara reciting these words stood in the presence of the Exalted One. To Mara who spoke thus, the Exalted One replied:

"O Evil One, kinsman of the heedless! You have come here for your own sake. "Even an iota of merit is of no avail. To them who are in need of merit it behoves you, Mara, to speak thus. "Confidence (Saddha), self-control (Tapo), perseverance (Viriya), and wisdom (Panna) are mine. Me who am thus intent, why do you question about life?

"Even the streams of rivers will this wind dry up. Why should not the blood of me who am thus striving dry up? "When blood dries up, the bile and phlegm also dry up. When my flesh wastes away, more and more does my mind get clarified? Still more do my mindfulness, wisdom, and concentration become firm? "While I live thus, experiencing the utmost pain, my mind does not long for lust! Behold the purity of a being! "Sense-desires (Kama) are your first army. The second is called Aversion for the Holy Life (Arati).

The third is Hunger and Thirst (Khuppipasa). The fourth is called Craving (Tanha). The fifth is Sloth and Torpor (Thina-Middha). The sixth is called Fear (Bhiru). The seventh is Doubt (Vicikiccha), and the eighth is Detraction and Obstinacy (Makkha-Thambha). The ninth is Gain (Labha), Praise (Siloka) and Honour (Sakkara), and that ill-gotten Fame (Yasa). The tenth is the extolling of oneself and contempt for others (Attukhamsanaparavambhana).

"This, Namuci, is your army, the opposing host of the Evil One. That army the coward does not overcome, but he who overcomes obtains happiness. "This Munja do I display! What boots life in this world! Better for me is death in the battle than that one should live on, vanquished! "Some ascetics and brahmins are not seen plunged in this battle.

They know not nor do they tread the path of the virtuous. "Seeing the army on all sides with Mara arrayed on elephant, I go forward to battle. Mara shall not drive me from my position. That army of yours, which the world together with gods conquers not, by my wisdom I go to destroy as I would an unbaked bowl with a stone. "Controlling my thoughts, and with mindfulness well-established, I shall wander from country to country, training many a disciple."Diligent, intent, and practising my teaching, they, disregarding you, will go where having gone they grieve not."

THE MIDDLE PATH

The ascetic Gotama was now fully convinced from personal experience of the utter futility of self-mortification which, though considered indispensable for Deliverance by the ascetic philosophers of the day, actually weakened one's intellect, and resulted in lassitude of spirit. He abandoned for ever this painful extreme as did he the other extreme of self-indulgence which tends to retard moral progress. He conceived the idea of adopting the Golden Mean which later became one of the salient features of his teaching. He recalled how when his father was engaged in ploughing, he sat in the cool shade of the rose-apple tree, absorbed in the contemplation of his own breath, which resulted in the attainment of the First Jhana (Ecstasy). Thereupon he thought: "Well, this is the path to Enlightenment."

He realized that Enlightenment could not be gained with such an utterly exhausted body: Physical fitness was essential for spiritual progress. So he decided to nourish the body sparingly and took some coarse food both hard and soft. The five favourite disciples who were attending on him with great hopes thinking that whatever truth the ascetic Gotama would comprehend, that would he impart to them, felt disappointed at this unexpected change of method. They thus left him and went to Isipatana, saying that "the ascetic Gotama had become luxurious, had ceased from striving, and had returned to a life of comfort." At a crucial time when help was most welcome, his companions deserted him leaving him alone. He was not discouraged, but their voluntary separation was advantageous to him though their presence during his great struggle was helpful to him. Alone, in sylvan solitudes, great men often realize deep truths and solve intricate problems.

DAWN OF TRUTH

Regaining his lost strength with some coarse food, he easily developed the First Jhana which he gained in his youth. By degrees he developed the second, third and fourth Jhanas as well. By developing the Jhanas he gained perfect one-pointedness of the mind. His mind was now like a polished mirror where everything is reflected in its true perspective. Thus with thoughts tranquillized, purified, cleansed, free from lust and impurity, pliable, alert, steady, and unshakable, he directed his mind to the knowledge as regards "The Reminiscence of Past Births" (Pubbenivasanussati Nana).

He recalled his varied lots in former existences as follows: first one life, then two lives, then three, four, five, ten, twenty, up to fifty lives; then a hundred, a thousand, a hundred thousand; then the dissolution of many world cycles, then the evolution of many world cycles, then both the dissolution and evolution of many world cycles. In that place he was of such a name, such a family, such a caste, such a dietary, such the pleasure and pain he experienced, such his life's end; Departing from there, he came into existence elsewhere. Then such was his name, such his family, such his caste, such his dietary, such the pleasure and pain he did experience, such life's end. Thence departing, he came into existence here.

Thus he recalled the mode and details of his varied lots in his former births. This, indeed, was the First Knowledge that he realized in the first watch of the night. Dispelling thus the ignorance with regard to the past, he directed his purified mind to "The Perception of the Disappearing and Reappearing of Beings" (Cutupapata Nana). With clairvoyant vision, purified and supernormal, he perceived beings disappearing from one state of existence and reappearing in another; he beheld the base and the noble, the beautiful and the ugly, the happy and the miserable, all passing according to their deeds.

He knew that these good individuals, by evil deeds, words, and thoughts, by reviling the Noble Ones, by being misbelievers, and by conforming themselves to the actions of the misbelievers, after the dissolution of their bodies and after death, had been born in sorrowful states. He knew that these good individuals, by good deeds, words, and thoughts, by not reviling the Noble Ones, by being right believers, and by conforming themselves to the actions of the right believers, after the dissolution of their bodies and after death, had been born in happy celestial worlds. Thus with clairvoyant supernormal vision he beheld the disappearing and the reappearing of beings. This, indeed, was the Second Knowledge that he realized in the middle watch of the night. Dispelling thus the ignorance with regard to the future, he directed his purified mind to "The Comprehension of the Cessation of Corruptions" (Asavakkhaya Nana).

He realized in accordance with fact:

"This is Sorrow (dukka)" "This, the Arising of Sorrow", "This, the Cessation Sorrow", "This, the Path leading to the Cessation of Sorrow". Likewise in accordance with fact he realized: "These are the Corruptions", "This, the Arising of Corruptions", "This, the Cessation of Corruptions", "This, the Path leading to the Cessation of Corruptions". Thus cognizing, thus perceiving, his mind was delivered from the Corruption of Sensual Craving; from the Corruption of Craving for Existence; from the Corruption of Ignorance.

Being delivered, He knew, "Delivered am I" and He realized, "Rebirth is ended; fulfilled the Holy Life; done what was to be done; there is no more of this state again." This was the Third Knowledge that He realized in the last watch of the night. Ignorance was dispelled, and wisdom arose; darkness vanished, and light arose.

CHARACTERISTICS OF THE BUDDHA

After a stupendous struggle of six strenuous years, in His 35th year the ascetic Gotama, unaided and unguided by any supernatural agency, and solely relying on His own efforts and wisdom, eradicated all defilements, ended the process of grasping, and, realizing things as they truly are by His own intuitive knowledge, became a Buddha - an Enlightened or Awakened One. Thereafter he was known as Buddha Gotama, one of a long series of Buddhas that appeared in the past and will appear in the future. He was not born a Buddha, but became a Buddha by His own efforts.

The Pali term Buddha is derived from "budh", to understand, or to be awakened. As He fully comprehended the four Noble Truths and as He arose from the slumbers of ignorance He is called a Buddha. Since He not only comprehends but also expounds the doctrine and enlightens others, He is called a Samma-Sambuddha -a Fully Enlightened One - to distinguish Him from Pacceka (Individual) Buddhas who only comprehend the doctrine but are incapable of enlightening others. Before His Enlightenment He was called Bodhisatta which means one who is aspiring to attain Buddhahood. Every aspirant to Buddhahood passes through the Bodhisatta Period - a period of intensive exercise and development of the qualities of generosity, discipline, renunciation, wisdom, energy, endurance, truthfulness, determination, benevolence and perfect equanimity.

In a particular era there arises only one Samma-Sambuddha. Just as certain plants and trees can bear only one flower even so one world-system (lokadhatu) can bear only one Samma-Sambuddha. The Buddha was a unique being. Such a being arises but rarely in this world, and is born out of compassion for the world, for the good, benefit, and happiness of gods and men. The Buddha is called "acchariya manussa" as He was a wonderful man. He is called "amatassa data" as He is the giver of Deathlessness. He is called "varado" as He is the Giver of the purest love, the profoundest wisdom, and the Highest Truth. He is also called Dhammassami as He is the Lord of the Dhamma (Doctrine).

As the Buddha Himself says, "He is the Accomplished One (Tathagata), the Worthy One (Araham), the Fully Enlightened One (Samma-Sambuddha), the creator of the unarisen way, the producer of the unproduced way, the proclaimer of the unproclaimed way, the knower of the way, the beholder of the way, the cognizer of the way." The Buddha had no teacher for His Enlightenment.

"Na me acariyo atthi" - A teacher have I not - are His own words. He did receive His mundane knowledge (from His lay teachers, but teachers He had none for His a supramundane knowledge which He himself realized by His own intuitive wisdom. If He had received His knowledge from another teacher or from another religious system such as Hinduism in which He was nurtured, He could not have said of Himself as being the incomparable teacher (aham sattha anuttaro). In His first discourse He declared that light arose in things not heard before.

During the early period of His renunciation He sought the advice of the distinguished religious teachers of the day, but He could not find what He sought in their teachings. Circumstances compelled Him to think for Himself and seek the Truth. He sought the Truth within Himself. He plunged into the deepest profundities of thought, and He realized the ultimate Truth which He had not heard or known before. Illumination came from within and shed light on things which He had never seen before. As He knew everything that ought to be known and as He obtained the key to all knowledge, He is called Sabbannu - the Omniscient One. This supernormal knowledge He acquired by His own efforts continued through a countless series of births.

Once a certain Brahmin named Dona, noticing the characteristic marks of the footprint of the Buddha, approached Him and questioned Him.

"Your Reverence will be a Deva?"

"No, indeed, brahmin, a Deva am I not," replied the Buddha.

"Then Your Reverence will be a Gandhabba?"

"No indeed, branmin, a Gandhabba am I not."

"A Yakkha then?"

"No, indeed, brahmin, not a Yakkha."

"Then Your Reverence will be a human being?"

"No indeed, brahmin, a human being am I not."

"Who, then, pray, will Your Reverence be?"

The Buddha replied that He had destroyed Defilements which condition rebirth as a Deva, Gandhabba, Yakkha, or a human being and added:

"As a lotus, fair and lovely,

By the water is not soiled,

By the world am I not soiled;

Therefore, brahmin, am I Buddha."

The Buddha does not claim to be an incarnation (Avatara) of Hindu God Vishnu, who, as the Bhagavadgita charmingly sings, is born again and again in different periods to protect the righteous, to destroy the wicked, and to establish the Dharma (right). According to the Buddha countless are the gods (Devas) who are also a class of beings subject to birth and death; but there is no one Supreme God, who controls the destinies of human beings and who possesses a divine power to appear on earth at different intervals, employing a human form as a vehicle. Nor does the Buddha call Himself a "Saviour" who freely saves others by his personal salvation.

The Buddha exhorts His followers to depend on themselves for their deliverance, since both defilement and purity depend on oneself. One cannot directly purify or defile another. Clarifying His relationship with His followers and emphasizing the importance of self- reliance and individual striving, the Buddha plainly states:

"You yourselves should make an exertion. The Tathagatas are only teachers."

The Buddha only indicates the path and method whereby He delivered Himself from suffering and death and achieved His ultimate goal. It is left for His faithful adherents who wish their release from the ills of life to follow the path. "To depend on others for salvation is negative, but to depend on one is positive." Dependence on others means a surrender of one's effort." "Be an island unto yourselves; be a refuge unto yourselves; seek no refuge in others."

These significant words uttered by the Buddha in His last days are very striking and inspiring. They reveal how vital is self-exertion to accomplish one's ends, and how superficial and futile it is to seek redemption through benignant saviours, and crave for illusory happiness in an afterlife through the propitiation of imaginary gods by fruitless prayers and meaningless sacrifices.

The Buddha was a human being. As a man He was born, as a Buddha He lived, and as a Buddha His life came to an end. Though human, He became an extraordinary man owing to His unique characteristics. The Buddha laid stress on this important point, and left no room for any one to fall into the error of thinking that He was an immortal being. It has been said of Him that there was no religious teacher who was "ever so godless as the Buddha, yet none was so god-like." In His time the Buddha was no doubt highly venerated by His followers, but He never arrogated to Himself any divinity.

THE BUDDHA'S GREATNESS

Born a man, living as a mortal, by His own exertion He attained the supreme state of perfection called Buddhahood, and without keeping His Enlightenment to Himself, He proclaimed to the world the latent possibilities and the invincible power of the human mind. Instead of placing an unseen Almighty God over man, and giving man a subservient position in relation to such a conception of divine power, He demonstrated how man could attain the highest knowledge and Supreme Enlightenment by his own efforts. He thus raised the worth of man. He taught that man can gain his deliverance from the ills of life and realize the eternal bliss of Nibbana without depending on an external God or mediating priests. He taught the egocentric, power seeking world the noble ideal of selfless service.

He protested against the evils of caste-system that hampered the progress of mankind and advocated equal opportunities for all. He declared that the gates of deliverance were open to all, in every condition of life, high or low, saint or sinner, who would care to turn a new leaf and aspire to perfection. He raised the status of down-trodden women, and not only brought them to a realization of their importance to society but also founded the first religious order for women.

For the first time in the history of the world He attempted to abolish slavery. He banned the sacrifice of unfortunate animals and brought them within His compass of loving kindness. He did not force His followers to be slaves either to His teachings or to Himself, but granted complete freedom of thought and admonished His followers to accept His words not merely out of regard for Him but after subjecting them to a thorough examination, "... as the wise would test gold by burning, cutting, and rubbing it on a piece of touchstone."

He comforted the bereaved mothers like Patacara and Kisagotami by His consoling words. He ministered to the deserted sick like Putigatta Tissa Thera with His own hands. He helped the poor and the neglected like Rajjumala and Sopaka and saved them from an untimely and tragic death. He ennobled the lives of criminals like Angulimala and courtesans like Ambapali. He encouraged the feeble, united the divided, enlightened the ignorant, clarified the mystic, guided the deluded, elevated the base, and dignified the noble. The rich and the poor, the saint and the criminal, loved Him alike. His noble example was a source of inspiration to all. He was the most compassionate and tolerant of teachers. His will, wisdom, compassion, service, renunciation, perfect purity, exemplary personal life, the blameless methods that were employed to propagate the Dhamma and His final success - all these factors have compelled about one fifth of the population of the world to hail the Buddha as the greatest religious teacher that ever lived on earth.

Paying a glowing tribute to the Buddha, Sri Radhakrishnan writes:

"In Gotama the Buddha we have a master mind from the East second to none so far as the influence on the thought and life of the human race is concerned and sacred to all as the founder of a religious tradition whose hold is hardly less wide and deep than any other. He belongs to the history of the worlds thought, to the general inheritance of all cultivated men, for, judged by intellectual integrity, moral earnestness, and spiritual insight, he is undoubtedly one of the greatest figures in history."

In the Three Greatest Men in History H.G. Wells states:

"In the Buddha you see clearly a man, simple, devout, lonely, battling for light, a vivid human personality, not a myth. He too gave a message to mankind universal in character. Many of our best modern ideas are in closest harmony with it. All the miseries and discontents of life are due, he taught, to selfishness.

Before a man can become serene he must cease to live for his senses or himself. Then he merges into a greater being. Buddhism in different language called men to self-forgetfulness 500 years before Christ. In some ways he was nearer to us and our needs. He was more lucid upon our individual importance in service than Christ and less ambiguous upon the question of personal immortality."

The Poet Tagore calls Him the Greatest Man ever born. In admiration of the Buddha, Fausboll, a Danish scholar says - "The more I know Him, the more I love Him." A humble follower of the Buddha would modestly say: The more I know Him, the more I love Him; the more I love Him, the more I know Him. In the memorable forenoon, immediately preceding the morn of His Enlightenment, as the Bodhisatta was seated under the Ajapala banyan tree in close proximity to the Bodhi tree, a generous lady, named Sujata, unexpectedly offered Him some rich milk rice, specially prepared by her with great care. This substantial meal He ate, and after His Enlightenment the Buddha fasted for seven weeks, and spent a quiet time, in deep contemplation, under the Bodhi tree and in its neighbourhood.

THE SEVEN WEEKS

First Week

Throughout the first week the Buddha sat under the Bodhi tree in one posture, experiencing the Bliss of Emancipation (Vimutti Sukha). After those seven days had elapsed, the Buddha emerged from the state of concentration, and in the first watch of the night, thoroughly reflected on

"The Dependent Arising" (Paticca Samuppada) in direct order thus: "When this (cause) exists, this (effect) is; with the arising of this (cause), this effect arises." Dependent on Ignorance (avijja) arise moral and immoral Conditioning Activities (sankhara).

Dependent on Conditioning Activities arises (Relinking) Consciousness (vinnana).

Dependent on (Relinking) Consciousness arise Mind and Matter (nama-rupa). Dependent on Mind and Matter arise the Six Spheres of Sense (salayatana). Dependent on the Six Spheres of Sense arises Contact (phassa).

Dependent on Contact arises Feeling (vedana).

Dependent on Feeling arises Craving (tanha).

Dependent on Craving arises Grasping (upadana).

Dependent on Grasping arises Becoming (bhava).

Dependent on Becoming arises Birth (jati).

Dependent on Birth arise Decay (jara), Death (marana), Sorrow (soka), Lamentation (parideva), Pain (dukkha) Grief (domanassa), and Despair (upayasa).

Thus does this whole mass of suffering originate? Thereupon the Exalted One, knowing the meaning of this, uttered, at that time, this paean of joy:

"When, indeed, the Truths become manifest unto the strenuous, meditative Brahmana, and then do all his doubts vanish away since he knows the truth together with its cause."

In the middle watch of the night the Exalted One thoroughly reflected on "The Dependent Arising" in reverse order thus: "When this cause does not exist, this effect is not; with the cessation of this cause, this effect ceases.

With the cessation of Ignorance, Conditioning Activities cease.

With the cessation of Conditioning Activities (Relinking) Consciousness ceases.

With the cessation of (Relinking) Consciousness, Mind and Matter cease.

With the cessation of Mind and Matter, the six Spheres of Sense cease.

With the cessation of the Six Spheres of Sense, Contact ceases.

With the cessation of Contact, Feeling ceases.

With the cessation of Feeling, Craving ceases.

With the cessation of Craving, Grasping ceases.

With the cessation of Grasping, Becoming ceases.

With the cessation of Becoming, Birth ceases.

With the cessation of Birth, Decay, Death, Sorrow, Lamentation, Pain, Grief, and Despair cease.

Thus does this whole mass of suffering cease. Thereupon the Exalted One, knowing the meaning of this, uttered, at that time, this paean of joy:

"When, indeed, the Truths become manifest unto the strenuous and meditative Brahmana, then all his doubts vanish away since he has understood the destruction of the causes."

In the third watch of the night, the Exalted One reflected on "The Dependent Arising" in direct and reverse order thus. "When this cause exists, this effect is; with the arising of this cause, this effect arises. When this cause does not exist, this effect is not; with the cessation of this cause, this effect ceases. Dependent on Ignorance arise Conditioning Activities and so forth. Thus does this whole mass of suffering arise. With the cessation of Ignorance, Conditioning Activities cease... and so forth. Thus does this whole mass of suffering cease.

Thereupon the Blessed One, knowing the meaning of this, uttered, at that time, this paean of joy:

"When indeed the Truths become manifest unto the strenuous and meditative Brahmana, then he stands routing the hosts of the Evil One even as the sun illumines the sky."

Second Week

The second week was uneventful, but He silently taught a great moral lesson to the world. As a mark of profound gratitude to the inanimate Bodhi tree that sheltered him during His struggle for Enlightenment, He stood at a certain distance gazing at the tree with motionless eyes for one whole week. Following His noble example, His followers, in memory of His Enlightenment, still venerate not only the original Bodhi tree but also its descendants.

Third Week

As the Buddha had not given up His temporary residence at the Bodhi tree the Devas doubted His attainment to Buddhahood. The Buddha read their thoughts, and in order to clear their doubts He created by His psychic powers a jewelled ambulatory (ratana camkamana) and paced up and down for another week.

Fourth Week

The fourth week He spent in a jewelled chamber (ratanaghara) contemplating the intricacies of the Abhidhamma (Higher Teaching). Books state that His mind and body were so purified when He pondered on the Book of Relations (Patthana), the seventh treatise of the Abhidhamma that six coloured rays emitted from His body.

Fifth Week

During the fifth week too the Buddha enjoyed the Bliss of Emancipation (Vimutti Sukha), seated in one posture under the famous Ajapala banyan tree in the vicinity of the Bodhi tree. When He arose from that transcendental state a conceited (huhunkajatiha) brahmin approached Him and after the customary salutations and friendly, greetings, questioned Him thus: "In what respect, O Venerable Gotama, does one become a Brahmana and what are the conditions that make a Brahmana?"

The Buddha uttered this paean of joy in reply:

"That brahmin who has discarded evil, without conceit (huhumka), free from Defilements, self-controlled, versed in knowledge and who has led the Holy Life rightly would call himself a Brahmana. For him there is no elation anywhere in this world." According to the Jataka commentary it was during this week that the daughters of Mara-Tanha, Arati and Raga made a vain attempt to tempt the Buddha by their charms.

Sixth week

From the Ajapala banyan tree the Buddha proceeded to the Mucalinda tree, where he spent the sixth week, again enjoying the Bliss of Emancipation. At that time there arose an unexpected great shower. Rain clouds and gloomy weather with cold winds prevailed for several days. Thereupon Mucalinda, the serpent-king, came out of his abode, and coiling round the body of the Buddha seven times, remained keeping his large hood over the head of the Buddha so that He may not be affected by the elements.

At the close of seven days Mucalinda, seeing the clear, cloudless sky, uncoiled him from around the body of the Buddha, and, leaving his own form, took the guise of a young man, and stood in front of the Exalted One with clasped hands.

Thereupon the Buddha uttered this paean of joy:

"Happy is seclusion to him who is contented, to him who has heard the truth, and to him who sees. Happy is goodwill in this world, and so is restraint towards all beings. Happy in this world is non-attachment, the passing beyond of sense-desires. The suppression of the 'I am' conceit is indeed the highest happiness."

Seventh week

The seventh week the Buddha peacefully passed at the Rajayatana tree, experiencing the Bliss of Emancipation.

One of the First Utterances of the Buddha

'Thro' many a birth in existence wandered I,

Seeking, but not finding, the builder of this house.

Sorrowful is repeated birth.

O house builder, thou art seen. Thou shalt build no house again.

All thy rafters are broken. Thy ridge-pole is shattered.

Mind attains the Unconditioned.

Achieved is the End of Craving.

At dawn on the very day of His Enlightenment the Buddha uttered this paean of joy (Udana) which vividly describes His transcendental moral victory and His inner spiritual experience. The Buddha admits His past wanderings in existence which entailed suffering, a fact that evidently proves the belief in rebirth.

He was compelled to wander and consequently to suffer, as He could not discover the architect that built this house, the body. In His final birth, while engaged in solitary meditation which He had highly developed in the course of His wanderings, after a relentless search He discovered by His own intuitive wisdom the elusive architect, residing no outside but within the recesses of His own heart. It was craving or attachment, a self-creation, a mental element latent in all. How and when this craving originated is incomprehensible. What is created by oneself can be destroyed by oneself. The discovery of the architect is the eradication of craving by attaining Arahantship, which in these verses is alluded to as "end of craving."

The rafters of this self-created house are the passions (kilesa) such as attachment (lobha) aversion (dosa), illusion (moha), conceit (mana), false views (ditthi), doubt (vicikiccha), sloth (thina), and restlessness (uddhacca), and moral shamelessness (ahirika), moral fearlessness (anottappa). The ridge-pole that supports the rafters represents ignorance the root cause of all passions. The shattering of the ridge-pole of ignorance by wisdom results in the complete demolition of the house. The ridge-pole and rafters are the material with which the architect builds this undesired house. With their destruction the architect is deprived of the material to rebuild the house which is not wanted. With the demolition of the house the mind, for which there is no place in the analogy attains the unconditioned state, which is Nibbana. Whatever that is mundane is left behind, and only the Supramundane State, Nibbana, remains.

THE SELF AND THE ANATTA DOCTRINE

It is on this very doctrine of Non-self (anatta) that all Abhidhamma thought converges and this is where it culminates. The elaborate and thorough treatment of Anatta is also the most important practical contribution of the Abhidhamma to the progress of the Buddha's disciple towards liberation. The Abhidhamma provides him with ample material for his meditations in the field of insight (vipassana), concerning Impermanence and Impersonality, and this material has been analysed down to the subtlest point and is couched in strictly philosophical language. There will certainly be many to whom the degree of analytical details found in the Suttas will be quite enough for them to understand Anatta, and sufficient for their use in meditative practice. But there are also minds that require repeated and varied demonstration and illustration of a truth before they are entirely satisfied and convinced.

There are also others who wish to push their analysis to the greatest detail possible and to extend it to the very smallest unit accessible; in order to make quite sure that even the realm of the infinitesimal, of the material and psychical 'atoms', does not hide any self or abiding substance. To such minds the Abhidhamma will be of great value. But also those who, in general, are satisfied with the expositions in the Suttas, may sometimes wish to investigate more closely a particular point that has roused their interest or presents difficulties. To them too the Abhidhamma will prove helpful.

Besides helping such individual cases, the Abhidhamma will in general render valuable aid in the slow and difficult change of thought and outlook from the view-point of 'self' to that of 'non-self'. Having once grasped intellectually the doctrine of non-self, one can certainly succeed in applying it to theoretical and practical issues if only one remembers it in time and deliberately directs one's thoughts and volitions accordingly. But except for such deliberate directing of thought, which in most cases will be relatively rare, the mind will continue to move in the old-accustomed ruts of 'I' and 'mine', 'self' and 'substance', which are deeply ingrained in our daily language and our modes of thinking; and our actions too will still continue to be frequently governed by our ancient egocentric impulses.

An occasional intellectual assent to the true outlook of Anatta will not effect great changes in that situation. The only remedy is for bad or wrong habits of action, speech and thinking to be gradually replaced by good and correct habits until the latter become as spontaneous as the former are now. It is therefore necessary that right thinking, that is, thinking in terms of Anatta, is made the subject of regular and systematic mental training until the power of wrong habits of thought is reduced and finally broken. The Abhidhamma in general, and in particular the various Triads and Dyads of terms as listed in the Matika, 'Schedule', of the Abhidhamma Pitaka, provide ample material for such 'fluency exercises' of right thinking. Familiarity with the application of the 'impersonal' view-point of the Abhidhamma and with the terminology by which it is expressed will exercise a considerable formative influence on the mind.

2

The Three Characteristics of Existence

A characteristic is a fact which tells us something about the nature of things. If a fact is sometimes connected with a things and sometimes not, then it is not a characteristic and will not help us very much to understand the nature of that thing. Heat, for example, is a fact. Heat is not characteristic of water, as water is not always hot. The heat of water depends upon other factors like sun or an electric stove. But heat is a characteristic of fire because fire is always hot and heat of fire does not depend on any other factors. Heat is always connected with fire and tells us something about the nature of fire. The Buddha taught that there are three characteristics of facts of existence. They are generally found in all that exists and so they can tell us something about the nature of existence. The three characteristics of existence taught by the Buddha are impermanence, suffering and impersonality.

IMPERMANENCE

The Buddha taught that all existence is impermanent because there is nothing internal or external whatsoever which is permanent, stable, lasting, not subject to decay and destruction, and forever the same. Everything changes continuously. Existence is like the flowing water of a river or the burning flame of a candle, which is never the same in two consecutive moments. Our body, for instance, is made up of material elements such as flesh, bones and blood, which are impermanent. From the moment of our birth, the body constantly undergoes change. The human mind, too, is dependent on many factors. It is in constant change. It is like a monkeys forever jumping about, never still for even a moment. The neither the body nor the mind is permanent and unchanging.

Science teaches that apparently permanent objects like the oceans, continents, mountain ranges and even the earth, the sun and the solar system are constantly changing and will some day become extinct. When all these are also subject to change and destruction, one cannot doubt the impermanence of life. Life can end at any moment. No one can avoid death and the destruction of the body. Understanding the characteristic of impermanence benefits people in two important ways: Firstly, it can improve human relationships and activities. Secondly, it can encourage people to follow the Noble Eightfold Path. Often people find that they make mistakes in their relationships with other because they fail to take into account the changes that constantly occur in themselves and others. Often friendships die because one or both parties fail to realize that their friend's personality, interests and attitudes have changed.

When one realizes that people and situation are impermanent and constantly changing, one will approach each moment of a relationship with an open mind. One will be able to react to each new situation without clinging to outdated ideas about people. Relationships can then develop fruitfully. Success in life depends on one's ability to adapt to change in situations and to make the most of new opportunities arising. Having understood that youth, health, material well-being and even life itself are impermanent, people should then make the most of that favorable circumstance while they last. This means that they need to practice the Noble Eightfold Path in order to achieve happiness and Enlightenment. The Buddha's last words were:

> "Subject to change are all things,
>
> Strive on with diligence."

SUFFERING

The Truth of suffering is the first of the Four Noble Truths taught by the Buddha. Suffering is a fact of life which people can see for themselves. It is one of the three characteristics of existence. Whatever is impermanent is also suffering. Everything which arises will last only for a time, then it decay and finally dies. Repeated birth and death is hard to endure, it disturbs one's peace and mind and is a cause of suffering. Thus old age, sickness and death which are evidence of the impermanence of life are forms of suffering.

Since people tend to cling to youth, heath, relationship and material achievements, the realization that these are impermanent, cause anxiety and fears. It is said that even the gods trembled when the Buddha reminded them that the heavens are also impermanent. Understanding that suffering is universal and inevitable enables one to face the realities of life with calmness of mind. One will be able to cope with old age, sickness and death without becoming disheartened or desperate. It also encourages people to look for solution to the problem of suffering just as Prince Siddhartha did.

IMPERSONALITY

People often think that there must be a personality or self that is real and permanent, otherwise they would not exist or experience things in life. However, the Buddha taught that there is no real, permanent and independent personality or self at all. This is the third characteristic of existence. If a permanent and independent self really existed, one should be able to identify it. Some people may say that the body is the self, or that mind is the self. However, both ideas are wrong. Both body and mind are impermanent, ever changing and subject to destruction. They depend on many factors for their existence. Neither body nor mind can possibly be the permanent and independent self.

If the body were the self, it would be able to will itself to be strong or fair. However the body grows tired, hungry and falls sick against its will, so the body cannot be the personality or self. Similarly, if the mind were the self, it would do whatever it wished. But the mind often runs away from what it knows to be right, and run after what is wrong. It becomes disturbed, distracted and excited against its will. Therefore the mind is also not the self. When people say, for instance, "I am going to work", they are just using a convenient name I for a collection of physical and mental factors. In reality, there is no I or self.

So long as people think that the self is permanent and independent, they are bound to be self centered and egoistic. Not only will feel constantly threatened by people and situations, but they will also feel compelled to protect themselves, their possessions, and even their opinions, at any cost. But once people realize that the self is just a convenient name for a collection of constantly changing physical and mental factors, they will no longer cling to it in fear and insecurity. They will find it easier to grow, learn, develop, and to be generous, kind and compassionate because they will no longer need to be constantly on the defensive. Understanding the fact of impersonality can help people deal more effectively with everyday situation. It encourages the cultivation of Good Conduct and helps one to progress towards happiness, peace and Enlightenment.

Impermanence, Suffering and impersonality are the three characteristic of existence. Whatever is impermanent is suffering, and whatever is impermanent and suffering is also without an independent self. Those who realize the truth of these three facts of existence will be able to overcome suffering because their minds are freed from delusions of permanence, pleasure and the self. According to the Buddhist tradition, all phenomena other than Nirvana are marked by three characteristics, sometimes referred to as the Dharma seals: impermanence, suffering, and no/not-self. According to tradition, after much meditation, the Buddha concluded that everything in the physical world (and everything in the phenomenology of psychology) is marked by these three characteristics:

- Anicca (Sanskrit anitya) or "impermanence". This refers not only to the fact that all conditioned things (sankhara) eventually cease to exist, but also that all conditioned things are in a constant state of flux. (Visualize a leaf growing on a tree. It dies and falls off the tree but is soon replaced by a new leaf.)
- Dukkha (Sanskrit duhkha) or "unsatisfactoriness" (or "disease"; also often translated "suffering", though this is somewhat misleading). Nothing found in the physical world or even the psychological realm can bring lasting deep satisfaction.
- Anatta (Sanskrit anatman) or "no-self" is used in the suttas both as a noun and as a predicative adjective to denote that phenomena are not, or are without, a permanent self, to describe any and all composite, consubstantial, phenomenal and temporal things, from the macrocosmic to microcosmic, be it matter pertaining to the physical body or the cosmos at large, as well as any and all mental machinations, which are impermanent.

There is often a fourth Dharma Seal mentioned:

- Nirvana is peace. Nirvana is the "other shore" from samsara.

Together the three characteristics of existence are called ti-lakkhana in Pali or tri-laksana in Sanskrit. By bringing the three (or four) seals into moment-to-moment experience through concentrated awareness, we are said to achieve wisdom – the third of the three higher trainings – the way out of samsara. Thus the method for leaving samsara involves a deep-rooted change in world view.

ANICCA

All compounded phenomena (things and experiences) are inconstant, unsteady, and impermanent. Everything we can experience through our senses is made up of parts, and its existence is dependent on external conditions. Everything is in constant flux, and so conditions and the thing itself is constantly changing. Things are constantly coming into being, and ceasing to be. Nothing lasts. The important point here is that phenomena arise and cease according to (complex) conditions and not according to our whims and fancy. While we have limited ability to effect change to our possessions and surroundings, experience tells us that our feeble attempts are no guarantee that the results of our efforts will be to our liking. More often than not, the results fall short of our expectations.

In Mahayana Buddhism, a caveat is added: one should indeed always meditate on the impermanence and transitory nature of compound structures and phenomena, but one must guard against extending this to the realm of Nirvana, where impermanence holds no sway. In this view, the ultimate nature of reality is free from the stains of dualistic thought, and should therefore not be labeled as 'one' or the 'other' (i.e. 'permanent' or 'impermanent'). Dzongsar Jamyang Khyentse Rinpoche states that in the four seals of the Mahayana, Nirvana should be viewed as "beyond extremes". Furthermore, he states that "In many philosophies or religions, the final goal is something that you can hold on to and keep. The final goal is the only thing that truly exists. But nirvana is not fabricated, so it is not something to be held on to. It is referred to as 'beyond extremes.'

We somehow think that we can go somewhere where we'll have a better sofa seat, a better shower system, a better sewer system, a nirvana where you don't even have to have a remote control, where everything is there the moment you think of it. But as I said earlier, it's not that we are adding something new that was not there before. Nirvana is achieved when you remove everything that was artificial and obscuring."

DUKKHA

Whatever is impermanent is subject to change. Whatever is subject to change is subject to suffering —The Buddha

Striving for what we desire, we may experience stress and suffering - dukkha. Getting what we desired, we may find delight and happiness. Soon after, the novelty may wear out and we may get bored with it. Boredom is a form of dissatisfaction (or suffering) and to escape from it, we divert ourselves from such boredom by indulging in a pursuit of new forms of pleasure. Sometimes not willing to relinquish objects that we are already uninterested in, we start to collect and amass possessions instead of sharing with others who may have better uses for them than we do. Boredom is a result of change: the change of our interest in that object of desire which so captivated us in the first place.

Change may also take place in the object of our desire as opposed to change from within. Silverware may become tarnished, a new dress worn thin or a gadget gone obsolete. Or it may become broken, causing us to grieve. In some cases it may get lost or stolen. In some cases, we may worry about such losses even before they happen. Husbands and wives worry about losing their spouses even though their partners are faithful. Unfortunately, sometimes our very worry and fear drives us to act irrationally, resulting in distrust and breaking up of the very relationship that we cherished so much. While we like changes such as becoming an adult when we are in our teens, we dislike the change called aging. While we strive for change to become rich, we fear the change of retrenchment.

We are selective in our attitude towards the transient nature of our very existence. Unfortunately, this transient nature is unselective. We can try to fight it, just as many have tried since beginningless time, only to have our efforts washed away through the passages of time. As a result, we continually experience dissatisfaction or suffering due to the very impermanence of compounded phenomena. Only in the realm of Nirvana - so Buddhism insists – can true and lasting happiness be found.

Nirvana is the opposite of the conditional, the transitory and the painful, so it does not result in disappointment or deterioration of the state of bliss. Nirvana is the refuge from the otherwise universal tyranny of change and suffering. In other schools of Buddhism, nirvana is not viewed as the goal, but merely as a projection from the state of samsara. According to these schools samsara (daily routine) and nirvana (perfection) are two sides of the same coin.

ANATTA

In Indian philosophy, the concept of a self is called âtman (that is, "soul" or metaphysical self), which refers to an unchanging, permanent essence conceived by virtue of existence. This concept and the related concept of Brahman, the Vedantic monistic ideal, which was regarded as an ultimate âtman for all beings, were indispensable for mainstream Indian metaphysics, logic, and science; for all apparent things there had to be an underlying and persistent reality, akin to a Platonic form. The Buddha rejected all concepts of âtman, emphasizing not permanence, but changeability. He taught that all concepts of a substantial personal self were incorrect, and formed in the realm of ignorance. The Buddha criticized conceiving theories even of a unitary soul or identity immanent in all things as unskillful in the Great Discourse on Causation.

In fact, according to the Buddha's statement in Khandha Samyutta 47, all thoughts about self are necessarily, whether the thinker is aware of it or not, thoughts about the five aggregates or one of them. In a number of major Mahayana sutras (e.g. the Mahaparinirvana Sutra, the Tathagatagarbha Sutra, the Srimala Sutra, among others), the Buddha is presented as clarifying this teaching by saying that, while the skandhas (constituents of the ordinary body and mind) are not the self, there does truly exist an eternal, unchanging, blissful Buddha-essence in all sentient beings, which is the uncreated and deathless Buddha-nature ("Buddha-dhatu") or "True Self" of the Buddha himself. The "tathagatagarbha"/ Buddha nature does not represent a substantial self; rather, it is a positive language expression of "sunyata" (emptiness) and represents the potentiality to realize Buddhahood through Buddhist practices; the intention of the teaching of tathagatagarbha (Buddha nature) is soteriological rather than theoretical.

This immaculate Buddhic Self (atman) is in no way to be construed as a mundane, impermanent, suffering "ego", of which it is the diametrical opposite. On the other hand, this Buddha-essence or Buddha-nature is also often explained as the potential for achieving Buddhahood, rather than an existing phenomenon one can grasp onto as being me or self. Anatta is discussed in the Questions of King Milinda, composed during the period of the Hellenistic Indo-Greek kingdom of the 2nd and 1 st centuries BCE. In this text, the monk Nagasena demonstrates the concept of absolute "non-Self" by likening human beings to a chariot and challenges the Greek king "Milinda" (Menander) to find the essence of the chariot. Nagasena states that just as a chariot is made up of a number of things, none of which are the essence of the chariot in isolation, without the other pieces, similarly no one part of a person is a permanent entity; we can be broken up into five constituents - body, sensations, ideation, mental formations and consciousness - the consciousness being closest to the permanent idea of "Self", but is ever-changing with each new thought according to this viewpoint.

According to some thinkers both in the East and the West, the doctrine of "non-Self", may imply that Buddhism is a form of nihilism or something similar. However, as thinkers like Nagarjuna have clearly pointed out, Buddhism is not simply a rejection of the concept of existence or meaning, but of the hard and fast distinction between existence and non-existence, or rather between being and no-thingness. Phenomena are not independent from causes and conditions and do not exist as isolated things as we perceive them to be.

The lack of a permanent, unchanging, substantial Self in beings and things does not mean that they do not experience growth and decay on the relative level. But on the ultimate level of analysis, one cannot distinguish an object from its causes and conditions or even distinguish between object and subject (an idea appearing relatively recently in Western science). Buddhism thus has much more in common with Western empiricism, pragmatism, anti-foundationalism, and even post structuralism than with nihilism.

In the Nikâyas, the Buddha and his disciples commonly question or declare "Is that which is impermanent, subject to change, subject to suffering fit to be considered thus: 'This I am, this is mine, this is my self'?" The question which the Buddha poses to his audience is whether compounded phenomena are fit to be considered as self, to which the audience agrees that it is unworthy to be considered so. And in relinquishing such an attachment to compounded phenomena, such a person gives up delight, desire and craving for compounded phenomena and is unbounded by its change. When completely free from attachments, craving or desire to the five aggregates, such a person experiences then transcends the very causes of suffering.

In this way, the insight wisdom or prajñâ of non-Self gives rise to cessation of suffering, and not an intellectual debate over whether a self exists or not. It is by realizing (not merely understanding intellectually, but making real in one's experience) the three marks of conditioned existence that one develops prajñâ, which is the antidote to the ignorance that lies at the root of all suffering.

INTERPRETATIONS OF THE THREE MARKS BY VARIOUS SCHOOLS

Some Buddhist traditions assert that Anatta pervades everything, and is not limited to personality, or soul. These traditions assert that Nirvana also has the quality of Anatta, but that Nirvana (by definition) is the cessation of Dukkha and Anicca.

In his Mulamadhyamakakarika (XXV: 19), Nagarjuna says:

There is not the slightest difference

Between Samsara and Nirvana

This verse points us to an interesting stress between dukkha and nirvana, through an argument based in Anatta. This specific stress can be seen to be the key to (and possibly source for the development of) the deity yogas of vajrayana. The sutra path enjoins us to identify the entire world (internally and externally) as samsara – a continual churning of suffering that nobody wants to be part of. Our practice is that of leaving the shores of samsara. On the other hand, we are told that unconditioned, enlightened activity is not actually different from samsara.

Whereas the deity yoga of vajrayana enjoins us to identify the entire world as nirvana – a continual play of enlightening activity that everyone wishes to be a part of. Our practice here is that of arriving at the shores of nirvana. At this level, the distinction between Sutra and Vajrayana remain that of view (departing vs. arriving), but basically the practitioner remains involved in undergoing a transformative development to his or her Weltanschauung, and in this context, these practices remain rooted in psychological change, grounded in the development of Samatha, or training in concentration.

However, there are certain practices in Tantra which are not solely concerned with psychological change; these revolve around the basic idea that it is possible to induce deep levels of concentration through psycho-physical methods as a result of special exercises. The purpose remains the same (to achieve liberating view), but the method involves a 'short cut' for the training in Samatha.

THE MAHAKARUNA OF THE BUDDHA

Siddhartha Gautama - the Buddha, a historic personage of the 6th century Before Christ has been extolled in Buddhist literature as a Super Human being, with extra-ordinary qualities and powers. With His extra-sensory perceptions He could describe the universe as it is now found to be by scientists of today. Although He could tread into any area of knowledge His doctrine was purposely narrowed down to what is required for the liberation from craving that tie us down to all sufferings imaginable. Of the Four Unchanging Truths discovered by the Enlightened One, the Buddha, the Truth of Suffering is the first, which may appear to the uninitiated as pessimism. The next Truth alerts us to the causes of this condition. Once the causes are identified the next Truth reveals that there is a path to liberation from sufferings. The

Fourth Truth is that one could indeed surpass this condition of suffering. The Buddha with His Great Compassion revealed these to the worldlings, particularly for the benefit of those who can grasp it, with a view to liberating them from this endless condition of suffering. Since His Enlightenment every single day was begun by Him, looking at the worldlings identifying one per day who deserves to be helped with priority. On one day it was Angulimala, the killer highwayman whose mother was to die at his hands that day. In his great compassion he not only prevented this but also helped the killer to get out of that rut and tread the path to complete liberation.

A sculptor in ancient Sri Lanka has expressed on stone this great compassion of the Buddha at the Galvihara in Polonnaruwa. In the Buddha Statue to the left of the reclining statue depicting the Parinirvana, the final departure from continued existence, stands this statue with arms folded on the breast, looking in a particular posture with half closed eyes as He would, on the creatures of the three realms of existence that are entangled in fetters of suffering. Considering the plight of these creatures He gave up His chance for complete liberation. He had to go through innumerable births before; aspiring to become the Buddha cultivated the extraordinary qualities required in this process, in births counting about five hundred going through many sufferings in various forms.

In His final birth, the Bodhisathva was born as Prince Siddhartha of the Gautama clan ruling in Kapilavasthu that was in land of modern Nepal. Though closer to His goal He led a princely life which He renounced when the time was ripe. A mind conditioned with materialistic consideration alone, may not be able to grasp the rationale of this great departure, the Abhiniskramana. Some have even used it to tarnish the greatness of this super human being, the Buddha. Bharatha (expanding beyond modern India with a large number of independent kingdoms wanting to be identified under that name) in the 6th century B.C. was going through a period of unprecedented emancipation. Youths both male and female went into homeless life in search of Truth about existence and deliverance from suffering.

Princess Yashodara perhaps at least had an idea about this background that conditioned her husband's thinking though she may not have been aware of his aspirations for Enlightenment as a Buddha coming through numerous previous births. Enmeshed in the narrow limits of a nucleus family one may not understand the extended family life that existed in that time. Though Prince Siddhartha's mother died seven days after His birth, He was breast fed and brought up with love and care by His foster mother Maha Prajapathi Gothami added to which was His father's great love. The decision to leave the palace was taken on the day His son was born, fourteen years after being happily married since begin wedded to Yashodara at the age of sixteen. He knew well that His wife and child shall only lose His Company which He had to sacrifice for the greater good for both of them as well as for all other beings of the three realms of existence.

He had the confidence that they shall be well looked after in the palace, unlike those of the present day, taking pride in the limited bonds of a nucleus family, depending mostly on the father, the bread winner, who spends His earnings for no one else of the extended family. The conditions were right for the Prince to be motivated by His Great Compassion for all beings of suffering and He made a sacrifice of His comforts and family bonds. Dhamma with the Four Unchanging Truths were then discovered by Him in the subsequent years of homelessness.

The benefits of this discovery was not only for the beings of that period for the Dhamma is timeless or 'Akalika'. Therefore it is for us too and for the posterity, depending on the degree of inclination and emancipation. If we have eyes only to see the glitter of modern living and be dazzled then we shall never see anything else. How far behind are the present day people in the spirit of spiritual exploration that existed in the Bharatha in the 6th century B.C. But we can make a decision even today and the path to complete liberation shall be revealed for us to tread, with the Great compassion of the Enlightened One, the Buddha.

3

The Significance of the Refuges

THE THREEFOLD REFUGE

After listening to the Buddha's Discourse called "Fear and Dread," the Brahman Jaanussoni becomes a lay follower of the Buddha, by taking the Threefold Refuge. The words used by him differ slightly from the usual formula in so far as in the latter the words "the Lord Gotama" are replaced by "the Buddha." Buddhaghosa's comment, here slightly abridged, runs as follows:

"I go for refuge to the Lord Gotama" (bhavantam Gotamam sarnam gacchaami). This means: The Lord Gotama is my refuge and my guiding ideal. I am going for refuge to the Lord Gotama. I resort to him, follow and honor him, in the sense of his being the Destroyer of Affliction and the Provider of Weal. Or: I know and understand him to be of such a nature.

This last explanation is based upon the fact that in the Pali language, the verbal roots denoting "going" (gati) may also have the meaning of "knowing" (buddhi). Therefore the words "I go for refuge to the Buddha" may also be taken to express the idea: "I know and understand him to be the refuge." "I go for refuge to the Dhamma." The word Dhamma, i.e., the Doctrine or the Law, is derived from the verb dhareti, to keep or to bear. In accordance with that derivation, the Dhamma may be regarded as refuge, because it keeps, upholds, and supports the beings by way of preventing their fall into the states of woe by way of enabling a life according to instruction (as given by the Dhamma), by way of attainment of the Path, and by realization of the extinction (of suffering). Accordingly, the Dhamma (meant in the formula of refuge) is the (supramundane) Noble Path as well as Nibbana. Besides, it is the attainment of the noble fruitions (of the stream-enterer, the once-returner, the non-returner, and the saint), and also the Dhamma of Learning (laid down in the Scriptures: pariyatti- Dhamma).

"I go for refuge to the Sangha." The Sangha is (here) the community of (holy) monks which is united by the communion of right view and virtue (ditthi-siila sanghaatena samhato' ti sangho). That is to say: the Sangha (meant in the formula of refuge) is the group of the eight noble beings (ariya-puggala: those in possession of 1) the path of stream-entry, 2) the fruition thereof, etc.). In order to gain proficiency with regard to this subject of "refuge," one should be acquainted with the following method of exposition, dealing with 1) the word sarana; 2) the going for refuge (saranaagamana); 3) Who is going for refuge?; 4) the divisions; 5) the results; 6) the defilements; 7) the breach.

1. As to the meaning of the word sara.na, the commentator relates it, not in the sense of a linguistic derivation, but for the purpose of exposition, to the verb sarati, "to crush," having the same meaning as himsati, "to kill." The refuge is explained in that way, because, for those who are taking that refuge, it kills and destroys danger and fear, suffering, and the defilements leading to evil destiny. The refuge is a name of the Triple Gem. Another explanation: The Buddha destroys fear in beings by promoting their happiness and by removing harm from them. The Dhamma does it by making the beings cross the wilderness of existence and by giving them solace. The Sangha does it by (enabling devotees) to obtain rich results even from small religious acts (like homage, offerings etc.)
2. The going for (or taking) refuge is a state of mind in

which defilements are destroyed owing to the faith in and veneration for, the Triple Gem; a state of mind which, without relying on others (apara-paccayo), proceeds by way of taking the Triple Gem as its guiding ideal (paraaya.na).

3. Who is going for refuge? It is a being endowed with a state of mind as described above.
4. The going for refuge has two main divisions: it may be mundane or supramundane.

The supramundane refuge is taken by those who have a (true) vision of the Noble Truth (dittha-sacca; i.e., by the eight noble beings). In the path-moment (of stream-entry, where any trace of the fetter of doubt has been removed), the supramundane refuge succeeds in exterminating any blemish that may still attach to the going for refuge. It has Nibbanaas its object, and in its function it comprises the entire Triple Gem (in that object of Nibbana).

The mundane refuge is taken by worldlings (puthujjanas; i.e., all those, monks or laymen, who are still outside of the four stages of sanctity). It succeeds in effecting a temporary repression of the blemishes attaching to their going for refuge. Its objects are the noble qualities of the Buddha, Dhamma, and Sangha. It consists in the acquisition of faith (saddhaa) in these three objects. It is this faith in the Triple Gem that is referred to when, among the ten meritorious acts (puññakiriyavatthu), the "straightening of views" (ditthujjukamma) is defined as Right Understanding rooted in faith (saddhaamuulika sammaa-ditthi).

This mundane refuge is of four kinds: (a) the surrender of self (atta-sanniyyaatanaa); (b) acceptance (of the Triple Gem) as one's guiding ideal (tapparaaya.nataa); (c) acceptance of discipleship (sissabhaavuupaagamana); (d) homage by prostration (pa.nipaata).

a. The Surrender of Self is expressed as follows:

"From today onward I surrender myself to the Buddha... to the Dhamma... to the Sangha."

Ajja aadim katvaa aham attaanam Buddhassa niyyaatemi Dhammassa Sanghassa'ti.

This is the giving over of one's self to the Triple Gem. It may also be done in this way:

"To the Exalted One I am giving my self, to the Dhamma I am giving my self, to the Sangha I am giving my self. I am giving them my life! Given is my self, given my life! Until my life ends, I am taking refuge in the Buddha! The Buddha is my refuge, my shelter and my protection."

Bhagavato attaanam pariccajaami. Dhammassa Sanghassa attaanam pariccajaami, jiivitañca pariccajaami. Pariccatto yeva me attaa, pariccattam yeva me jiivitam. Jiivita pariyantikam Buddham saranam gacchaami. Buddho me saranam lenam taanan'ti.

b. The Acceptance of the Guiding Ideal.

"From today onward the Buddha is my Guiding Ideal, the Dhamma, and the Sangha. Thus may you know me!"

Ajja aadim katvaa aham Buddhaparayano Dhammaparayano Sanghaparayano. Iti mam dharetha.

It is illustrated by the following verse spoken by Alavaka:

"From village to village, from town to town I'll wend my way, lauding the Enlightened One and the perfection of His Law." — Samyutta Nikaya 1.10 (v. 192)

Thus the acceptance of the guiding ideal by Alavaka and others has to be understood as equaling their going for refuge.

c. The Acceptance of Discipleship:

"From today onward I am the Disciple of the Buddha, the Dhamma, and the Sangha. Thus may you know me!"

Ajja aadim katvaa aham Buddhassa antevaasiko Dhammassa Sanghassa. Iti mam dharetha.

This is illustrated by the following passage expressing Kassapa's acceptance of discipleship that has to be understood as equaling his going for refuge:

"Fain would I see the Master, The Exalted One, him I would wish to see! Fain would I see the Blessed One! The Exalted One, him would I wish to see! Fain would I see the Enlightened One! The Exalted One, him I would wish to see!

"Then I prostrated myself before the Exalted One and addressed him thus: The Exalted One, O Lord, is my Master, and I am his disciple!"

d. Homage by Prostration:

"From today onward I shall give respectful greeting, devoted attendance, the añjali-salutation (by folding the palms and raising the hands) and homage only to those three: the Buddha, the Dhamma, and the Sangha. Thus may you know me!"

Ajja aadim katvaa aham abhivadana-paccutthana-añjalikamma-saamicikammam Buddhadiinam yeva tinnam vatthuunam karomi. Iti mam dharetha.

This way of going for refuge consists in showing deep humility towards the Buddha, Dhamma, and the Sangha. (It is illustrated by the Brahman Brahmayu's homage after his being deeply stirred by a stanza spoken by the Buddha.)

Homage by prostration may be of four kinds: being paid towards (senior) relatives, out of fear, towards one's teacher, and towards those deserving highest veneration. Only the latter case – i.e., the prostration before those worthy of highest veneration – is to be regarded as "going for refuge"; the three other cases do not count as such. Only if referring to the highest (in one's scale of values), refuge is taken or broken, respectively.

Therefore if a member of the Sakya or Koliya clan worships the Buddha, thinking: "He is our relative," no refuge is taken in that case. Or, one may think: "The recluse Gotama is honored by kings and has great influence. If he is not worshipped, he might do me harm." If, thinking thus, one worships out of fear, no refuge is taken in that case. Furthermore, a person remembers to have learned something from the Blessed One while he was a Bodhisatta, an aspirant to Buddhahood; or, after his attaining Buddhahood, one has received from the Master advice relating to worldly knowledge. If for these reasons, one regards the Buddha as one's teacher and worships him, no refuge is taken, in that case too. But if one pays worship to the Buddha in the conviction "This is the most venerable being in the world," only by such a one is refuge taken.

On the other hand, the going for refuge remains unbroken in the following situations. A male or female lay devotee, who has taken refuge in the Triple Gem, worships a (senior) relative, thinking: "He is my kinsman." Even if that relative is a recluse of another faith, the refuge in the Triple Gem is unbroken; still less can it be said to be broken if it is not a recluse or a priest. When prostrating before a king, out of fear: "If he who is honored by the whole country is not worshipped, he will do me harm!"- in that case too the refuge is unbroken. If one has learned any science, art, or craft even from a non-Buddhist, and one worships him in his capacity as one's teacher, in that case too the refuge remains unbroken.

5. Results. The fruit of the supramundane refuge, in the sense of being its karmic result (vipaaka-phala), is the four fruitions of monkhood (saamañña-phala), viz. the fruition of stream-entry, etc. The fruit in the sense of advantage or blessing (aanisamsa-phala) is the destruction of suffering; further, the blessings mentioned in the following scriptural passage:

"It is impossible, O monks, that a person endowed with insight (ditthi-sampanno - i.e., stream-enterer, etc.) should regard any conditioned thing as permanent, enjoyable, or an ego; that he should take the life of his mother, his father, or a saint; that, with a thought of hate, he should shed the blood of the Blessed One; that he should cause a split in the community of monks; that he should choose another teacher. There is no possibility of that."

But the fruit of the mundane refuge is only the attainment of favorable rebirth, and the attainment of property and enjoyment.

6. Defilements. In three cases the mundane refuge is defiled and without great brightness and radiating influence: if

connected with ignorance, doubt, and wrong views. The supramundane refuge is free from any defilement.

7. A breach of the mundane refuge might be blamable or blameless. It is blamable when occurring as a going for refuge by self-surrender, etc., to other religious masters: in that case the breach will have undesirable results. The breach is blameless at the time of death, as it will not cause any karmic result. The supramundane refuge is without breach. Even in another existence a holy disciple will not turn to another master.

THOUGHTS AND COMMENTS

In all Buddhist lands the followers of the Enlightened One profess their allegiance to him and his liberating doctrine by the ancient, simple, and yet so touching formula of "taking refuge or, more literal and more expressive, by going for refuge to the Triple Gem. The going for refuge, as this figurative expression itself suggests, should be a conscious act, not the mere profession of a theoretical belief, still less the habitual rite of traditional piety. The protecting refuge exists, but we have to go to it by our own effort. It will not come to us by itself, while we stay put. The Buddha, as He repeatedly declared, is only the teacher, "pointing out the Way."

Therefore, the going for refuge, expressive of Buddhist faith (saddhaa), is in the first place a conscious act of will and determination, directed towards the goal of liberation. Hereby the conception of faith as a mere passive waiting for "saving grace" is rejected. In the Commentary, translated above, there is the remarkable statement that the expression "going for refuge" is meant to convey, in addition, the idea of "knowing" and "understanding." The points to the second aspects of going for refuge as a conscious act of understanding. Hereby unthinking credulity and blind faith based on external authority are rejected.

The commentator emphasizes this aspect by describing the going for refuge as a state of mind, not relying on others (aparapaccaya). On many occasions the Master warned his disciples not to accept his teachings out of mere trust in him, but only after personal experience, practice, and reflection. Here it may suffice to remember the famous Sermon to the Kalamas:

"Do not go by hearsay, or by tradition, or by people's tales, or by the authority of Scriptures. Do not go by reasoning, or by logic and methodical investigations, or by approval of speculative views, nor moved by reverence, nor by the thought: 'The Recluse is my teacher!'" –Anguttara Nikaya 3.65

It is a threefold knowledge that is, or should be, implied in the act of going for refuge. It is a knowledge answering the following questions: Is this world of ours really such a place of danger and misery that there is a need for taking refuge? Does such a refuge actually exist? And what is its nature? There are many who do not see any need for a refuge. Being well pleased with themselves and with the petty, momentary happiness of their life, they are fully convinced that "all is well with the world." They do not wish, or are not able, to look beyond their narrow horizon. For them neither the Buddha nor any other great religious teacher has yet appeared. But the majority of men know very well, by their own bitter experience, the hard and cruel face of the world which is only temporarily hidden by a friendly mask.

There are some others who, sufficiently aware of a fellow being's actual existence, add to that personal experience by observation of other lives. And there are a still smaller number of people who are able to reflect wisely on both experience and observation. Particularly to those latter ones "whose eyes are less covered by dust," life will appear as a vast ocean of suffering, of unfathomable depth, on the surface of which beings swim about for a little while, or navigate in their fragile nutshells of which they are very proud. True, there are spells of calm on the waters when it is pleasant to float upon a smooth sea, or to prove and to enjoy the strength of one's body by a long swim. But those with open eyes and minds are not deceived by these short moments of respite: they know the overpowering fierceness of a storm-swept sea; they know the dangerous currents and whirlpools in it, and the demons and monsters of the deep.

They know that, even under the most favorable conditions, the feeble strength of man will soon be exhausted by the impact of life's elemental forces. The vicissitudes of life give no chance of maintaining permanently, during the unlimited sequence of transformations, even the lowest degree of happiness, even the lowest standard of moral worth. There is nothing to gain by traversing ever anew the infinite expanse of life's ocean, in any of its regions. There is only the same senseless repetition of the ups and downs, of ebb and tide. Faced by the ever-present perils of life and by its essential monotony, there will be only the one cry for refuge in a heart and mind that has truly grasped its situation within the world. A refuge is the one great need of all life and "going to it" the one sane act demanded by that situation.

But granting its necessity, does a refuge from the world's ills actually exist? The Buddhist affirms it and proves by that affirmation to be anything but a pessimist. The refuge to which he turns his steps is the triad of the Buddha, his Doctrine, and the Fraternity of holy disciples. Being what is most precious and most pure, it has been called "The Triple Gem." But the fact that it provides the final refuge and not only a temporary shelter, cannot otherwise be proved than through the actual attainment of that refuge by those who are going to it. The Triple Gem has objective existence as an impersonal idea or ideal as long as it is known and cherished. In so far it is doubtlessly a still persisting and active source of energy for the world. But it is transformed from an impersonal idea to a personal refuge only to the extent of its being realized in one's own mind and manifested in one's own life. Therefore the existence of the Triple Gem in its characteristic nature as a refuge cannot be proven to others than those who find this refuge in themselves by their own efforts.

The refuge becomes and grows by the process of going to it.

By effort, earnestness and self-control

Let the wise man make for him an island

Which no flood can overwhelm. - Dhammapada 25

The refuge exists for us only in so far as something within ourselves responds and corresponds to it.

Therefore the Sixth Zen Patriarch said:

"Let each of us take refuge to the Triple Gems within our mind!"

With regard to the first refuge, in the Buddha, the Master himself said, shortly after His Enlightenment:

Like me the conquerors will be

Who have attained to the defilements' end?

Majjhima Nikaya 26, Ariya-pariyesana-sutta

Concerning the second refuge, in the Dhamma, the Buddha said shortly before his decease:

"Be ye islands unto yourselves, be ye a refuge unto yourselves! Take no other refuge! The Dhamma be your island, the Dhamma be your refuge; Take no other refuge!"

Digha Nikaya 16, Maha-parinibbana-sutta

In the commentarial literature it is said (in reference to another passage, but applicable to the one just quoted):

The Dhamma is called "self" (atta) because, in the case of a wise one, the Dhamma is not different from himself and because it pertains to his personal existence.

Tika to Maha-Satipatthana-Sutta

The third refuge, the Sangha, being the community of holy disciples, is the great and inspiring model for emulation. The actual foundation of that refuge is the capacity inherent in all beings to become one of the eight noble beings who form the Sangha of the refuge. We turn now to the third subject of the knowledge implied in taking refuge, i.e., to the ultimate nature of the threefold refuge.

We have seen that the refuge becomes attainable and even perceptible only by way of the living roots, by the actual foundations it has within the average mind. Like the lotus, it arises within the waters of worldly existence; there it develops and from there it takes its nourishment. But what is still immersed in the ocean of worldliness and suffering cannot be the ultimate refuge, the place of safety and bliss. It must not only assuage, but finally transcend, the world of danger, fear and ill, like the lotus that rises above the surface of the water and remains unsullied by it. Therefore the consummate refuge meant in the traditional formula is of supramundane nature-lokuttara i.e., world-transcending.

Consequently, the first refuge is not the recluse Gotama, but the Buddha as the personification of world-transcending enlightenment (bodhi). In the Vimamsaka Sutta it is said of the Noble Disciple: "He believes in the Enlightenment of the Exalted One." The Dhamma of the second refuge is not the faint, fragmentary, or even distorted picture of the Doctrine as mirrored in the mind of an unliberated worldling (puthujjana). It is the supramundane Eightfold Path and its consummation in Nibbana. The commentator underlines the supramundane nature of the second refuge by saying that the Dhamma, as an object of learning (pariyatti Dhamma), is only in so far included in the refuge as it arises in the Holy Disciple together with the fruition of stream-entry, etc.; i.e., only in so far as it is a formulation of that consummate knowledge acquired on the four stages of sanctity.

The Sangha of the third refuge is not the all-inclusive congregation of monks, having all the weaknesses of its single members and sharing in the shortcomings attaching to any human institution. It is rather the fraternity of holy disciples, not necessarily monks, who are united by the invisible tie of common attainment to the four stages of sanctity. In other words, it is likewise of supramundane nature. It is the assurance of possible progress to the world-transcending heights of a mind made holy and pure. By this threefold knowledge, about the need, existence, and nature of the refuge, the Going to that refuge becomes a conscious act of understanding.

This knowledge and understanding forms the firm basis of the third, the emotional, aspect of taking refuge, having, as it were, three facets: confidence, devotion, and love. The knowledge of the existence of a refuge provides the basis for a firm and justified confidence, for the calmness of inner assurance, and the strength of conviction. The knowledge of the need for a refuge instills unswerving devotion to it; and the understanding of its sublime nature fills the heart with love towards the highest that can be conceived. Confidence is the firmness in faith; devotion is the patient endurance in loyal service and effort; and love adds the element of ardor, warmth, and joy.

In the sense of these three constituents, the going for refuge is also a conscious act of wise faith. We may now define the going for refuge as a conscious act of will directed towards liberation, based upon knowledge and inspired by faith; or briefly: a conscious act of determination, understanding, and devotion. These three aspects of taking refuge have their counterparts in the volitional, rational, and emotional sides of the human mind. Therefore, for a harmonious development of character, the cultivation of all three is required.

Will, understanding, and faith support each other in their common task; will, transformed into purposive action, frees faith from the barrenness and dangers of emotional self-indulgence; it prevents intellectual understanding from stopping short at mere theoretical appreciation. Will harnesses the energies of both emotion and intellect to actual application. Understanding gives direction and method to will; it provides a check to the exuberance of faith and gives to it its true contents. Faith keeps will from slackening, and is the vitalizing and purposive factor in intellectual understanding.

The presence of these three aspects is the distinguishing feature of true Buddhist faith (saddha). In the conception of faith as found in all other world religions, only the emotional aspect is stressed (assurance, devotion, and love). The two other aspects will and understanding, are absent, or in an undeveloped state, being impeded by the dictates of the creed. The element of self-responsible will is supplanted by the postulate of obedience, by authoritarian guidance, and by submission to the will of a God. Understanding is replaced by dogmatic belief, demanding or implying a sacrifice of intellect.

Against such a one-sided emphasis on emotional faith, Buddhism moves from the very beginning of its spiritual training towards wholeness and completeness, i.e., towards a harmonious development of mental faculties. Therefore the act of going for refuge in its true sense, is accomplished only if there is connected with it at least a minimal degree of purposeful will and genuine understanding. Only in that case, faith (saddha) will have the quality of a "seed" attributed to it by the Buddha, i.e., of a seed productive of further growth. The element of will in that seed of faith will grow until maturing into the irrepressible desire for liberation (muñcitu-kamyataa-ñaña) which is one of the advanced stages of Insight.

The element of initial understanding in true faith will grow into penetrative wisdom that will finally transform the assurance of faith into the inner certitude conferred by realization. Taking refuge by way of thoughtless recital of the formula is a degradation of that venerable ancient practice. It deprives it of its true significance and of its efficacy. "Going for refuge" should be the expression of a genuine inner urge, in the same way as, in ordinary life; one may be urged by the awareness of a great danger to seek without delay the refuge of a place of safety. When taking refuge, one should always keep in mind the implications of this act, as outlined above.

This will be, at the same time, a beneficial training in right mindfulness. One should always ask oneself how the presently undertaken act of going for refuge could be translated into terms of will and understanding. Seeing that the house of our life is ablaze, it will not do merely to worship the safety and freedom that beckons outside, without making an actual move to reach it. The first step in that direction of safety and freedom is taking refuge in the right way, i.e., as a conscious act of determination, understanding, and devotion.

In the commentarial passage translated above, a precious document of ancient Buddhist practice is preserved, showing the thoughtful and discriminating way in which the devotees of old took refuge in the Triple Gem. Four different formulas are mentioned, given in what seems to be a descending order beginning from the highest form, the complete self-surrender, and ending with the lowest, the homage by prostration. It is greatly to be regretted that the information we can derive from the commentarial passage in which these formulas are embedded, is rather scanty.

Many questions that come to mind are left unanswered, as for instance: Have these four formulas been used instead of the traditional one, or in addition to it? By whom and on which occasions have the three lower kinds been used? Have they been administered to the devotees in a similar fashion as it is done today in the case of the traditional formula? Those three lower kinds, namely, have in common the last sentence, being a call to witness: "Thus may you know me!" (Iti mamdharetha). Does the plural form used in the Pali sentence, refer to an assembly of devotees that witnessed the act or, what seems to be more probable, was it merely a respectful way of addressing the spiritual teacher (guru) or the monk who may have administered that special formula of refuge, perhaps as a kind of initiation? In any case, the concluding "call to witness" gives to those utterances a strong emphasis and the solemnity of a vow distinguishing it from the general formula of refuge.

The commencing words ("From today onward...") too are stressing that character of a definite and personal dedication, as distinguished from an impersonal ritual. They mark the day of the first utterance as initiating a new period in the life of the devotee. Both the beginning and the end of these three modes of refuge are an echo of the earliest formulas of conversion, reported in the Suttas: "I take refuge in the Lord Gotama, the doctrine and the community of monks! May the Lord Gotama know of me as an upasaka! From today, as long as life lasts, I have taken refuge!" (...upaasakam mam bhavam Gotama dharetu, ajjatagge panupetam saranam gatam.)

The commentator explains the three lower modes of refuge merely by reference to scriptural passages which do not enlighten us very much. From this fact we may conclude that in Buddhaghosa's time and environment those modes of refuge were no longer a living practice, but only a reminiscence for which explanation had to be sought in literature. Otherwise the commentator would certainly have dealt with them in greater detail and probably illustrated them by some stories which he is usually so fond of relating. The fourth and highest mode of refuge has obviously been more familiar at that time and was probably still in use by those undergoing strenuous meditative practice, as evinced by a passage in the Visuddhimagga which we shall quote later.

But despite the lack of authentic information, the following facts become sufficiently clear from the formulae themselves. The ancient devotees who coined and used them have been obviously very sensitive as to the deep significance of that act of going for refuge, perceiving it as a most momentous step, decisive for life. By making a fourfold distinction demanding a definite and personal choice, they made provision for saving the performance of that act from becoming a soulless habit.

The ancient devotees knew well the implication of that apparently simple act and have been aware of the sacred responsibilities resulting from it. They knew that taking refuge is actually consummated only by a complete self-surrender to the Triple Gem, without any reservations. In the lesser modes of the act, there is still something of the presumed self that is kept back; it is a going for refuge with reservations. Nevertheless these lesser modes too are definite steps towards the Highest, and should be consciously cultivated. As in any harmonious mental development, here too the higher level will not exclude the lower one but absorb it into its wider compass. In trying to obtain a clearer picture of those four modes, we shall therefore start not from the highest, but from the lowest level.

Homage is the mental attitude, and the bodily and verbal expression, of reverence, resulting from the recognition and appreciation of something higher than oneself. It breaks through the first and hardest shell of pride and self-contented ignorance that knows of nothing better than one's own petty self. When encountering something higher, animals and undeveloped men - "primitive" or "civilized" - will mostly react by distrust, fear, flight, attack, resentment, hostility, persecution, etc., because they can view that higher form of life only as something different, alien, and therefore suspect. It is the sign of a truly developed human mind that it meets the higher with due respect, with admiration, and the wish to emulate. Recognition and appreciation of something higher is therefore the preliminary condition of spiritual growth, and true respect, resulting from it, forms the basis of moral education too. Kungfutse names respect (li) as the first of qualities of "human heartedness" (jen).

Therefore in man's relation to the Highest, i.e., the Triple Gem, true homage comes first. As a way of taking refuge, homage is the spontaneous expression of the deep emotion felt when becoming aware of the existence and significance of the supreme refuge. It is the emotional reaction in gratitude, veneration, and joy when feeling the full weight of the tremendous fact that there is actually a refuge from this universe of suffering. Therefore the commentator's illustration of this mode of taking refuge is not the habitual act of worship by confirmed devotees, but the highly emotional conversion of an aged Brahman who, deeply stirred, prostrates himself before the Exalted One, embracing and kissing his feet.

Homage represents the emotional side of taking refuge, being its aspect as a conscious act of faith. Through its single-heartedness and humility, the act of doing homage by body, speech, and mind, prepares the disciple emotionally for complete self-surrender. It is an indispensable step to it, but, being deficient with regard to understanding and determination, it requires the supplementation by the following two stages.

While homage is still a distant and one-sided relationship to the Supreme, the devotee still being in the outer court of the sanctuary, the acceptance of discipleship is a direct approach to it. Through the process of learning, a mutual relationship is established, or we may even say, a gradual and partial identification of teacher, teaching, and pupil takes place. Here the mind of the disciple goes for refuge to supreme wisdom, and becomes gradually permeated by it.

Through respect and humility acquired by true homage, the disciple has earned for himself the right of entry into the sanctuary of wisdom. Only if approached in that attitude of respect and humility, the guru, the spiritual teacher of the East, will impart his knowledge, as these qualities are the first indication that the disciple is ready to receive. If refuge is taken in the sense of discipleship, life becomes a constant act of learning, i.e., of adapting the mind to the standards set by the Buddha, the Dhamma, and the Sangha. It is the character of the wise man that he is always willing and anxious to learn.

The acceptance of discipleship represents the rational side of taking refuge which is here a conscious act of understanding. It supplies the full and satisfying reasons for the act of homage, and adds, in that way, to the strength and loyalty of devotion. But man is not always devotee or learner. There remains much in life that cannot be mastered easily by faith and understanding alone. It requires a strong will and determination, as well as the skill of long experience, to change the course of the manifold habitual activities of life into the direction of the refuge. This task of making the refuge gradually the center of one's life is performed by the third mode of taking refuge.

In accepting the Triple Gem as his guiding ideal the disciple pledges himself to subordinate gradually all the essential activities of his life to the ideals embodied in the Triple Gem. He vows to give all his strength to the task of impressing this sacred threefold seals upon his personal life and upon his environment too, as far as he is able to overcome its resistance. The threefold refuge in its aspect as the guiding ideal or as the determining factor of life calls for complete dedication in the sphere of external activities.

This, at least, is what we tentatively suggest as the meaning of this third variety of taking refuge, called in Pali tapparayanata. In putting forward this suggestion, we followed the trend of our previous thoughts about the three constituents of Buddhist faith, and we took up, in addition, the hint given in the illustrative passage quoted by the commentary in this connection. The canonical text to which that quotation belongs, tells of two deities who, after their conversion, vow to go through the world as "divine missionaries" of the Dhamma. This example given by the commentary may be taken as representative of the general task of establishing the sovereignty if the Triple Gem in one's own and in others' hearts.

But this dedication to the service of the Triple Gem is still not the highest form of taking refuge to which the disciple should aspire. Still there exists in the disciple's mind a difference between the noble objective and the person working for it. The delusive ego has been retained: it rejoices at the success of the work, and grieves when it fails. In a subtle way, the work, instead of the Triple Gem, becomes the refuge. If identification of self and work is not complete the ego, as it were, hides in the work, and evades the call for full surrender to the true refuge. Progress beyond this step is possible only if the service of the guiding ideal is done in a highly detached way, without looking for any reward.

This detached attitude towards work will be one of the many fruits of complete self-surrender to the Triple Gem. This last and highest form of refuge taken by the worldling is without reservations. If true understanding has told us before that nothing can be gained in samsara (which is the objective aspect of self), then, consequently, nothing can be lost by the surrender of self (which is the subjective aspect of samsara). Though this surrender of self is only the surrender of a delusion, it is a very hard sacrifice as all of us know. But if ever we wish to be free of the bonds of samsara, this self-surrender has to be done at one time or another, and therefore it may as well be done today as tomorrow.

The highest prize is won only by the highest stake, by the sacrifice of that illusive self that has assumed so much power that it requires the highest effort to break it. In taking refuge by way of self-surrender the disciple, in his modest way, will follow the example of the Exalted One who, in his last great struggle before Enlightenment, addressed his inner opponent, personified as Mara, with the following words: "It's Muñja grass I wear! Shame be on life! Fain in the battle I would die, than to live further as a vanquished one!" The Muñja grass was the crest of those ancient Indian warriors who entered battle with the vow "to do or to die." It should be the symbol of the spiritual warrior too. If any reservations, regrets, or reluctances are retained there will be merely a half-hearted attempt, instead of a single-minded effort which alone can bring victory.

If the grave step of taking refuge by self-surrender has once been taken, a feeling of lightness, unconcernedness, and fearlessness will enter the heart of the disciple. A self that has been renounced cannot and need not have any fear for a life that has been surrendered and that is kept now only on trust for the definite purpose of being used for the highest realization. Therefore in the early days of the Dhamma, those of determined mind who entered the "field of spiritual action" (kammatthana) - i.e., who took up a subject of meditation to be cultivated up to sainthood - they used to start their work by taking the vow of self-surrender, as advised by the following passage of the Visuddhi Magga:

"Having approached his noble friend (i.e., the meditation master) the meditator should first surrender himself to the Buddha, the Exalted One, or to his teacher, and then, possessed of a strong desire and a high resolve, he should ask for the subject of meditation. His surrender of self to the Buddha should be as follows:

'This personal existence of mine, I offer to thee, O Exalted One!' (Imaahm bhagavaa attabhaavam tumhaakam pariccajaami). Because one who, without such a surrender of self, lives in lonely places will be unable to stand firm against fearful objects that approach him. He might return to the village, and, associated with lay folk, might take up a search that is wrongful and come to distress. But to one who has surrendered his self, no fear arises even when approached by fearful objects. Only gladness will arise in him when he reflects: 'Hast thou not, O wise man, on that earlier day surrendered thyself to the Buddha?'

"And again, in surrendering himself to his teacher, he should say, 'This personal existence of mine, reverend sir, I offer to thee!' Because, without such a surrender of self, he will be unruly, stubborn, unwilling to accept advice; he will go about at his own will without asking the teacher's leave. And the teacher will favor him neither with material nor with spiritual help and will not instruct him in difficult books. Not receiving this twofold favor, he will become unvirtuous, or return to lay life."

This way of taking refuge by self-surrender is, of course, still far from the complete abolishing of egotism and self-delusion, but it is a powerful means to that end. It may mark the transition from the worldly or mundane refuge to which it still belongs, to the supramundane refuge at which it aims. The formulae of self-surrender, as given in our commentarial text, differ even in their external form from the three lesser modes of refuge in so far as they lack that concluding "call to witness," characteristic of the other modes. From that we may conclude that this gravest of all vows was to be taken in the secrecy of one's heart, as befits the sacredness of that resolve.

Here the presence of a witness as a kind of moral support for keeping the vow should no more be required; such a requirement would only prove that it is premature to take this step. Any publicity to it would only detract from the supreme dignity of the vow, and would render its observance more difficult by making the disciple too self-conscious or even proud. Needless to say, a deliberate parading of the vow would defeat its very purpose by reinstating the self that was to be surrendered. The longer formula of self-surrender enlarging upon the short sentence in the Visuddhimagga has been rendered here into a Western language for the first time; and also its Pali original seems to have evoked little attention in our day. If we reproduce that formula here, in the hope that it will be received with the reverence due to that precious document of ancient devotion hallowed by the efforts and achievements of those may have practiced in accordance with it.

We add the earnest request not to make use of it lightly for the purpose of ordinary devotion and not to take the vow rashly on the spur of a moment's enthusiasm. This solemn pledge should be taken only after having tested one's strength and perseverance for a long time, by minor observances and renunciations. We should beware of making those highest things of the spirit cheap and common by approaching them in too facile a way; by talking too glibly about them, or by taking them into our hands and dropping them again when interest fades or our feeble fingers get tired. Therefore, if we are not sure of our strength, we should not take upon ourselves the severe demands of Self-surrender, but take our refuge by way of those lesser modes. For these will likewise prove to be powerful helpers to high spiritual achievements.

In making an actual and intelligent use of that fourfold devotional Road of the Ancients, we shall preserve the most popular religious practice in the Buddhist world, the going for refuge, from becoming stale and ineffective. We shall be able to turn it into a strong, life-giving current of devotion that will carry us one day to the Isle of Final Peace, to Nibbana, where the refugee and refuge are merged into one.

THE FIRST REFUGE: THE BUDDHA

The first step in entering the Buddhist path is going for refuge to the Triple Gem, and the first of the three gems that we approach as refuge is the Buddha, the Enlightened One. Because the act of going for refuge to the Buddha marks the beginning of a new chapter in our life, it is worth our while to repeatedly pause and reflect upon the significance of this momentous step. Too often we are prone to take our first steps for granted. Yet it is only if we review these steps from time to time in a deepening awareness of their implications that we can be sure the following steps we take will bring us closer to our desired destination. The going for refuge to the Buddha is not a single action which occurs only once and is then completed with absolute finality.

It is, or should be, a continually evolving process which matures in tandem with our practice and understanding of the Dhamma. To go for refuge does not imply that at the outset we already possess a clear grasp of the dangers that make a refuge necessary or of the goal toward which we aspire. Comprehension of these matters grows gradually over time. But to the extent that we have actually gone for refuge with sincere intent, we should make an earnest effort to sharpen and deepen our understanding of the objects to which we have turned as the basis for our deliverance. In going for refuge to the Buddha it is most essential at the outset to clarify our conception of what a Buddha is and how he functions as a refuge. If such clarification is lacking, our sense of refuge can easily become tainted by erroneous views.

We may ascribe to the Buddha a status he never claimed for himself, as when we regard him as the incarnation of a god, as the emanation of the Absolute, or as a personal savior. On the other hand, we may detract from the exalted status to which the Buddha is properly entitled, as when we regard him simply as a benevolent sage, as an unusually astute Asiatic philosopher, or as a genius of meditative technology. A correct view of the Buddha's nature would see him in terms of the title he assigned to himself: as a Fully Self-Enlightened One (samma sambuddha). He is self-enlightened because he has awakened to the essential truths of existence entirely on his own, without a teacher or guide. He is fully enlightened because he has comprehended these truths completely, in all their ramifications and implications.

And as a Buddha he has not only fathomed these truths himself, but has also taught them to the world so that others may awaken from the long sleep of ignorance and attain the fruits of liberation. Taking refuge in the Buddha is an act anchored in a particular historical individual: the recluse Gotama, the scion of the Sakyan clan, who lived and taught in the Ganges valley in the fifth century B.C. When we take refuge in the Buddha, we rely upon this historical individual and the body of instruction that stems from him. It is important to stress this point in view of the fashionable notion that taking refuge in the Buddha means that we take refuge in "the Buddha-mind within ourselves" or in "the universal principle of enlightenment."

Such ideas, allowed to go unchecked, can lead to the belief that anything we contrive in the flights of our imagination can qualify as true Dhamma. To the contrary, the Buddhist tradition insists that when we go for refuge to the Buddha, we place ourselves under the guidance of one who is distinctly different from ourselves, one who has scaled heights that we have barely begun to glimpse. But when we rely upon the recluse Gotama as our refuge, we do not apprehend him merely as a particular individual, a wise and sensible sage.

We apprehend him rather as a Buddha. It is his Buddhahood - his possession of the full range of excellent qualities that come with perfect enlightenment - that makes the recluse Gotama a refuge. In any cosmic epoch, a Buddha is that being that first breaks through the dark mass of ignorance encompassing the world and rediscovers the lost path to Nibbana, the cessation of suffering. He is the pioneer, the trailblazer, who discovers the path and proclaims the path so that others, by following his tracks, may extinguish their ignorance, arrive at true wisdom, and break the fetters that tie them to the round of repeated birth and death.

For the refuge in the Buddha to be genuine, it must be accompanied by a commitment to the Buddha as an incomparable teacher, as unexcelled and unsurpassed. Strictly speaking, the historical Buddha is not unique since there have been earlier Fully Enlightened Ones who have arisen in past epochs and there will be others who will arise in future epochs as well. But in any one world system it is impossible for a second Buddha to arise while the teaching of another Buddha is still extant, and thus in terms of human history we are justified in regarding the Buddha as a unique teacher, unequalled by any other spiritual teacher known to humanity.

It is this readiness to recognize the Buddha as "the unsurpassed trainer of persons to be tamed, the teacher of gods and humans" that is the hallmark of an authentic act of taking refuge in the Buddha.

The Buddha serves as a refuge by teaching the Dhamma. The actual and final refuge, embedded within the Dhamma as refuge, is Nibbana, "the deathless element free from clinging, the sorrowless state that is void of stain" (Itiv. 51). The Dhamma as refuge comprises the final goal, the path that leads to that goal, and the body of teachings that explain the practice of the path. The Buddha as refuge has no capacity to grant us liberation by an act of will. He proclaims the path to be traveled and the principles to be understood. The actual work of walking the path is then left to us, his disciples.

The proper response to the Buddha as refuge is trust and confidence. Trust is required because the doctrine taught by the Buddha runs counter to our innate understanding of us and our natural orientation toward the world. To accept this teaching thus tends to arouse an inner resistance, even to provoke a rebellion against the changes it requires us to make in the way we lead our lives. But when we place trust in the Buddha we open ourselves to his guidance. By going to him for refuge we show that we are prepared to recognize that our inherent tendencies to self-affirmation and grasping are in truth the cause of our suffering. And we are ready to accept his counsel that to become free from suffering, these tendencies must be controlled and eliminated.

Confidence in the Buddha as our refuge is initially awakened when we contemplate his sublime virtues and his excellent teaching. It grows through our undertaking of the training. At first our confidence in the Buddha may be hesitant, punctured by doubts and perplexity. But as we apply ourselves to the practice of his path, we find that our defilements gradually lessen, that wholesome qualities increase, and with this comes a growing sense of freedom, peace and joy. This experience confirms our initial trust, disposing us to advance a few steps further. When at last we see the truth of the

Dhamma for ourselves, the refuge in the Buddha becomes inviolable. Confidence then becomes conviction, the conviction that the Blessed One is "the speaker, the proclaimer, the bringer of the good, the giver of the Deathless, the lord of the Dhamma, the Tathagata."

THE SECOND REFUGE: THE DHAMMA

The second source of refuge is the Dharma as external means taking the Dharma as your path. You recognize that the way you can attain the state of Buddhahood, the way that you can follow the example of the Buddha, is by practicing the Dharma which was taught by the Buddha. So when you go for refuge to the Dharma as external, you are going for refuge to the methods of the path by which one frees oneself from mental affliction.

This is called Sat-dharma, or genuine Dharma. Dharma as symbol traditionally consists of books, letters, speech and thought. Traditionally, we have the Buddhist Canon, and then we have all kinds of other expressions of the speech aspect of Dharma, such as audio-dharma, video-dharma, hard copy dharma, CD Rom dharma, and one last thing, floppy dharma. (Rinpoche laughs) No, floppy disk dharma. I have lots of those.

You trust these as a path which means that you trust that the practice of Dharma will increase your compassion. The Dharma is a necessary vehicle or method on our path to enlightenment. It is like a toolbox to liberation. In order to fix something like a screw, whether you have to loosen the screw or tighten the screw, we need a screwdriver and various different tools. In a similar way, we need the Dharma, as the external teachings of the Buddha, in order to work with our problems, to fix them and find our solutions.

Traditionally, the Dharma is said to be like a ship. If you want to cross a lake or an ocean, you have to rely on a ship. Dharma is like the boat or ship which helps you across. It helps you travel faster and not sink in this ocean of samsara. So Dharma is the path, Dharma is the words and wisdom of

Buddha, and Dharma is simply one's own understanding, experience, and realization. Our relationship with the Dharma is like our relationship with a boat or ship. After we have crossed the water, there's no need for us to carry the boat or ship. Therefore, after we have crossed the ocean of samsara, then we no more take refuge in Dharma. We have realized the nature of Dharma. We have become Dharma. We are inseparable with Dharma. That is the second refuge in the outer sense.

THE THIRD REFUGE: THE SANGHA

The third source of refuge is the jewel of the Sangha or the community of noble, realized beings. This refuge also has the same external, symbolic aspect. The external aspect of the Sangha to which one goes for refuge is first and foremost the retinue of Lord Buddha endowed with wisdom. From the Mahayana point of view, this refers to Bodhisattvas like Arya Manjushri, Avalokitesvara and so forth, and from the Hinayana point of view, the great arhats such as Mahakasyapa, Ananda, and Shariputra. The Sangha of ordinary individuals refers to all of those who have transmitted the Dharma, the teachings of Buddha, as an unbroken succession or lineage through time up to the present day through their wisdom and compassion. We take refuge in the noble Sangha as our companion on the path.

Without their help, there's no way we can really enter the path. Historically, they are the people who received teachings from the Buddha and then collected all of these teachings and put them on paper. Without the noble Sangha, we would not have any words, any literature of Dharma right now. Therefore, we take refuge in the Sangha as our companion because, without them, we wouldn't have the physical body of the Dharma. Without them, we wouldn't have the genuine lineage of the Dharma, the realization of the Dharma, or the path of the Dharma. From the time of the noble Sangha up until now, the time of our present great masters, we have the continuity of the teachings, continuity of the enlightened path.

4

Sanctions of Moral Conduct
The Precepts

THE FIVE PRECEPTS

The Five Precepts (Pali: pañca-sîla; Sanskrit: pañca-[+la) constitute the basic Buddhist code of ethics, undertaken by lay followers of the Buddha Gautama in the Theravada and Mahayana traditions. The Five Precepts are commitments to abstain from killing, stealing, sexual misconduct, lying and intoxication. Undertaking the five precepts is part of both lay Buddhist initiation and regular lay Buddhist devotional practices. They are not formulated as imperatives, but as training rules that laypeople undertake voluntarily to facilitate practice.

PALI TEXTS

Pali literature provides the scriptures and commentary for traditional Theravadin practice.

PALI TRAINING RULES

The following are the five precepts (pañca-sikkhâpada) or five virtues (pañca-sîla) rendered in English and Pali:

1. I undertake the training rule to abstain from taking life. 'PâGâtipâtâ veramani sikkhâpadam samâdiyâmi.'
2. I undertake the training rule to abstain from taking what is not given. 'Adinnâdânâ veramani sikkhâpadam samâdiyâmi.'

3. I undertake the training rule to abstain from sexual misconduct today. 'Kâmesu micchâcâra veramani sikkhâpadam samâdiyâmi.'
4. I undertake the training rule to abstain from false speech. 'Musâvâda veramani sikkhâpadam samâdiyâmi.'
5. I undertake the training rule to abstain from drinks [and drugs] that cause heedlessness. 'Surâ-meraya-majja-pamâdammhânâ veramani sikkhâpadam samâdiyâmi.'

ELABORATION

In the Pali Canon, the following typifies elaborations that frequently accompany these identified training rules:

There is the case where a certain person, abandoning the taking of life, abstains from the taking of life. He dwells with his rod laid down, his knife laid down, scrupulous, merciful, and compassionate for the welfare of all living beings. Abandoning the taking of what is not given, he abstains from taking what is not given. He does not take, in the manner of a thief, things in a village or a wilderness that belong to others and have not been given by them. Abandoning sensual misconduct, he abstains from sensual misconduct. He does not get sexually involved with those who are protected by their mothers, their fathers, their brothers, their sisters, their relatives, or their Dhamma; those with husbands, those who entail punishments, or even those crowned with flowers by another man.

There is the case where a certain person, abandoning false speech, abstains from false speech. When he has been called to a town meeting, a group meeting, a gathering of his relatives, his guild, or of the royalty, if he is asked as a witness, "Come & tell, good man, what you know": If he doesn't know, he says, "I don't know." If he does know, he says, "I know." If he hasn't seen, he says, "I haven't seen." If he has seen, he says, "I have seen." Thus he doesn't consciously tell a lie for his own sake, for the sake of another, or for the sake of any reward. Abandoning false speech, he abstains from false speech. According to the Buddha, killing, stealing, sexual misconduct and lying are never skillful.

MOTIVATION

In the Abhisandha Sutta (AN 8.39), the Buddha said that undertaking the precepts is a gift to oneself and others:

In [undertaking the five precepts], he gives freedom from danger, freedom from animosity, freedom from oppression to limitless numbers of beings. In giving freedom from danger, freedom from animosity, freedom from oppression to limitless numbers of beings, he gains a share in limitless freedom from danger, freedom from animosity, and freedom from oppression.

This is the... gift, the... great gift - original, long-standing, traditional, ancient, unadulterated, unadulterated from the beginning - that is not open to suspicion, will never be open to suspicion, and is unfaulted by knowledgeable contemplatives and priests.

This is the... reward of merit, reward of skillfulness, nourishment of happiness, celestial, resulting in happiness, leading to heaven, leading to what is desirable, pleasurable, & appealing; to welfare & to happiness. In the next canonical discourse, the Buddha described the minimal negative consequences of breaking the precepts.

TRADITIONAL PRAXIS

The laity undertakes to follow these training rules at the same time as they become Buddhists. In Mahayana countries a lay practitioner who has undertaken the precepts is called an upasaka. In Theravada countries any lay follower is in theory called an upasaka (or upasika, feminine), though in practice everyone is expected to take the precepts anyway. Additionally, traditional Theravada lay devotional practice (puja) includes the daily taking of refuge in the Triple Gem and undertaking to observe the five precepts.

INTERPRETATIONS

The precepts are considered differently in a Mahayana context to that of the Theravada school of thought. According to Theravada, killing, stealing, sexual misconduct and lying are never skillful. Some schools of Mahayana Buddhism disagree with this. For example, they might condone the act of murdering a mass murderer. Contemporary Theravada scholar-monk Bhikkhu Bodhi takes that position that, while non-dualistic philosophies assert that enlightened beings are beyond the proscriptions of conventional moral codes, in the Pali Canon the Buddha's teaching maintains a clear distinction between moral and immoral behaviors, a distinction that applies as much to the arahant as to the layperson.

THE EIGHT PRECEPTS

As a part of the tradition, in Buddhist countries, the laity wishing to cultivate a pure mind does observe the eight precepts. Usually, these people follow the five basic precepts at all times. These five precepts are already extremely beneficial on their own. They are so natural that many people being inclined to a virtuous living; do observe them without being aware of it. Being zealous in improving their conduct and being detached from things deemed to be relatively futile, some people have had the habit to observe the eight precepts for an approximate one day period weekly.

Buddhist countries following the lunar calendar, it will be about new moon, full moon and half-moon days. Admittedly, anyone can undertake the observance of the eight precepts any day whatsoever (for example each Sunday) or even better, at any time, as it is the case regarding nuns. Usually, yogís who come to do a retreat in a meditation centre are requested to follow these eight precepts. What are these eight precepts meant for? Their usefulness is so obvious: To purify one's mind. To train it to be more aware of things, to be less indulging into bad or useless things.

All this to enable us to perform good actions. In fact, those are not so much good things that ought to be done, but essentially evil ones to be avoided. Indeed, it is not that much about good things that ought to be performed, but essentially bad things that ought to be avoided. The simple fact to refrain from committing these evil actions is a good action indeed. Good actions mainly lie in doing from time to time little efforts that lie in avoiding bad habits, bad reflexes, and bad things. The secret of a clean country doesn't lie that much in not cleaning it but in not making it dirty instead. Well, what does apply to a country also does in the same way concerning our own mind.

Doesn't Buddha teach us that the greatest, the best, the most beneficial, the most honorable among all good actions is the mental noticing? In other parlance, the minimum effort that lies in observing the perceptions as they do appear. This direct insight into reality, obtained by this mere sustenance of attention, in Pali, Buddha calls it "vipassaná". At a time during which we turn our attention to a physical or mental object, which action do we perform? None! We just give to the mind the opportunity to know, to see directly, face to face, the object that appears. That is to say what is being perceived: What is heard, what is touched, what is seen, what is smelt, what is tasted and what is thought? On the other hand, at this moment, during which we simply turn our attention on the sensation that is being perceived, we do abstain. We do abstain from everything as a whole. We do nothing else except abstaining.

Thus, the eight precepts lie in abstaining from all things that can be detrimental, unhealthy, and painful to us or our environment. All these precepts are extremely easy to observe as all we have to do is not to do. All the difficulties only lie in the fact to avoid doing detrimental things, to prevent one from indulging into bad habits, that, according to the various classes of individuals, can be less strongly ingrained in these latter. Besides, all the job of mental purification mainly rests on this point, whether for monks or lay men. It is a training aimed at avoiding bad habits. Each of these precepts corresponds to a very specific spirit. They are reference points that are of precious help in our daily lives. They do enable us to develop a right and virtuous conduct.

To observe these precepts, once the refuge into Buddha, Dhamma and saμgha has been taken, what are sufficient lies in reciting them one by one, in Pali. So that each one could understand what he does recite, here is a summarized meaning of these precepts:

All these precepts are ending by the words: "veramaši sikkhápadaμ samádhiyámi." Which could be translated by: "I will refrain from doing this, so as to develop a good conduct."

THE EIGHT PRECEPTS

1st Precept

"Pánátipátá veramani sikkhápadam samádhiyámi." "I will abstain from being harmful to living beings."

That is to say: I will not kill; I will cause injuries to other beings, whatever and whoever they are. Not even to the mosquitoes that bite me.

2nd Precept

"Adinnádáná veramani sikkhápadam samádhiyámi." "I will abstain from stealing."

That is to say: I will not appropriate others' property; I will not take possession of that which has not been given to me. I will not even take the metro, even for a station distance, without paying.

3rd Precept

Abrahmacariyá veramani sikkhápadam samádhiyámi." "I will abstain from all sexual practices."

That is to say: No copulation, no masturbation. I will even avoid indulging in petting.

Beware: When we only deal with the five precepts, the 3rd thus becomes:

"Kamesu miccacara veramani sikkhápadam samádhiyámi." "I will abstain from all inconvenient sexual practices."

That is to say: I will not commit adultery; I will not indulge into any illegal sexual relationship, neither through prostitution, etc.

4th Precept

"Musávádá veramani sikkhápadam samádhiyámi." "I will abstain from uttering lies."

That is to say: I will not lie; I will be honest while facing all situations. Whatever one might think and whatever the intention underlying it might be, a lie will always bear a negative result. I will even avoid speaking ill of anyone, swearing and indulging in vain talks. (this precept is perhaps the most difficult to observe).

5th Precept

"Surámeraya majjapamáda háná veramani sikkhápadam samádhiyámi." "I will refrain from intoxicating drinks and drugs which lead to carelessness."

That is to say: I will not consume any substance likely to intoxicate my body or my mind, such as alcohol, drugs, tobacco, etc. I will even avoid drinking too much coffee. Due to health reasons, the medicines are authorised.

6th Precept

"Vikálabhojaná veramani sikkhápadam samádhiyámi." "I will abstain from eating after noon time."

That is to say: I will never consume any solid foods after the solar noon (which, in Paris, befalls around 1:30 P.M. during the summer time and around 12:30 A.M. during the winter time) and this, until the following dawn. During this period, I will no even drink milk, which is considered as a solid food, as it is very nourishing. In case of severe hunger or a great lack of energy, honey, molasses, liquid sugars, oil and butter are also authorised.

7th Precept

"Nacca gíta vádita visukadassaná málá gandha vilepana dhárana mandana vibhúsanattháná veramani sikkhápadam samádhiyámi." "I will abstain from listening or playing music, songs, wearing flowers, jewellery and other ornaments."

That is to say: I will not listen to some music, I will not watch any show whatsoever, I will not watch films, neither go for entertainment, nor read any fashion magazines, play games, etc. I will not wear perfumes; I will not arrange my body for an aesthetic purpose (make up, fashion clothes, sophisticated hair dressing, jewellery, etc.) I will even avoid dressing myself in an attractive way. For health reasons, skin care products are authorised.

8th Precept

"Mala-gandha-vilepana-dharana-mandana-vibhusanatthana veramani sikkhapadam samadiyami."

I undertake the precept to refrain from wearing garlands, using perfumes, and beautifying the body with cosmetics.

9th Precept

"Uccásayana mahásayana veramani sikkhápadam samádhiyámi." "I will refrain from lining or seating on high and luxurious places."

That is to say: I will not sit or lie down on places located higher than those of the noble ones (bhikkhu, bhikkhuní or sámašera, kings, etc.) or in places reserved for these beings.

THE 10TH PRECEPTS

The Flower Garland (Avatamsaka) Sutra says:

1. Bodhisattvas that abide in this stage are by nature completely free from the killing of living things. They are without brutality or the need to use weapons, and they do not harbor feelings of anger and resentment. With humility, they are full of good will and forgiveness towards living beings, only wishing for their welfare. These Bodhisattvas do not even have thoughts of distressing living beings, much less think of turning these thoughts into doing actual harm.

2. By nature Bodhisattvas do not steal. They are always perfectly satisfied with their own possessions and, with kindness and good will towards others they do not encroach upon their belongings. If they think about the possessions of others, they never have a thought of taking them. They would never even think of taking a single blade of grass that was not given to them, much less any other possession.
3. By nature Bodhisattvas do not commit acts of sexual immorality. They are satisfied with their own spouses and do not seek those of others. They do not bear any thoughts of desire or lust for others' spouses or lovers, much less act on these thoughts or have sexual relations with them.
4. By nature Bodhisattvas do not speak falsely. They speak the truth, saying what so is and what is appropriate to the occasion. Even in their dreams they do not desire to use words to deceive or cover up the truth, much less actually do so consciously.
5. By nature Bodhisattvas do not have a double tongue. They do not wish to sow dissension among living beings, or to distress or harm them in any way. They do not accuse others to put them down, nor do they speak behind their back. They do not try to break up those who are together and they do not try to increase the rift between those that are divided. They do not rejoice or take pleasure in divisiveness, and do not use speech that will cause it, whether it is true or not.
6. By nature Bodhisattvas do not have a hateful mouth. This is speech that is poisonous and injurious, coarse and rude, hurtful to others, speech that makes others angry and hateful, and speech that is openly or covertly mean, cheap and low, unpleasant to hear, angry and hateful, like a fire burning the mind, tied up in resentment, hot and distressful, impossible to care for or like, and capable of harming themselves and others. Having completely forsaken this speech and freed themselves from it, they always speak with words that are comforting and kind, soft and gentle, pleasing and nice to hear. They give joy

to those that hear them and skillfully reach people's heart. Their speech is graceful and refined, authoritative, loved and enjoyed by all people, and makes the body and mind rejoice.

7. By nature Bodhisattvas do not have dissembling speech that is silken and flowery. Their speech of is always intentional and judicious, appropriate to the occasion, truthful, meaningful, logical and reasonable, carefully considered, thoughtful and well measured. Even when telling a joke, Bodhisattvas are always intentional and judicious, and they are never prattling nonsense.
8. By nature Bodhisattvas are without greedy desire for the wealth or belongings of others. They do not seek or wish for it.
9. By nature Bodhisattvas are free from anger and hatred. For living beings they always inspire a mind of kindness and desire to benefit, and they offer empathy, joy, friendship, and acceptance. They are ever free of anger, resentment, malice and the heat of distress. They are always considerate and act with benevolence, kindness and the desire to care for and be of benefit to others.
10. And, being free of false views, Bodhisattvas abide in the True Path of Enlightenment. Not practicing in divination, fortune-telling or the making of evil hexes, their views are straight and true, and without deception or flattery. Their resolute faith is in the Buddha, the Dharma and the Sangha.

Bodhisattva Mahasattvas unceasingly keep and embrace the tenfold path of good karmic deeds like this and make this thought:

"No living beings fall into the destiny of hell without the making of the ten karmic deeds that are not good, and therefore I must cultivate the true practice for myself and encourage others to cultivate the true practice as well."

Why is this so? This is because it is impossible to make others cultivate it if one does is unable to cultivate it oneself.

These Bodhisattva Mahasattvas further make these thoughts:

- The paths of the ten karmic deeds that are not good cause the spiritual realms of hell, brutality and hunger.
- The paths of the ten good karmic deeds cause the spiritual realms of personality and heaven, up to the crown of existence (the Akanishta Heaven, the highest of the 25 states of existence in the threefold realm of Life & Death).
- This path of the higher grade of ten good karmic deeds is further cultivated with the wisdom of spiritual learning. But in being narrow-minded, fearing the threefold realm, being deficient in compassion and only understanding after hearing from others, one attains the vehicle of the spiritual disciple (Sravaka).
- This path of the higher grade of ten good karmic deeds is further cultivated and purified so that one awakens oneself without the teachings of others. Being inadequate in the skillfulness of ways and means but very deeply understanding the causality of spirituality (the Dharma) one attains the vehicle that is the Solitary Awakening (Pratyekabuddha).
- This path of the higher grade of ten good karmic deeds is further cultivated and purified so that the one is broadminded and limitless, full of compassion and empathy, skillful in the management of ways and means, inspired by great vows, and not forsaking living beings. One seeks the great wisdom of the Buddhas, the Bodhisattva stages of purity and healing, and the pure cultivation of all the perfections (Paramitas). One attains the broad and great practice of the Bodhisattva.
- With the supreme path of the highest ten good karmic deeds there are all kinds of purity up to the realization of the ten spiritual powers, the four kinds of fearlessness and the attainment of all of the enlightenment of the Buddhas. Therefore I now practice these ten good deeds and make all purified and fulfilled

The Bodhisattvas must study the ways and means like this. These Bodhisattva Mahasattvas also make this thought:

"The path of these ten bad deeds causes hell in the worst case, brutality in the middle case, and hunger in the least case."

1. The sin of killing living beings can make living beings fall into hell, brutality and hunger. In human life, two kinds of retribution are attained: #1 A short life #2 Much sickness
2. The sin of stealing can make living beings fall into the three evil roads. In human life, two kinds of retribution are attained: #1 Poverty #2 Shared possession of property and lack of ownership
3. The sin of sexual immorality can make living beings fall into the three evil roads. In human life, two kinds of retribution are attained: #1 An unfaithful spouse #2 Untrusting followers
4. The sin of false speech can make living beings fall into the three evil roads. In human life, two kinds of retribution are attained: #1 Much slander #2 The deception of others
5. The sin of a double tongue can make living beings fall into the three evil roads. In human life, two kinds of retribution are attained: #1 Disobedience & loss of followers #2 Intimates and family that are corrupt and evil
6. The sin of an evil mouth can make living beings fall into the three evil roads. In human life, two kinds of retribution are attained: #1 Always hearing evil voices #2 Arguments
7. The sin of silken, flowery speech can make living beings fall into the three evil roads. In human life, two kinds of retribution are attained: #1 Lack of people's trust #2 Lack of clarity in one's speech
8. The sin of greedy desire can make living beings fall into the three evil roads. In human life, two kinds of retribution are attained: #1 Dissatisfaction #2 Endless ambition

9. The sin of anger and hatred can make living beings fall into the three evil roads. In human life, two kinds of retribution are attained: #1 Always suffering other people's merits and defects #2 Constantly suffering other people's distress and malice
10. The sin of false views can make living beings fall into the three evil roads. In human life, two kinds of retribution are attained: #1 Living in schools of false views #2 Minds that are crooked and deceitful

The ten bad karmic deeds are able to produce this great host of limitless and boundless sufferings. Therefore Bodhisattvas make this thought. "I must completely forsake the path of the ten bad deeds and abide with peace and contentment in the garden of the Dharma by means of the ten good deeds. With oneself abiding in its midst, one encourages others to do so as well.

5

The Underlying Ideals of the Moralities

RELATING THE PRECEPTS TO THE REFUGES

The Buddha's teaching can be thought of as a kind of building with its own distinct foundation, stories, stairs, and roof. Like any other building the teaching also has a door, and in order to enter it we have to enter through this door. The door of entrance to the teaching of the Buddha is the going for refuge to the Triple Gem - that is, to the Buddha as the fully enlightened teacher, to the Dhamma as the truth taught by him, and to the Sangha as the community of his noble disciples. From ancient times to the present the going for refuge has functioned as the entranceway to the dispensation of the Buddha, giving admission to the rest of the teaching from its lowermost story to its top. All those who embrace the Buddha's teaching do so by passing through the door of taking refuge, while those already committed regularly reaffirm their conviction by making the same threefold profession:

Buddham saranam gacchami (I go for refuge to the Buddha);

Dhammam saranam gacchami (I go for refuge to the Dhamma);

Sangham saranam gacchami (I go for refuge to the Sangha).

As slight and commonplace as this step might seem, especially in comparison with the lofty achievements lying beyond, its importance should never be underestimated, as it is this act which imparts direction and forward momentum to the entire practice of the Buddhist path. Since the going for refuge plays such a crucial role it is vital that the act be properly understood both in its own nature and in its implications for future development along the path. To open up the process of going for refuge to the eye of inner understanding, we here present an examination of the process in terms of its most significant aspects. These will be dealt with under the following eight headings: the reasons for taking refuge; the existence of a refuge; the identification of the refuge objects; the act of going for refuge; the function of going for refuge, methods of going for refuge; the corruption and breach of the going for refuge; and the similes for the refuges.

THE REASONS FOR TAKING REFUGE

When it is said that the practice of the Buddha's teaching starts with taking refuge, this immediately raises an important question. The question is: "What need do we have for a refuge?" A refuge is a person, place, or thing giving protection from harm and danger. So when we begin a practice by going for refuge, this implies that the practice is intended to protect us from harm and danger.

Our original question as to the need for a refuge can thus be translated into another question: "What is the harm and danger from which we need to be protected?" If we look at our lives in review we may not see ourselves exposed to any imminent personal danger. Our jobs may be steady, our health good, our families well-provided for, our resources adequate, and all this we may think gives us sufficient reason for considering ourselves secure. In such a case the going for refuge becomes entirely superfluous.

To understand the need for a refuge we must learn to see our position as it really is; that is, to see it accurately and against its total background. From the Buddhist perspective the human situation is similar to an iceberg: a small fraction of its mass appears above the surface, the vast substratum remains below, hidden out of view. Owing to the limits of our mental vision our insight fails to penetrate beneath the surface crust, to see our situation in its underlying depths. But there is no need to speak of what we cannot see; even what is immediately visible to us we rarely perceive with accuracy. The Buddha teaches that cognition is subservient to wish. In subtle ways concealed from ourselves our desires condition our perceptions, twisting them to fit into the mould they themselves want to impose. Thus our minds work by way of selection and exclusion. We take note of those things agreeable to our pre-conceptions; we blot out or distort those that threaten to throw them into disarray.

From the standpoint of a deeper, more comprehensive understanding the sense of security we ordinarily enjoy comes to view as a false security sustained by unawareness and the mind's capacity for subterfuge. Our position appears impregnable only because of the limitations and distortions of our outlook. The real way to safety, however, lies through correct insight, not through wishful thinking. To reach beyond fear and danger we must sharpen and widen our vision. We have to pierce through the deceptions that lull us into a comfortable complacency, to take a straight look down into the depths of our existence, without turning away uneasily or running after distractions.

When we do so, it becomes increasingly clear that we move across a narrow footpath at the edge of a perilous abyss. In the words of the Buddha we are like a traveler passing through a thick forest bordered by a swamp and precipice; like a man swept away by a stream seeking safety by clutching at reeds; like a sailor crossing a turbulent ocean; or like a man pursued by venomous snakes and murderous enemies.

The dangers to which we are exposed may not always be immediately evident to us. Very often they are subtle, camouflaged, difficult to detect. But though we may not see them straightaway the plain fact remains that they are there all the same. If we wish to get free from them we must first make the effort to recognize them for what they are. This, however, calls for courage and determination. On the basis of the Buddha's teaching the dangers that make the quest for a refuge necessary can be grouped into three general classes: (1) the dangers pertaining to the present life; (2) those pertaining to future lives; and (3) those pertaining to the general course of existence. Each of these in turn involves two aspects: (A) and objective aspect which is a particular feature of the world; and (B) a subjective aspect which is a corresponding feature of our mental constitution. We will now consider each of these in turn.

THE DANGERS PERTAINING TO THE PRESENT LIFE

Objective Aspect

The most obvious danger confronting us is the sheer fragility of our physical body and its material supports. From the moment we are born we are subject to disease, accident, and injury. Nature troubles us with disasters such as earthquakes and floods, societal existence with crime, exploitation, repression, and the threat of war. Events on the political, social, and economic fronts rarely pass very long without erupting into crisis. Attempts at reform and revolution always wind up repeating the same old story of stagnation, violence, and consequent disillusionment. Even in times of relative tranquillity the order of our lives is never quite perfect. Something or other always seems to be getting out of focus. Snags and predicaments follow each other endlessly.

Even though we might be fortunate enough to escape the serious adversities there is one we cannot avoid. This is death. We are bound to die, and with all our wealth, expertise, and power we still stand helpless before our inevitable mortality. Death weighs upon us from the time we are born. Every moment brings us closer to the inescapable. As we are drawn along, feeling secure in the midst of our comforts, we are like a man walking across a frozen lake, believing himself safe while the ice is cracking underfoot. The dangers hanging over us are made even more problematic by their common feature of uncertainty. We have no knowledge when they will take place.

If we knew calamity is going to hit we could at least prepare in advance to resign ourselves stoically. But we do not enjoy even this much edge on the future. Because we lack the benefit of foreknowledge our hopes stand up straight, moment after moment, coupled with a vague presentiment that any second, in a flash, they can suddenly be dashed to pieces. Our health might be stricken down by illness, our business fail, our friends turn against us, and our loved ones die - we do not know. We can have no guarantee that these reversals will not come upon us. Even death is only certain in that we can be sure it will strike and exactly when it will strike still remains uncertain.

Subjective Aspect

The adversities just sketched are objective features built into the world's constitution. On the one side there are calamity, crisis, and predicament, on the other the radical uncertainty pervading them. The subjective aspect of the danger pertaining to the present life consists in our negative response to this twofold liability. The element of uncertainty tends to provoke in us a persistent disquietude running beneath our surface self-assurance. At a deep interior level we sense the instability of our reliances, their transience and vulnerability to change and this awareness produces a nagging apprehensiveness which rises at times to a pitch of anxiety. The source of our disquietude we may not always be able to pinpoint, but it remains lurking in the undercurrent of the mind - an unlocalized fear that our familiar supports will suddenly be stripped away, leaving us without our usual frame of reference.

This anxiety is sufficient disturbance in itself. Yet often our fears are confirmed. The course of events follows a pattern of its own independently of our will, and the two do not necessarily coincide. The world thrown up illness, loss, and death strike when the time is ripe. When the course of events clashes with our will the outcome is pain and dissatisfaction. If the conflict is small we become angry, upset, depressed, or annoyed; if it is great we undergo anguish, grief, or despair. In either case a fundamental disharmony emerges from the cleavage between desire and the world, and the result, for us, is suffering.

The suffering that arises is not significant solely in itself. It has a symptomatic value, pointing to some more deeply grounded malady underlying it. This malady lies in our attitude towards the world. We operate out of a mental frame built up of expectations, projections, and demands. We expect reality to conform to our wishes, to submit to our mandates, to confirm our preconceptions, but this it refuses to do. When it refuses we meet pain and disappointment, born from the conflict between expectation and actuality.

To escape this suffering one of the two must change, our will or the world. Since we cannot alter the nature of the world to make it harmonize with our will, the only alternative is to change ourselves, by putting away attachment and aversion towards the world. We have to relinquish our clinging, to stop hankering and grasping, to learn to view the fluctuation of events with a detached equanimity free from the swing of elation and dejection.

The mind of equanimity, poised beyond the play of worldly opposites, is the highest safety and security, but to gain this equanimity we stand in need of guidance. The guidance available cannot protect us from objective adversity. It can only safeguard us from the dangers of a negative response - from anxiety, sorrow, frustration, and despair. This is the only protection possible, and because it grants us this essential protection such guidance can be considered a genuine refuge. This is the first reason for going for refuge - the need for protection from negative reactions to the dangers besetting us here and now.

THE DANGERS PERTAINING TO FUTURE LIVES

Objective aspect

Our liability to harm and danger does not end with death. From the perspective of the Buddha's teaching the event of death is the prelude to a new birth and thus the potential passageway to still further suffering. The Buddha teaches that all living beings bound by ignorance and craving are subject to rebirth so long as the basic drive to go on existing stands intact, the individualized current of existence continues on after death inheriting the impressions and dispositions accumulated in the previous life. There is no soul to transmigrate from one life to the next, but there is an ongoing stream of consciousness which springs up following death in a new form appropriate to its own dominant tendencies. Rebirth, according to Buddhism, can take place in any of six realms of becoming. The lowest of the six is the hells, regions of severe pain and torment where evil actions receive their due expiation.

Then comes the animal kingdom where suffering prevails and brute force is the ruling power. Next is the realm of "hungry ghosts" (petavisaya), shadowy beings afflicted with strong desires they can never satisfy. Above them is the human world, with its familiar balance of happiness and suffering, virtue and evil. Then is the world of the demi-gods (asuras), titanic beings obsessed by jealousy and ambition and at the top stands the heavenly worlds inhabited by the devas or gods. The first three realms of rebirth - the hells, the animal kingdom, and the realm of ghosts - together with the asuras, are called the "evil destinations" (duggati) or "plane of misery" (apayabhumi). They receive these names because of the preponderance of suffering found in them. The human world and the heavenly worlds are called, in contrast, the "happy destinations" (sugati) since they contain a preponderance of happiness.

Rebirth in the evil destinations is considered especially unfortunate not only because of the intrinsic suffering they involve, but for another reason as well. Rebirth there is calamitous because escape from the evil destinations is extremely difficult. A fortunate rebirth depends on the performance of meritorious actions, but the beings in the evil destinations find little opportunity to acquire merit; thence the suffering in these realms tends to perpetuate itself in a circle very difficult to break. The Buddha says that if a yoke with a single hole was floating at random on the sea, and a blind turtle living in the sea were to surface once every hundred years - the likelihood of the turtle pushing his neck through the hole in the yoke would be greater than that of a being in the evil destinations regaining human status. For these two reasons - because of their inherent misery and because of the difficulty of escaping from them - rebirth in the evil destinations is a grave danger pertaining to the future life, from which we need protection.

Subjective Aspect

Protection from a fall into the plane of misery cannot be obtained from others. It can only be obtained by avoiding the causes leading to an unfortunate rebirth. The cause for rebirth into any specific plane of existence lays in our kamma, that is, our willed actions and volitions. Kamma divides into two classes, the wholesome and the unwholesome. The former are actions motivated by detachment, kindness, and understanding, the latter actions motivated by greed, hatred and delusion. These two classes of kamma generate rebirth into the two general planes of existence: wholesome kamma brings rebirth into the happy destinations, unwholesome kamma brings rebirth into the evil destinations. We cannot obliterate the evil destinations themselves; they will continue on as long as the world itself endures. To avoid rebirth in these realms we can only keep watch over ourselves, by controlling our actions so that they do not spill over into the unwholesome courses leading to a plunge into the plane of misery. But to avoid generating unwholesome kamma we need help and that for two principal reasons.

First, we need help because the avenues of action open to us are so varied and numerous that we often do not know which way to turn. Some actions are obviously wholesome or unwholesome, but others are difficult to evaluate, throwing us into perplexity when we run up against them. To choose correctly we require guidance - the clear indications of one who knows the ethical value of all actions and the pathways leading to the different realms of being. The second reason we need help is because, even when we can discriminate right from wrong, we are often driven to pursue the wrong against our better judgment. Our actions do not always follow the counsel of our dispassionate decisions. They are often impulsive, driven by irrational urges we cannot master or control. By yielding to these drives we work our own harm even while helplessly watching ourselves do so.

We have to gain mastery over our mind, to bring our capacity for action under the control of our sense of higher wisdom. But this is a task which requires discipline. To learn the right course of discipline we need the instructions of one who understands the subtle workings of the mind and can teach us how to conquer the obsessions which drive us into unhealthy self-destructive patterns of behavior. Because these instructions and the one who gives them help protect us from future harm and suffering, they can be considered a genuine refuge. This is the second reason for going for refuge - the need to achieve mastery over our capacity for action so as to avoid falling into the evil destinations in future lives.

THE DANGERS PERTAINING TO THE GENERAL COURSE OF EXISTENCE

Objective Aspect

The perils to which we are exposed are immensely greater than those just discussed. Beyond the evident adversities and misfortunes of the present life and the risk of a fall into the plane of misery, there is a more fundamental and comprehensive danger running through the entire course of worldly existence. This is the intrinsic unsatisfactoriness of samsara- the cycle of becoming, the round of birth, aging and death, which has been revolving through beginningless time. Rebirth does not take place only once, leading to an eternity in the life to come.

The life-process repeats itself over and over, the whole pattern spelling itself out again and total with each new turn: each single birth issues in decay and death, each single death gives way to a new birth. Rebirth can be fortunate or miserable, but wherever it occurs no halt is made to the revolution of the wheel. The law of impermanence imposes its decree upon the entire domain of sentient life; whatever arises must eventually cease. Even the heavens provide no outlet; life there also ends when the kamma that brought a heavenly birth is exhausted, to be followed by a re-arising in some other plane, perhaps in the miserable abodes.

Because of this pervasive transience all forms of conditioned existence appear to the eye of wisdom as essentially dukkha, unsatisfactory or suffering. None of our supports and reliances is exempt from the necessity to change and pass away. Thence what we resort to for comfort and enjoyment is in reality a concealed form of suffering; what we rely on for security is itself exposed to danger; what we turn to for protection itself needs to be protected. Nothing that we want to hold to can be held onto forever, without perishing: "It is crumbling away, it is crumbling away, and therefore it is called 'the world'."

Youth issues in old age, health in sickness, life in death. All union ends in separation, and in the pain that accompanies separation. But to understand the situation in its full depth and gravity we must multiply it by infinity. From time without beginning we have been transmigrating through the round of existence, encountering the same experiences again and again with vertiginous frequency: birth, aging, sickness and death, separation and loss, failure and frustration.

Repeatedly we have made the plunge into the plane of misery; times beyond counting we have been animal, ghost, and denizen of hell. Over and over we have experienced suffering, violence, grief, despair. The Buddha declares that the amount of tears and blood we have shed in the course of our samsaric wandering is greater than the waters in the ocean; the bones we have left behind could form a heap higher than the Himalaya Mountains. We have met this suffering countless times in the past, and as long as the causes of our cycling in samsara are not cut off we risk meeting more of the same in the course of our future wandering.

Subjective aspect

To escape from these dangers there is only one way of release: to turn away from all forms of existence, even the most sublime. But for the turning away to be effective we must cut off the causes that hold us in bondage to the round. The basic causes that sustain our wandering in samsara lie within us. We roam from life to life, the Buddha teaches, because we are driven by a profound insatiable urge for the perpetuation of our being. This urge the Buddha calls bhava-tanha, the craving for existence. While craving for existence remains operative, even if only latently, death itself is no barrier to the continuation of the life-process. Craving will bridge the vacuum created by death, generating a new form of existence determined by the previously accumulated storage of kamma. Thus craving and existence sustain each other in succession.

Craving brings forth a new existence; the new existence gives the ground for craving to resume its search for gratification. Underlying this vicious nexus which links together craving and repeated existence is a still more primordial factor called "ignorance" (avijja). Ignorance is a basic unawareness of the true nature of things, a beginningless state of spiritual unknowing. The unawareness operates in two distinct ways: on one side it obscures correct cognition; on the other it creates a net of cognitive and perceptual distortions. Owing to ignorance we see beauty in things that are really repulsive, permanence in the impermanent, pleasure in the unpleasurable, and selfhood in selfless, transient, unsubstantial phenomena.

These delusions sustain the forward drive of craving. Like a donkey chasing a carrot suspended from a cart, dangling before its face, we rush headlong after the appearances of beauty, permanence, pleasure and selfhood, only to find ourselves still empty-handed, more tightly entangled in the samsaric round. To be freed from this futile and profitless pattern it is necessary to eradicate the craving that keeps it in motion, not merely temporarily but permanently and completely. To eradicate craving the ignorance which supports it has to be dislodged, for as long as ignorance is allowed to weave its illusions the ground is present for craving to revive. The antidote to ignorance is wisdom (pañña). Wisdom is the penetrating knowledge which tears aside the veils of ignorance in order to "see things as they really are." It is not mere conceptual knowledge, but an experience that must be generated in ourselves; it has to be made direct, immediate and personal.

To arouse this wisdom we need instruction, help, and guidance - someone who will teach us what we must understand and see for ourselves, and the methods by which we can arouse the liberating wisdom that will cut the cords binding us to repeated becoming. Since those who give this guidance, and the instructions themselves, provide protection from the perils of transmigration they can be considered a genuine refuge. This is the third reason for going for refuge - the need for deliverance from the pervasive unsatisfactoriness of Samsara.

THE EXISTENCE OF A REFUGE

To realize that the human situation impels the search for a refuge is a necessary condition for taking refuge, but is not in itself a sufficient condition. To go for refuge we must also become convinced that an effective refuge actually exists. But before we can decide on the existence of a refuge we first have to determine for ourselves exactly what a refuge is. The dictionary defines "refuge" as a shelter or protection from danger and distress, a person or place giving such protection, and an expedient used to obtain such protection. These tallies with the explanation of the Pali word sarana, meaning "refuge", which has come down in the Pali commentaries. The commentaries gloss the word sarana with another word meaning "to crush" (himsati), explaining that "when people have gone for refuge, then by that very going for refuge it crushes, dispels, removes, and stops their fear, anguish, suffering, risk of unhappy rebirth and defilement."

These explanations suggest two essential qualifications of a refuge. (1) First, a refuge must be itself beyond danger and distress. A person or thing subject to danger is not secure in it, and thus cannot give security to others. Only what is beyond fear and danger can be confidently relied upon for protection. (2) Second, the purported refuge must be accessible to us. A state beyond fear and danger that is inaccessible is irrelevant to our concerns and thus cannot function as a refuge. In order for something to serve as a refuge it must be approachable, capable of giving protection from danger. From this abstract determination of the qualifications of a refuge we can return to the concrete question at hand. Does there exist a refuge able to give protection from the three types of dangers delineated above: from anxiety, frustration, sorrow and distress in the present life; from the risk of an unhappy destination after death; and from continued transmigration in samsara?

The task of working out an answer to this question has to be approached cautiously. We must recognize at once that an objectively verifiable, publicly demonstrable answer cannot be given. The existence of a refuge, or the specification of a particular refuge, cannot be proven logically in an irrefutable manner binding on all. The most that can be done is to adduce cogent grounds for believing that certain persons or objects possess the qualifications of a refuge. The rest depends upon faith, a confidence born out of trust, at least until that initial assent is transformed into knowledge by means of direct experience. But even then the verification remains inward and personal, a matter of subjective appropriation rather than of logical proof or objective demonstration.

From the Buddhist perspective there are three refuges which together make available complete protection from danger and distress. These three are the Buddha, the Dhamma, and the Sangha. The three are not separate refuges each sufficient in itself; rather they are interrelated members of a single effective refuge which divides into three by way of a distinction in the characteristics and functions of its members. Why such a distinction is necessary becomes clear if we consider the order in which the three are presented. The Buddha comes first because he is a person. Since we are persons we naturally look to another person for guidance, inspiration, and direction. When it is ultimate deliverance that is at stake, what we look for in the first place is a person who has himself reached complete freedom from danger and can lead us to the same state of safety.

This is the Buddha, the enlightened one, who comes first in the triad for the reason that he is the person who discovers, achieves, and proclaims the state of refuge. In the second place we need that state of refuge itself, the state beyond fear and danger; then we need a path leading to this goal; and also we need a set of instructions guiding us along the path. This is the Dhamma, which as we will see has this threefold denotation. Then, in the third place, we need persons who began like ourselves - as ordinary people troubled by afflictions - and by following the way taught by the guide reached the state of safety beyond fear and danger. This is the Sangha, the community of spiritual persons who have entered the path, realized the goal, and can now teach the path to others.

Within the triad each member works in harmony with the other two to make the means of deliverance available and effective. The Buddha serves as the indicator of refuge. He is not a savior who can bestow salvation through the agency of his person. Salvation or deliverance depends upon us, upon our own vigor and dedication in the practice of the teaching. The Buddha is primarily a teacher, an expounder of the path, who points out the way we ourselves must tread with our own energy and intelligence. The Dhamma is the actual refuge. As the goal of the teaching the Dhamma is the state of security free from danger; as the path it is the means for arriving at the goal; and as the verbal teaching it is the body of instructions describing the way to practice the path. But to make effective use of the means at our disposal we need the help of others who are familiar with the path. Those who know the path make up the Sangha, the helpers in finding refuge, the union of spiritual friends who can lead us to our own attainment of the path.

This triadic structure of the three refuges can be understood with the aid of a simple analogy. If we are ill and want to get well we need a doctor to diagnose our illness and prescribe a remedy; we need medicine to cure our illness; and we need attendants to look after our requirements. The doctor and attendants cannot cure us. The most they can do for us is to give us the right medicine and make sure that we take it. The medicine is the actual remedy which restores our health. Similarly, when seeking relief from suffering and distress, we rely on the Buddha as the physician who can find out the cause of our illness and show us the way to get well; we rely on the Dhamma as the medicine which cures our afflictions; and we rely on the Sangha as the attendants who will help us take the medicine. To get well we have to take the medicine. We can't just sit back and expect the doctor to cure us all by himself. In the same way, to find deliverance from suffering, we have to practice the Dhamma, for the Dhamma is the actual refuge which leads to the state of deliverance.

IDENTIFICATION OF THE OBJECTS OF REFUGE

The fruitfulness of the act of taking refuge is proportional to the depth and precision with which we understand the nature of the refuge-objects. Therefore these objects have to be identified with precision and correctly understood. Each refuge-object has a double layer of signification, one concrete and mundane, the other intangible and supramundane. The two are not entirely distinct, but intermesh in such a way that the former acts as a vehicle for the latter. An examination of each refuge in turn will make clear what their twofold signification is and how they interfuse.

The Buddha

The Buddha as refuge can be considered first. On one level the word "Buddha" refers to a particular figure - the man Siddhattha Gotama who lived in India in the fifth century B.C. When we take refuge in the Buddha, we take refuge in this person, for he is the teacher of the Dhamma and the historical founder of Buddhism. However, in going to him for refuge, we do not take refuge in him merely in his concrete particularity. We rely upon him as the Buddha, the enlightened one, and this has a significance transcending the limits of what can be given by empirical, historical fact. What enables the Buddha to function as a refuge is his actualization of a supramundane attainment. This attainment is the state of Buddhahood or perfect enlightenment, a state which has been realized by other persons in the past and will be realized again in the future.

Those who realize this state are Buddhas. When we take refuge in the Buddha we rely upon him as a refuge because he embodies this attainment in himself. It is his Buddhahood that makes the Buddha a refuge. But what is the Buddhahood of the Buddha? In brief the Buddhahood of the Buddha is the sum total of the qualities possessed by that person named Gotama which make him a Buddha. These qualities can be summed up as the abandonment of all defects and the acquisition of all virtues. The defects abandoned are the defilements (kilesa) together with their residual impressions (vasana). The defilements are afflictive mental forces which cause inner corruption and disturbance and motivate unwholesome actions. Their principle members are greed, hatred, and delusion; from these all the secondary defilements derive.

In the Buddha these defilements have been abandoned totally, completely, and finally. They are abandoned totally in that all defilements have been destroyed with none remaining. They are abandoned completely in that each one has been destroyed at the root, without residue. And they have been abandoned finally in that they can never arise again in the future. The virtues acquired by the Buddha are very numerous, but two stand out as paramount: great wisdom (mahapañña) and great compassion (maha-karuna). The great wisdom of the Buddha has two aspects - extensiveness of range and profundity of view. Through the extensive range of his wisdom the Buddha understands the totality of existent phenomena; through his profundity of view he understands the precise mode of existence of each phenomenon.

The Buddha's wisdom does not abide in passive contemplation but issues in great compassion. Through his great compassion the Buddha comes forth to work for the welfare of others. He takes up the burden of toiling for the good of sentient beings, actively and fearlessly, in order to lead them to deliverance from suffering. When we go for refuge to the Buddha we resort to him as the supreme embodiment of purity, wisdom and compassion, the peerless teacher who can guide us to safety out of the perilous ocean of samsara.

The Dhamma

The Dhamma too involves a double reference. At the elementary level the word "Dhamma" signifies the teaching of the Buddha - the conceptually formulated, verbally expressed set of doctrines taught by or deriving from the historical figure Gotama. This teaching, called "the transmission" (agama), is contained in the Tipitaka or three collections of scripture and in the commentaries and expository works which explain them. The three collections are the Vinayapitaka, the Suttapitaka, and the Abhi Dhammapitaka. The Vinayapitaka collects together all the monastic rules and regulations detailing the discipline for Buddhist monks and nuns. The Suttapitaka contains the discourses of the Buddha expounding his doctrine and the practice of his path.

The Abhi Dhammapitaka presents an exposition of the sphere of actuality from the standpoint of a precise philosophical understanding which analyzes actuality into its fundamental constituting elements and shows how these elements lock together through a network of conditional relations. The verbally transmitted Dhamma contained in the scriptures and commentaries serves as the conduit to a deeper level of meaning communicated through its words and expressions. This is the Dhamma of actual achievement (adhigama), which comprises the path (magga) and the goal (attha). The goal is the final end of the teaching, Nibbana, the complete cessation of suffering, the unconditioned state outside and beyond the round of impermanent phenomena making up samsara.

This goal is to be reached by a specific path, a course of practice bringing its attainment, namely the noble eightfold path - right views, right intentions, right speech, right action, right livelihood, right effort, right mindfulness, and right concentration. The path divides into two stages, a mundane path and a supramundane path. The mundane path is the course of application developed when its factors are cultivated in daily life and in periods of intensified practice. The supramundane path is a state of wisdom-consciousness that arises when all the requisite conditions for realization are fully matured, usually at the peak of intensified practice. This path actually represents a state in the experience of enlightenment, having the dual function of realizing Nibbana and eradicating defilements.

The supramundane path comes only in momentary breakthroughs which, when they occur, effect radical transformations in the structure of the mind. These breakthroughs are four in number, called the four paths. The four divide according to their ability to cut the successively subtler "fetters" causing to samsara. The first path, the initial breakthrough to enlightenment, is the path of stream-entry (sotapattimagga), which eradicates the fetters of ego-affirming views, doubt, and clinging to rites and wrong observances. The second, called the path of the once-returner (sakadagamimagga), does not cut off any fetters but weakens their underlying roots. The third, the path of the non-returner (anagamimagga), eliminates the fetters of sensual desire and ill-will.

And the forth, the path of arahatship (arahattamagga), eradicates the five remaining fetters - desire for existence in the spheres of fine material and immaterial being, conceit, restlessness, and ignorance. Each path-moment is followed immediately by several moments of another supramundane experience called fruition (phala), which comes in four stages corresponding to the four paths. Fruition marks the enjoyment of the freedom from defilement effected by the preceding path-moment. It is the state of release or experiential freedom which comes when the fetters are broken. Earlier it was said that the Dhamma is the actual refuge. In the light of the distinctions just drawn this statement can now be made more precise. The verbal teaching is essentially a map, a body of instructions and guidelines. Since we have to rely on these instructions to realize the goal, the teaching counts as an actual refuge, but it is so in a derivative way. Thus we can call it an actual but indirect refuge.

The mundane path is direct, since it must be practiced, but because it serves principally as preparation for the supramundane path its function is purely provisional; thus it is an actual and direct but provisional refuge. The supramundane path apprehends Nibbana, and once attained leads irreversibly to the goal; thence it may be called an actual, direct, and superior refuge. However, even the supramundane path is a conditioned phenomenon sharing the characteristic of impermanence common to all conditioned phenomena. Moreover, as a means to an end, it possesses instrumental value only, not intrinsic value. Thus its status as a refuge is not ultimate. Ultimate status as a refuge belongs exclusively to the goal, to the unconditioned state of Nibbana, which therefore among all three refuges can alone be considered the refuge which is actual, direct, superior, and ultimate. It is the final resort, the island of peace, the sanctuary offering permanent shelter from the fears and dangers of samsaric becoming.

The Sangha

At the conventional or mundane level the Sangha signifies the Bhikkhu-Sangha, the order of monks. The Sangha here is an institutional body governed by formally promulgated regulations. Its doors of membership are open to any candidate meeting the required standards. All that is needed to enter the Sangha is to undergo ordination according to the procedure laid down in the Vinaya, the system of monastic discipline. Despite its formal character, the order of monks fulfills an indispensable role in the preservation and perpetuation of the Buddha's dispensation. In an unbroken lineage extending back over twenty-five hundred years, the monastic order has served as the custodian of the Dhamma.

The mode of life it makes possible permits it to exercise this function. The Buddha's dispensation, as we suggested, possesses a twofold character; it is a path of practice leading to liberation from suffering, and also a distinctive set of doctrines embedded in scriptures expounding the details of this path. The Sangha bears the responsibility for maintaining both aspects of the dispensation. Its members assume the burden of continuing the tradition of practice with the aim of showing that the goal can be realized and deliverance attained. They also take up the task of preserving the doctrines, seeing to it that the scriptures are taught and transmitted to posterity free from distortion and misinterpretation. For these reasons the institutional Sangha is extremely vital to the perpetuation of the Buddha's teaching. However, the order of monks is not itself the Sangha which takes the position of the third refuge.

The Sangha which serves as refuge is not an institutional body but an unchartered spiritual community comprising all those who have achieved penetration of the innermost meaning of the Buddha's teaching. The Sangha-refuge is the ariyan Sangha, the noble community, made up exclusively of ariyans, person of superior spiritual stature. Its membership is not bound together by formal ecclesiastical ties but by the invisible bond of a common inward realization. The one requirement for admission is the attainment of this realization, which in itself is sufficient to grant entrance. Though the way of life laid down for the monastic order, with its emphasis on renunciation and meditation, is most conducive to attaining the state of an ariyan, the monastic Sangha and the ariyan Sangha are not coextensive. Their makeup can differ, and that for two reasons: first, because many monks - the vast majority in fact - are still worldlings (puthujjana) and thence cannot function as a refuge; and second, because the ariyan Sangha can also include laymen. Membership in the ariyan Sangha depends solely on spiritual achievement and not on formal ordination. Anyone - layman or monk - who penetrates the Buddha's teaching by direct vision gains admission through that very attainment itself.

The membership of the ariyan Sangha comprises eight types of persons, which unite into four pairs. The first pair consists of the person standing on the path of stream-entry and the stream-enterer, who has entered the way to deliverance and will attain the goal in a maximum of seven lives; the second pair of the person standing on the path of the once-returner and the once-returner, who will return to the human world only one more time before reaching the goal; the third pair of the person standing on the path of the non-returner and the non-returner, who will not come back to the human world again but will take rebirth in a pure heavenly world where he will reach the final goal; and the fourth pair of the person standing on the path of arahatship and the arahant, who has expelled all defilements and cut off the ten fetters causing bondage to samsara.

The eight persons can be divided in another way into two general classes. One consists of those who, by penetrating the teaching, have entered the supramundane path to liberation but still must practice further to arrive at the goal. These include the first seven types of ariyan persons, who are collectively called "trainees" or "learners" (sekha) because they are still in the process of training. The second class comprises the arahats, who have completed the practice and fully actualized the goal. These are called "beyond training" (asekha) because they have no further training left to undertake. Both the learners and the arahats have directly understood the essential import of the Buddha's teaching for them. The teaching has taken root in them, and to the extent that any work remains to be done they no longer depend on others to bring it to its consummation. By virtue of this inner mastery these individuals possess the qualifications needed to guide others towards the goal. Hence the ariyan Sangha, the community of noble persons, can function as a refuge.

THE ACT OF GOING FOR REFUGE

To enter the door to the teaching of the Buddha it is not enough merely to know the reference of the refuge-objects. The door of entrance to the teaching is the going for refuge to the Buddha, the Dhamma, and the Sangha. To understand what the refuge-objects mean is one thing, to go to them for refuge is another, and it is the going for refuge alone that constitutes the actual entrance to the dispensation. But what is the going for refuge? At first glance it would seem to be the formal commitment to the Triple Gem expressed by reciting the formula of refuge, for it is this act which marks the embracing of the Buddha's teaching. Such an understanding, however, would be superficial. The treatises make it clear that the true going for refuge involves much more than the reciting of a pre-established formula. They indicate that beneath the verbal profession of taking refuge there runs concurrently another process that is essentially inward and spiritual. This other process is the mental commitment to the taking of refuge.

The going for refuge, as defined by the commentaries, is in reality an occasion of consciousness: "It is an act of consciousness devoid of defilements, (motivated) by confidence in and reverence for (the Triple Gem), taking (the Triple Gem) as the supreme resort." That the act is said to be "devoid of defilements" stresses the need for sincerity of aim. Refuge is not pure if undertaken with defiled motivation - out of desire for recognition, pride, or fear of blame. The only valid motivation for taking refuge is confidence and reverence directed towards the Triple Gem. The act of consciousness motivated by confidence and reverence occurs "taking the Triple Gem as the supreme resort," (parayana). That the Triple Gem is taken as the "supreme resort" means that it is perceived as the sole source of deliverance.

By turning to the threefold refuge as supreme resort, the going for refuge becomes an act of opening and self-surrender. We drop our defenses before the objects of refuge and open ourselves to their capacity to help. We surrender our ego, our claim to self-sufficiency, and reach out to the refuge-objects in the trust that they can guide us to release from our confusion, turmoil, and pain. Like any other act of consciousness the going for refuge is a complex process made up of many factors. These factors can be classified by way of three basic faculties: intelligence, volition, and emotion. To bring the act of going for refuge into clearer focus we will take the mental process behind the outer act, divide it by way of these faculties, and see how each contributes to its total character. That is, we will examine the going for refuge as an act of intelligence, will, and emotion.

Before doing this, however, one word of caution is necessary. Any particular phenomenon represents far more than is immediately visible even to a deeply probing inspection. A seed, for example, has a much greater significance than the grain of organic matter that meets the eye. On one side it collects into itself the entire history of the trees that went into its making; on the other it points beyond to the many potential trees locked up in its hull. Similarly the act of consciousness involved in taking refuge represents the crystallization of a vast network of forces extending backwards, forwards, and outwards in all directions. It simultaneously stands for the many lines of experience converging upon its formation out of the dim recesses of the past, and the potential for future lines of development barely adumbrated in its own immediate content. This applies equally to the act of taking refuge as a whole and to each of its constituting factors: both the whole and its parts must be seen as momentary concretions with a vast history, past and future, hidden from our sight.

Therefore what emerges out of an analytical scrutiny of the refuge-act should be understood to be only a fraction of what the act implies by way of background and future evolution. Turning to the act of taking refuge itself, we find in the first place that it is an act of understanding. Though inspired by reverence and trust, it must be guided by vision, by an intelligent perceptivity which protects it from the dangers of blind emotion. The faculty of intelligence steers the act of refuge towards the actualization of its inner urge for liberation. It distinguishes the goal from the distractions, and prevents the aspirant from deviating from his quest for the goal to go in pursuit of futile ends. For this reason we find that in the formulation of the noble eightfold path right view is given first. To follow the path we must see where it leads from, where it goes, and the steps that must be taken to get from the one point to the other.

In its initial form the faculty of intelligence involved in taking refuge comprehends the basic unsatisfactoriness of existence which makes reliance on a refuge necessary. Suffering has to be seen as a pervasive feature infecting our existence at its root, which cannot be eliminated by superficial palliatives but only by a through going treatment. We must come to see further that the causes of our dissatisfaction and unrest lie within ourselves, in our clinging, craving, and delusions, and that to get free from suffering we must follow a course which extinguishes its causes. The mind also has to grasp the reliability of the refuge-objects. Absolute certainty as to the emancipating power of the teaching can only come later, with the attainment of the path, but already at the outset an intelligent conviction must be established that the refuge-objects are capable of providing help.

To this end the Buddha has to be examined by investigating the records of his life and character; his teaching searched for contradictions and irrationalities; and the Sangha approached to see if it is worthy of trust and confidence. Only if they pass these tests can they be considered dependable supports for the achievement of our ultimate aim. Intelligence comes into play not only with the initial decision to take refuge, but throughout the entire course of practice. The growth of understanding brings a deeper commitment to the refuges, and the deepening of the inner refuge facilitates the growth of understanding. The climax of this process of reciprocal development is the attainment of the supramundane path. When the path arises, penetrating the truth of the teaching, the refuge becomes irreversible, for it has been verified by direct experience.

The going for refuge is also an act of volition. It results from a voluntary decision free from coercion or outside pressures. It is a choice that must be aparappaccaya, "not compelled by others." This freely chosen act brings about a far-reaching restructuring of volition. Whereas previously the will might have been scattered among a multitude of interests and concerns, when the taking of refuge gains ascendency the will becomes ordered in a unified way determined by the new commitment. The spiritual ideal comes to the center of the inner life, expelling the less crucial concerns and relegating the others to a position subordinate to its own direction. In this way the act of refuge brings to the mind a harmonization of values, which now ascend to and converge upon the fundamental aspiration for deliverance as the guiding purpose of all activity.

The act of taking refuge also effects a deep-seated reversal in the movement of the will. Before refuge is taken the will tends to move in an outward direction, pushing for the extension of its bounds of self-identity. It seeks to gain increasing territory for the self, to widen the range of ownership, control and domination. When refuge is sought in the teaching of the Buddha the ground is laid for this pattern to be undermined and turned around. The Buddha teaches that our drive for self-expansion is the root of our bondage. It is a mode of craving, of grasping and clinging, leading headlong into frustration and despair. When this is understood the danger in egocentric seeking comes to the surface and the will turns in the opposite direction, moving towards renunciation and detachment. The objects of clinging are gradually relinquished, the sense of "I" and "mine" withdrawn from the objects to which it has attached itself. Ultimate deliverance is now seen to lie, not in the extension of the ego to the limits of infinity, but in the utter abolition of the ego-delusion at its base.

The third aspect of going for refuge is the emotional. While going for refuge requires more than emotional fervor, it also cannot come to full fruition without the inspiring upward pull of the emotions. The emotions entering into the refuge act are principally three: confidence, reverence, and love. Confidence (pasada) is a feeling of serene trust in the protective power of the refuge-objects, based on a clear understanding of their qualities and functions. Confidence gives rise to reverence (gaurava), a sense of awe, esteem, and veneration born from a growing awareness of the sublime and lofty nature of the Triple Gem. Yet this reverence does not remain cool, formal, and aloof. As we experience the transforming effect of the Dhamma on our life, reverence awakens (pema). Love adds the element of warmth and vitality to the spiritual life. It kindles the flame of devotion, coming to expression in acts of dedicated service by which we seek to extend the protective and liberative capacity of the threefold refuge to others.

THE FUNCTION OF GOING FOR REFUGE

The going for refuge is the door of entrance to the teaching of the Buddha. It functions in the context of the teaching as the entranceway to all the practices of the Buddhist discipline. To engage in the practices in their proper setting we have to enter them through the door of taking refuge, just as to go into a restaurant and have a meal we have to enter through the door. If we merely stand outside the restaurant and read the menu on the window we may come away with a thorough knowledge of the menu but not with a satisfied appetite. Similarly, by merely studying and admiring the Buddha's teaching we do not enter upon its practice. Even if we abstract certain elements of practice for our personal use without first taking refuge, our efforts cannot count as the actual practice of the Buddha's teaching. They are only practices derived from the teaching, or practices in harmony with the teaching, but so long as they are not conjoined with a mental attitude of taking refuge in the Triple Gem they have not yet become the practice of the Buddha's teaching.

To bring out the significance of going for refuge we can consider a contrast between two individuals. One meticulously observes the moral principles embedded in the five precepts (pañcasila). He does not formally undertake the precepts in the context of Buddhist ethical practice but spontaneously conforms to the standards of conduct they enjoin through his own innate sense of right and wrong; that is, he follows them as part of natural morality. We might further suppose that he practices meditation several hours a day, but does this not in the framework of the Dhamma but simply as a means to enjoy peace of mind here and now. We can further suppose that this person has met the Buddha's teaching, appreciates it and respects it, but does not feel sufficiently convinced to acknowledge its truth or find himself impelled to go for refuge.

On the other hand let us suppose there is another person whose circumstances prevent perfect observance of the precepts and who cannot find leisure for practicing meditation. But though he lacks these achievements, from the depths of his heart, with full sincerity, understanding, and dedication of purpose he has gone for refuge to the Triple Gem. Comparing these two persons we can ask whose mental attitude is of greater long-term spiritual value - that of the person who without going for refuge observes the moral principles embedded in the five precepts and practices meditation several hours a day, or that of the other person who cannot accomplish these practices but has sincerely gone for refuge to the Buddha, Dhamma, and Sangha. No clear pronouncement on this case is found in the suttas and commentaries, but enough indication is given to support an intelligent guess.

On this basis we would say that the mental attitude of the second person, who has gone for refuge with clear understanding and sincerity of heart, is of greater long-term spiritual value. The reason for such a judgment is as follows. As a result of his moral and meditative practices the first individual will enjoy peace and happiness in his present life, and will accumulate merit which will lead to a favorable rebirth in the future. However, when that merit ripens, it will become exhausted and expend its force without leading to further spiritual development. When the fortunate rebirth resulting from the merit comes to an end, it will be followed by rebirth in some other plane, as determined by stored-up kamma, and the person will continue to revolve in the cycle of existence. His virtuous undertakings do not contribute directly to the transcending of the samsaric round.

On the other hand the person, who has sincerely gone for refuge to the Triple Gem, without being capable of higher practices, still lays the foundation for spiritual progress in future lives merely by his heartfelt act of seeking refuge. Of course he has to reap the results of his kamma and cannot escape them by taking refuge, but all the same the mental act of going for refuge, if it is truly the focus of his inner life, becomes a powerful positive kamma in itself. It will function as a link tending to bring him into connection with the

Buddha's dispensation in future lives, thereby aiding his chances for further progress. And if he fails to reach deliverance within the dispensation of the present Buddha it will very likely lead him to the dispensations of future Buddhas, until he eventually reaches the goal. Since this all comes about through the germination of that mental act of going for refuge, we can understand that the taking of refuge is very essential.

The importance of going for refuge can be further gauged through a textual simile comparing faith to a seed. Since faith is the motivating force behind the act of refuge, the analogy may be transferred to the refuge-act itself. We explained earlier that the mental act of going for refuge calls into play three cardinal faculties - understanding, will, and emotion. These three faculties are already present even in that very simple, basic act of seeking refuge, contained there as seeds with the potential to develop into the flowers and fruits of the Buddhist spiritual life. The understanding that leads a man to go for refuge - the understanding of the danger and fearfulness of samsaric existence - this is the seed for the faculty of wisdom which eventually issues in direct penetration of the four noble truths. The element of volition is the seed for the will to renunciation - the driving force that impels a man to renounce his craving, enjoyments, and egoistic clingings in order to go forth in search of liberation.

It functions as well as the seed for the practice of right effort, the sixth factor of the noble eightfold path, by which we strive to abandon unwholesome impure mental states and to cultivate the wholesome and pure states. Devotion and reverence for the Triple Gem - these become the seed for the germination of "unwavering confidence" (aveccappasada), the assurance of a noble disciple whose confidence in the Buddha, Dhamma, and Sangha can never be shaken by any outside force. In this way the simple act of going for refuge serves as the threefold seed for the development of the higher faculties of right understanding, right effort, and unshakable confidence. From this example we can again understand the taking of refuge to be very essential.

THE METHODS OF GOING FOR REFUGE

The methods of going for refuge divide into two general kinds: the superior or supramundane going for refuge and the common or mundane going for refuge. The supramundane going for refuge is the going for refuge of a superior person, that is, of an ariyan disciple who has reached the supramundane path leading irreversibly to Nibbana. When such a person goes for refuge to the Triple Gem, his going for refuge is a superior refuge, unshakable and invincible. The ariyan person can never again, through the remainder of his future births (which amount to a maximum of only seven), go for refuge to any other teacher than the Buddha, to any other doctrine than the Dhamma, or to any other spiritual community than the Sangha. The Buddha says that the confidence such a disciple places in the Triple Gem cannot be shaken by anyone in the world, that it is firmly grounded and immovable.

The common way of going for refuges is the way in which ordinary persons, the vast majority below the ariyan plane, go for refuge to the Triple Gem. This can be subdivided into two types: the initial going for refuge and the recurrent going for refuge. The initial going for refuge is the act of formally going for refuge for the first time. When a person has studied the basic principles of the Buddha's teaching, undertaken some of its practices, and become convinced of its value for his life, he may want to commit himself to the teaching by making an outer profession of his conviction. Strictly speaking, as soon as there arises in his mind an act of consciousness which takes the Buddha, Dhamma, and Sangha as his guiding ideal, that person has gone for refuge to the Triple Gem and become a Buddhist lay disciple (upasaka).

However, within the Buddhist tradition it is generally considered to be insufficient under normal circumstances to rest content with merely going for refuge by an internal act of dedication. If one has sincerely become convinced of the truth of the Buddha's teaching, and wishes to follow the teaching, it is preferable, when possible, to conform to the prescribed way of going for refuge that has come down in the Buddhist tradition. This way is to receive the three refuges from a bhikkhu, a Buddhist monk who has taken full ordination and remains in good standing in the monastic Order. After one has decided to go for refuge, one should seek out a qualified monk - one's own spiritual teacher or another respected member of the Order - discuss one's intentions with him, and make arrangements for undergoing the ceremony. When the day arrives one should come to the monastery or temple bringing offerings such as candles, incense, and flowers for the shrine room and a small gift for the preceptor.

After making the offerings one should, in the presence of the preceptor, join the palms together in respectful salutation (anjali), bow down three times before the image of the Buddha, and pay respects to the Buddha, Dhamma, and Sangha, as represented by the images and symbols in the shrine. Then, kneeling in front of the shrine, one should request the bhikkhu to give the three refuges. The bhikkhu will reply: "Repeat after me" and then recite:

Buddham saranam gacchami (I go for refuge to the Buddha);

Dhammam saranam gacchami (I go for refuge to the Dhamma);

Sangham saranam gacchami (I go for refuge to the Sangha).

Dutiyampi Buddham saranam gacchami (A second time I go for refuge to the Buddha).

Dutiyampi Dhammam saranam gacchami (A second time I go for refuge to the Dhamma).

Dutiyampi Sangham saranam gacchami (A second time I go for refuge to the Sangha).

Tatiyampi Buddham saranam gacchami (A third time I go for refuge to the Buddha).

Tatiyampi Dhammam saranam gacchami (A third time I go for refuge to the Dhamma).

Tatiyampi Sangham saranam gacchami (A third time I go for refuge to the Sangha).

The candidate should repeat each line after the bhikkhu. At the end the bhikkhu will say: Saranagamanam sampunnam "The going for refuge is completed." With this one formally becomes a lay follower of the Buddha, and remains such so long as the going for refuge stands intact. But to make the going for refuge especially strong and definitive, the candidate may confirm his acceptance of the refuge by declaring to the monk: "Venerable sir, please accept me as a lay disciple gone for refuge from this day forth until the end of my life." This phrase is added to show one's resolution to hold to the three refuges as one's guiding ideal for the rest of one's life. Following the declaration of the refuges, the bhikkhu will usually administer the five precepts, the ethical observances of abstaining from taking life, stealing, sexual misconduct, false speech, and intoxicants.

By undergoing the formal ceremony of taking refuge one openly embraces the teaching of the Buddha and becomes for the first time a self-declared follower of the Master. However, going for refuge should not be an event which occurs only once in a lifetime and then is allowed to fade into the background. Going for refuge is a method of cultivation, a practice of inner development which should be undertaken regularly, repeated and renewed every day as part of one's daily routine. Just as we care for our body by washing it each morning, so we should also take care of our mind by implanting in it each day the fundamental seed for our development along the Buddhist path, that is, the going for refuge. Preferably the going for refuge should be done twice each day, with each refuge repeated three times; but if a second recitation is too difficult to fit in, as a minimum one recitation should be done every day, with three repetitions of each refuge.

The daily undertaking of the refuges is best done in a shrine room or before a household altar with a Buddha-image. The actual recitation should be preceded by the offering of candles, incense, and possibly flowers. After making the offerings one should make three salutations before the Buddha-image and then remain kneeling with the hands held out palms joined. Before actually reciting the refuge formula it may be helpful to visualize to oneself the three objects of refuge arousing the feeling that one is in their presence. To represent the Buddha one can visualize an inspiring picture or statue of the Master. The Dhamma can be represented by visualizing, in front of the Buddha, three volumes of scripture to symbolize the Tipitaka, the three collections of Buddhist scriptures.

The Dhamma can also be represented by the Dhammacakka, the "wheel of Dhamma," with its eight spokes symbolizing the noble eightfold path converging upon Nibbana at the hub; it should be bright and beautiful, radiating a golden light. To represent the Sangha one can visualize on either side of the Buddha the two chief disciples, Sariputta and Moggallana; alternatively, one can visualize around the Buddha a group of monks, all of them adepts of the teaching, arahats who have conquered the defilements and reached perfect emancipation. Generating deep faith and confidence, while retaining the visualized images before one's inner eye, one should recite the refuge-formula three times with feeling and conviction. If one is undertaking the practice of meditation it is especially important to recite the refuge-formula before beginning the practice, for this gives needed inspiration to sustain the endeavor through the difficulties that may be encountered along the way.

For this reason those who undertake intensive meditation and go off into solitude preface their practice, not with the usual method of recitation, but with a special variation: Aham attanam Buddhassa niyyatemi Dhammassa Sanghassa, "My person I surrender to the Buddha, Dhamma, and Sangha." By surrendering his person and life to the Triple Gem the yogin shields him against the obstacles which might arise to impede his progress and safeguards him against egoistic clinging to the attainments he might reach. However, this variation on the refuge-formula should not be undertaken lightly, as its consequences are very serious. For ordinary purposes it is enough to use the standard formula for daily recitation.

CORRUPTIONS AND BREACH OF THE REFUGE

Corruptions of the refuge are factors that make the going for refuge impure, insincere, and ineffective. According to the commentaries there are three factors that defile the going for refuge - ignorance, doubt, and wrong views. If one does not understand the reasons for going for refuge, the meaning of taking refuge, or the qualities of the refuge-objects, this lack of understanding is a form of ignorance which corrupts the going for refuge. Doubt corrupts the refuge insofar as the person overcome by doubt cannot settle confidence firmly in the Triple Gem. His commitment to the refuge is tainted by inner perplexity, suspicion, and indecision. The defilement of wrong views means a wrong understanding of the act of refuge or the refuge-objects.

A person holding wrong views goes for refuge with the thought that the refuge act is a sufficient guarantee of deliverance; or he believes that the Buddha is a god with the power to save him, or that the Dhamma teaches the existence of an eternal self, or that the Sangha functions as an intercessory body with the ability to mediate his salvation. Even though the refuge act is defiled by these corruptions, as long as a person regards the Triple Gem as his supreme reliance his going for refuge is intact and he remains a Buddhist follower. But though the refuge is intact, his attitude of taking refuge is defective and has to be purified. Such purification can come about if he meets a proper teacher to give him instruction and help him overcome his ignorance, doubts, and wrong views.

The breach of the refuge means the breaking or violation of the commitment to the threefold refuge. A breach of the refuge occurs when a person who has gone for refuge comes to regard some counterpart to the three refuges as his guiding ideal or supreme reliance. If he comes to regard another spiritual teacher as superior to the Buddha, or as possessing greater spiritual authority than the Buddha, then his going for refuge to the Buddha is broken. If he comes to regard another religious teaching as superior to the Dhamma, or resorts to some other system of practice as his means to deliverance, then his going for refuge to the Dhamma is broken. If he comes to regard some spiritual community other than the ariyan Sangha as endowed with supramundane status, or as occupying a higher spiritual level than the ariyan Sangha, then his going for refuge to the Sangha is broken.

In order for the refuge-act to remain valid and intact, the Triple Gem must be recognized as the exclusive resort for ultimate deliverance: "For me there is no other refuge, the Buddha, Dhamma, and Sangha are my supreme refuge." Breaking the commitment to any of the three refuge-objects breaks the commitment to all of them, since the effectiveness of the refuge-act requires the recognition of the interdependence and inseparability of the three. Thus by adopting an attitude which bestows the status of a supreme reliance upon anything outside the Triple Gem, one cut off the going for refuge and relinquishes one's claim to be a disciple of the Buddha, Dhamma and Sangha. In order to become valid once again the going for refuge must be renewed, preferably by confessing one's lapse and then by once more going through the entire formal ceremony of taking refuge.

THE SIMILES FOR THE REFUGES

In the traditional Indian method of exposition no account or treatment of a theme is considered complete unless it has been illustrated by similes. Therefore we conclude this explanation of going for refuge with a look at some of the classical similes for the objects of refuge. Though many beautiful similes are given in the texts, from fear of prolixity we here limit ourselves to four.

The first simile compares the Buddha to the sun, for his appearance in the world is like the sun rising over the horizon. His teaching of the true Dhamma is like the net of the sun's rays spreading out over the earth, dispelling the darkness and cold of the night, giving warmth and light to all beings. The Sangha is like the beings for whom the darkness of night has been dispelled, who go about their affairs enjoying the warmth and radiance of the sun.

The second simile compares the Buddha to the full moon, the jewel of the night-time sky. His teaching of the Dhamma is like the moon shedding its beams of light over the world, cooling off the heat of the day. The Sangha is like the persons who go out in the night to see and enjoy the refreshing splendor of the moonlight. In the third simile the Buddha is likened to a great raincloud spreading out across the countryside at a time when the land has been parched with a long summer's heat.

The teaching of the true Dhamma is like the downpour of the rain, which inundates the land giving water to the plants and vegetation. The Sangha is like the plants - the trees, shrubs, bushes, and grass - which thrive and flourish when nourished by the rain pouring down from the cloud.

The fourth simile compares the Buddha to a lotus flower, the paragon of beauty and purity. Just as a lotus grows up in a muddy lake, but rises above the water and stands in full splendor unsoiled by the mud, so the Buddha, having grown up in the world, overcomes the world and abides in its midst untainted by its impurities. The Buddha's teaching of the true Dhamma is like the sweet perfumed fragrance emitted by the lotus flower, giving delight to all. And the Sangha is like the host of bees who collect around the lotus, gather up the pollen, and fly off to their hives to transform it into honey.

TAKING THE PRECEPTS

Going for refuge to the Triple Gem - the Buddha, the Dhamma, and the Sangha - is the door of entrance to the Buddha's teaching. To enter the teaching we have to pass through this door, but once we have made the initial commitment by taking refuge it is necessary to go further and to put the teaching into actual practice. For the Buddha's teaching is not a system of salvation by faith. It is essentially a path leading to Nibbana, the end of suffering. At the outset we need a certain degree of faith as the incentive for entering the path, but progress towards the goal depends primarily upon our own energy and intelligence in following the path through each of its successive stages.

The teaching takes the attainment of deliverance away from every external resort and places it into our own hands. We have to realize the goal for ourselves, within ourselves, by working upon ourselves with the guidance of the Buddha's instructions. The path of liberation that the Buddha points to is the threefold training in moral discipline (sila), concentration (samadhi), and wisdom (pañña). These three divisions of the path rise up each in dependence upon its predecessor - concentration upon moral discipline and wisdom upon concentration. The foundation for the entire path, it can be seen, is the training in moral discipline. Because this first section of the path plays such a pivotal role it is vitally important for the serious practitioner to obtain a clear understanding of its essential meaning and the way it is to be practiced.

To aid the development of such an understanding we here present an explanation of the training in Sila or moral discipline, giving special attention to its most basic form as the observance of the five precepts (pañcasila). The subject will be dealt with under the following headings: (I) the essential meaning of sila; (II) the five precepts individually explained; (III) the eight precepts; (IV) the benefits of sila; (V) the undertaking of sila; (VI) the breach of sila; and (VII) the similes for sila.

THE ESSENTIAL MEANING OF SILA

The Pali word for moral discipline, sila, has three levels of meaning: (1) inner virtue, i.e., endowment with such qualities as kindness, contentment, simplicity, truthfulness, patience, etc.; (2) virtuous actions of body and speech which express those inner virtues outwardly; and (3) rules of conduct governing actions of body and speech designed to bring them into accord with the ethical ideals. These three levels are closely intertwined and not always distinguishable in individual cases. But if we isolate them, Sila as inner virtue can be called the aim of the training in moral discipline, Sila as purified actions of body and speech the manifestation of that aim, and Sila as rules of conduct the systematic means of actualizing the aim. Thus Sila as inner virtue is established by bringing our bodily and verbal actions into accord with the ethical ideals, and this is done by following the rules of conduct intended to give these ideals concrete form.

The Buddhist texts explain that Sila has the characteristic of harmonizing our actions of body and speech. Sila harmonizes our actions by bringing them into accord with our own true interests, with the well-being of others, and with universal laws. Actions contrary to Sila lead to a state of self-division marked by guilt, anxiety, and remorse. But the observance of the principles of Sila heals this division, bringing our inner faculties together into a balanced and centered state of unity. Sila also brings us into harmony with other men. While actions undertaken in disregard of ethical principles lead to relations scarred by competitiveness, exploitation, and aggression, actions intended to embody such principles promote concord between man and man - peace, cooperation, and mutual respect.

The harmony achieved by maintaining Sila does not stop at the social level, but leads our actions into harmony with a higher law - the law of kamma, of action and its fruit, which reigns invisibly behind the entire world of sentient existence. The need to internalize ethical virtue as the foundation for the path translates itself into a set of precepts established as guidelines to good conduct. The most basic set of precepts found in the Buddha's teaching is the pañcasila, the five precepts, consisting of the following five training rules:

1. The training rule of abstaining from taking life;
2. The training rule of abstaining from taking what is not given;
3. The training rule of abstaining from sexual misconduct;
4. The training rule of abstaining from false speech; and
5. The training rule of abstaining from fermented and distilled intoxicants which are the basis for heedlessness.

These five precepts are the minimal ethical code binding on the Buddhist laity. They are administered regularly by the monks to the lay disciples at almost every service and ceremony, following immediately upon the giving of the three refuges. They are also undertaken afresh each day by earnest lay Buddhists as part of their daily recitation. The precepts function as the core of the training in moral discipline. They are intended to produce, through methodical practice, that inner purity of will and motivation which comes to expression as virtuous bodily and verbal conduct. Hence the equivalent term for precept, sikkhapada, which means literally "factor of training," that is, a factor of the training in moral discipline. However, the formulation of ethical virtue in terms of rules of conduct meets with an objection reflecting an attitude that is becoming increasingly widespread. This objection, raised by the ethical generalist, calls into question the need to cast ethics into the form of specific rules.

It is enough; it is said, simply to have good intentions and to let ourselves be guided by our intuition as to what is right and wrong. Submitting to rules of conduct is at best superfluous, but worse tends to lead to a straightjacket conception of morality, to a constricting and legalistic system of ethics. The Buddhist reply is that while moral virtue admittedly cannot be equated flatly with any set of rules, or with outward conduct conforming to rules, the rules are still of value for aiding the development of inner virtue. Only the very exceptional few can alter the stuff of their lives by a mere act of will. The overwhelming majority of men have to proceed more slowly, with the help of a set of stepping stones to help them gradually cross the rough currents of greed, hatred, and delusion. If the process of self-transformation which is the heart of the Buddhist path begins with moral discipline, then the concrete manifestation of this discipline is in the lines of conduct represented by the five precepts, which call for our adherence as expedient means to self-transformation.

The precepts are not commandments imposed from without, but principles of training each one takes upon himself through his own initiative and endeavors to follow with awareness and understanding. The formulas for the precepts do not read: "Thou shalt abstain from this and that." They read: "I undertake the training rule to abstain from the taking of life," etc. The emphasis here, as throughout the entire path, is on self-responsibility. The precepts engender virtuous dispositions by a process involving the substitution of opposites. The actions prohibited by the precepts - killing, stealing, adultery, etc. - are all motivated by unwholesome mental factors called in Buddhist terminology the "defilements" (kilesa). By engaging in these actions knowingly and willingly we reinforce the grip of the defilements upon the mind to the point where they become our dominant traits. But when we take up the training by observing the precepts we then put a brake upon the current of unwholesome mental factors. There then takes place a process of "factor substitution" whereby the defilements are replaced by wholesome states which become increasingly more deeply ingrained as we go on with the training.

In this process of self-transformation the precepts draw their efficacy from another psychological principle, the law of development through repetition. Even though at first a practice arouses some resistance from within, if it is repeated over and over with understanding and determination, the qualities it calls into play pass imperceptibly into the makeup of the mind. We generally begin in the grip of negative attitudes, hemmed in by unskillful emotions. But if we see that these states lead to suffering and that to be free from suffering we must abandon them, then we will have sufficient motivation to take up the training designed to counter them. This training starts with the outer observance of sila, and then proceeds to internalize self-restraint through meditation and wisdom. At the start to maintain the precepts may require special effort, but by degrees the virtuous qualities they embody will gather strength until our actions flow from them as naturally and smoothly as water from a spring.

The five precepts are formulated in accordance with the ethical algorithm of using oneself as the criterion for determining how to act in relation to others. In Pali the principle is expressed by the phrase attanam upamam katva, "consider oneself as similar to others and others as similar to oneself." The method of application involves a simple imaginative exchange of oneself and others. In order to decide whether or not to follow a particular line of action, we take ourselves as the standard and consider what would be pleasant and painful for us. Then we reflect that others are basically similar to ourselves, and so, what is pleasant and painful to us is also pleasant and painful to them; thus just as we would not want others to cause pain for us, so we should not cause pain for others. As the Buddha explains:

In this matter the noble disciple reflects: 'Here am I, fond of my life, not wanting to die, fond of pleasure and averse from pain. Suppose someone should deprive me of my life, it would not be a thing pleasing or delightful to me. If I, in my turn, were to deprive of his life one fond of life, not wanting to die, one fond of pleasure and averse from pain, it would not be a thing pleasing or delightful to him. For that state which is not pleasant or delightful to me must be not pleasant or delightful to another: and a state undear and unpleasing to me how could I inflict that upon another?' As a result of such reflection he himself abstains from taking the life of creatures and he encourages others so to abstain, and speaks in praise of so abstaining. - Samyuttanikaya, 55, No. 7

This deductive method the Buddha uses to derive the first four precepts. The fifth precept, abstaining from intoxicants, appears to deal only with my relation to myself, with what I put into my own body. However, because the violation of this precept can lead to the violation of all the other precepts and to much further harm for others, its social implications are deeper than is evident at first sight and bring it into range of this same method of derivation. Buddhist ethics, as formulated in the five precepts, is sometimes charged with being entirely negative. It is criticized on the ground that it is a morality solely of avoidance lacking any ideals of positive action. Against this criticism several lines of reply can be given. First of all it has to be pointed out that the five precepts, or even the longer codes of precepts promulgated by the Buddha, do not exhaust the full range of Buddhist ethics.

The precepts are only the most rudimentary code of moral training, but the Buddha also proposes other ethical codes inculcating definite positive virtues. The Mangala Sutta, for example, commends reverence, humility, contentment, gratitude, patience, generosity, etc. Other discourses prescribe numerous family, social, and political duties establishing the well being of society. And behind all these duties lie the four attitudes called the "immeasurables" - loving-kindness, compassion, sympathetic joy, and equanimity. But turning to the five precepts themselves, some words have to be said in defense of their negative formulation. Each moral principle included in the precepts contains two aspects - a negative aspect, which is a rule of abstinence, and a positive aspect, which is a virtue to be cultivated. These aspects are called, respectively, varitta (avoidance) and caritta (positive performance). Thus the first precept is formulated as abstaining from the destruction of life, which in itself is a varitta, a principle of abstinence.

But corresponding to this, we also find in the descriptions of the practice of this precept a caritta, a positive quality to be developed, namely compassion. Thus in the suttas we read: "The disciple, abstaining from the taking of life, dwells without stick or sword, conscientious, full of sympathy, desirous of the welfare of all living beings." So corresponding to the negative side of abstaining from the destruction of life, there is the positive side of developing compassion and sympathy for all beings. Similarly, abstinence from stealing is paired with honesty and contentment, abstinence from sexual misconduct is paired with marital fidelity in the case of lay people and celibacy in the case of monks, abstinence from falsehood is paired with speaking the truth, and abstinence from intoxicants is paired with heedfulness.

Nevertheless, despite this recognition of a duality of aspect, the question still comes up: if there are two sides to each moral principle, why is the precept worded only as abstinence? Why don't we also undertake training rules to develop positive virtues such as compassion, honesty, and so forth? The answer to this is twofold. First, in order to develop the positive virtues we have to begin by abstaining from the negative qualities opposed to them. The growth of the positive virtues will only be stunted or deformed as long as the defilements are allowed to reign unchecked. We cannot cultivate compassion while at the same time indulging in killing, or cultivate honesty while stealing and cheating. At the start we have to abandon the unwholesome through the aspect of avoidance. Only when we have secured a foundation in avoiding the unwholesome can we expect to succeed in cultivating the factors of positive performance.

The process of purifying virtue can be compared to growing a flower garden on a plot of uncultivated land. We don't begin by planting the seeds in expectation of a bountiful yield. We have to start with the duller work of weeding out the garden and preparing the beds. Only after we have uprooted the weeds and nourished the soil can we plant the seeds in the confidence that the flowers will grow healthily. Another reason why the precepts are worded in terms of abstinence is that the development of positive virtues cannot be prescribed by rules. Rules of training can govern what we have to avoid and perform in our outer actions but only ideals of aspiration, not rules, can govern what develops within ourselves. Thus we cannot take up a training rule to always love towards others. To impose such a rule is to place ourselves in a double bind since inner attitudes are just simply not so docile that they can be determined by command. Love and compassion are the fruits of the work we do on ourselves inwardly, not of assenting to a precept.

What we can do is to undertake a precept to abstain from destroying life and from injuring other beings. Then we can make a resolution, preferably without much fanfare, to develop loving-kindness, and apply ourselves to the mental training designed to nourish its growth. One more word should be added concerning the formulation of the precepts. Despite their negative wording, even in that form the precepts are productive of tremendous positive benefits for others as well as for oneself. The Buddha says that one who abstains from the destruction of life gives immeasurable safety and security to countless living beings. How the simple observance of a single precept leads to such a result is not immediately obvious but calls for some thought.

Now by myself I can never give immeasurable safety and security to other beings by any program of positive action. Even if I were to go on protest against all the slaughterhouses in the world, or to march against war continuously without stopping, by such action I could never stop the slaughter of animals or ensure that war would come to an end. But when I adopt for myself the precept to abstain from the destruction of life, then by reason of the precept I do not intentionally destroy the life of any living being. Thus any other being can feel safe and secure in my presence; all beings are ensured that they will never meet harm from me. Of course even then I can never ensure that other living beings will be absolutely immune from harm and suffering, but this is beyond anyone's power. All that lies within my power and the sphere of my responsibility are the attitudes and actions that emanate from myself towards others. And as long as these are circumscribed by the training rule to abstain from taking life, no living being need feel threatened in my presence, or fear that harm and suffering will come from me.

The same principle applies to the other precepts. When I undertake the precept to abstain from taking what is not given, no one has reason to fear that I will steal what belongs to him; the belongings of all other beings are safe from me. When I undertake the precept to abstain from sexual misconduct, no one has reason to fear that I will try to transgress against his wife. When I undertake the precept to abstain from falsehood, then anyone who speaks with me can be confident that they will hear the truth; my word can be regarded as trustworthy and reliable even in matters of critical importance. And because I undertake the precept of abstaining from intoxicants, then one can be assured that the crimes and transgression that result from intoxication will never be committed by me. In this way, by observing the five precepts I give immeasurable safety and security to countless beings simply through these five silent but powerful determinations established in the mind.

ABSTINENCE FROM TAKING LIFE

The first of the five precepts reads in Pali, Panatipata veramani sikkhapadam samadiyami; in English, "I undertake the training rule to abstain from taking life." Here the word pana, meaning that which breathes, denotes any living being that has breath and consciousness. It includes animals and insects as well as men, but does not include plants as they have only life but not breath or consciousness. The word "living being" is a conventional term, an expression of common usage, signifying in the strict philosophical sense the life faculty (jivitindriya). The word atipata means literally striking down, hence killing or destroying. Thus the precept enjoins abstinence (veramani) from the taking of life. Though the precept's wording prohibits the killing of living beings, in terms of its underlying purpose it can also be understood to prohibit injuring, maiming, and torturing as well.

The Pali Buddhist commentaries formally define the act of taking life thus: "The taking of life is the volition of killing expressed through the doors of either body or speech, occasioning action which results in the cutting off of the life faculty in a living being, when there is a living being present and (the perpetrator of the act) perceives it as a living being". The first important point to note in this definition is that the act of taking life is defined as volition (cetana). Volition is the mental factor responsible for action (kamma); it has the function of arousing the entire mental apparatus for the purpose of accomplishing a particular aim, in this case, the cutting off of the life faculty of a living being. The identification of the transgression with volition implies that the ultimate responsibility for the act of killing lies with the mind, since the volition that brings about the act is a mental factor.

The body and speech function merely as doors for that volition, i.e., as channels through which the volition of taking life reaches expression. Killing is classified as a bodily deed since it generally occurs via the body, but what really performs the act of killing is the mind using the body as the instrument for actualizing its aim. A second important point to note is that killing need not occur directly through the body. The volition to take life can also express itself through the door of speech. This means that the command to take life, given to others by way of words, writing, or gesture, is also considered a case of killing. One who issues such a command becomes responsible for the action as soon as it achieves its intention of depriving a being of life.

A complete act of killing constituting a full violation of the precept involves five factors: (1) a living being; (2) the perception of the living being as such; (3) the thought or volition of killing; (4) the appropriate effort; and (5) the actual death of the being as a result of the action. The second factor ensures that responsibility for killing is incurred only when the perpetrator of the act is aware that the object of his action is a living being. Thus if we step on an insect we do not see, the precept is not broken because the perception or awareness of a living being is lacking. The third factor ensures that the taking of life is intentional. Without the factor of volition there is no transgression, as when we kill a fly while intending simply to drive it away with our hand. The fourth factor holds that the action must be directed to the taking of life, the fifth that the being dies as a result of this action. If the life faculty is not cut off, a full violation of the precept is not incurred, though in harming or injuring living beings in any way its essential purpose will be violated.

The taking of life is distinguished into different types by way of its underlying motivation. One criterion for determining the motivation is the defilement principally responsible for the action. Acts of killing can originate from all three unwholesome roots - from greed, hatred, and delusion. As the immediate cause concomitant with the act of killing, hatred together with delusion functions as the root since the force which drives the act is the impulse to destroy the creature's life, a form of hatred. Any of the three unwholesome roots, however, can serve as the impelling cause or decisive support (upanissaya paccaya) for the act, operating over some span of time. Though greed and hatred are always mutually exclusive at a single moment, the two can work together at different moments over an extended period to occasion the taking of life. Killing motivated primarily by greed is seen in such cases as killing in order to gain material benefits or high status for one, to eliminate threats to one's comfort and security, or to obtain enjoyment as in hunting and fishing for sport.

Killing motivated by hatred is evident in cases of vicious murder where the motive is strong aversion, cruelty, or jealousy. And killing motivated by delusion can be seen in the case of those who perform animal sacrifices in the belief that they are spiritually wholesome or who kill followers of other religions with the view that this is a religious duty. Acts of taking life are differentiated by way of their degree of moral gravity. Not all cases of killing are equally blameworthy. All are unwholesome, a breach of the precept, but the Buddhist texts make a distinction in the moral weight attached to different kinds of killing. The first distinction given is that between killing beings with moral qualities (guna) and killing beings without moral qualities. For all practical purposes the former are human beings, the latter animals, and it is held that to kill a fellow human being is a more serious matter ethically than to kill an animal.

Then within each category further distinctions are drawn. In the case of animals the degree of moral gravity is said to be proportional to the animal, to kill a larger animal being more blameworthy than to kill a smaller one. Other factors relevant to determining moral weight are whether the animal has an owner or is ownerless, whether it is domestic or wild, and whether it has a gentle or a vicious temperament. The moral gravity would be greater in the former three alternatives, less in the latter three. In the killing of human beings the degree of moral blame depends on the personal qualities of the victim, to kill a person of superior spiritual stature or one's personal benefactors being more blameworthy than to kill a less developed person or one unrelated to oneself. The three cases of killing selected as the most culpable are matricide, parricide, and the murder of an arahant, a fully purified saint.

Another factor determinative of moral weight is the motivation of the act. This leads to a distinction between premeditated murder and impulsive killing. The former is murder in cold blood, intended and planned in advance, driven either by strong greed or strong hatred. The latter is killing which is not planned in advance, as when one person kills another in a fit of rage or in self-defense. Generally, premeditated murder is regarded as a graver transgression than impulsive killing, and the motivation of hatred as more blameworthy than the motivation of greed. The presence of cruelty and the obtaining of sadistic pleasure from the act further increase its moral weight. Other factors determinative of moral gravity are the force of the defilements accompanying the act and the amount of effort involved in its perpetration, but limitations of space prohibit a full discussion of their role.

ABSTINENCE FROM TAKING WHAT IS NOT GIVEN

The second precept reads: Adinnadana veramani sikkhapadam samadiyami, "I undertake the training rule to abstain from taking what is not given." The word adinna, meaning literally "what is not given," signifies the belongings of another person over which he exercises ownership legally and blamelessly (adandaraho anupavajjo). Thus no offense is committed if the article taken has no owner, e.g., if logs are taken to make a fire or stones are gathered to build a wall. Further, the other person has to have possession of the article taken legally and blamelessly; that is, he has to have the legal right over the article and also has to be blameless in his use of it. This latter phrase apparently becomes applicable in cases where a person gains legal possession of an article but does so in an improper way or uses it for unethical purposes.

In such cases there might be legitimate grounds for depriving him of the item, as when the law requires someone who commits a misdemeanor to pay a fine or deprives a person of some weapon rightfully his which he is using for destructive purposes. The act of taking what is not given is formally defined thus: "Taking what is not given is the volition with thievish intent arousing the activity of appropriating an article belonging to another legally and blamelessly in one who perceives it as belonging to another." As in the case of the first precept the transgression here consists ultimately in volition. This volition can commit the act of theft by originating action through body or speech; thus a transgression is incurred either by taking something directly by oneself or else indirectly, by commanding someone else to appropriate the desired article. The fundamental purpose of the precept is to protect the property of individuals from unjustified confiscation by others. Its ethical effect is to encourage honesty and right livelihood.

According to the commentaries, for a complete breach of the precept to be committed five factors must be present: (1) an article belonging to another legally and blamelessly; (2) the perception of it as belonging to another; (3) the thought or intention of stealing; (4) the activity of taking the article; and (5) the actual appropriation of the article. By reason of the second factor there is no violation in taking another's article if we mistakenly perceive it as our own, as when we might confuse identical-looking coats, umbrellas, etc. The third factor again provides a safeguard against accidental appropriation, while the fifth asserts that to fall into the class of a transgression the action must deprive the owner of his article. It is not necessary that he be aware that his possession is missing, only that it be removed from his sphere of control even if only momentarily.

Taking what is not given can be divided into many different kinds of violation. We might mention some of the most prominent. One is stealing, that is, taking what is not given, secretly, without the knowledge of the owner, as in housebreaking, a midnight bank theft, pickpocketing, etc. Another type is robbery, taking what is not given by force, either by snatching someone's belongings away from him or by compelling him to hand them over by means of threats. A third type is fraudulence, laying false claims or telling lies in order to gain someone else's possessions. Still another is deceit, using deceptive means to deprive someone of an article or to gain his money as when storekeepers use false weights and measures or when people produce counterfeit bills for use.

The violation of this precept need not amount to a major crime. The precept is subtle and offers many opportunities for its breach, some of them seemingly slight. For example, transgression will be incurred when employees take goods belonging to their employers, pocketing small items to which they have no right with the thought that the company will not miss them; when using another's telephone to make long-distance calls without his consent, letting him cover the bill; in bringing articles into a country without declaring them to customs in order to avoid paying duty on them; in idling away time on the job for which one is being paid in the expectation that one has been working diligently; in making one's employees work without giving them adequate compensation, etc.

By way of its underlying roots, the act of taking what is not given can precede either from greed or hatred, both being coupled with delusion. Stealing by reason of greed is the obvious case, but the offense can also be driven by hatred. Hatred functions as the motive for stealing when one person deprives another of an article not so much because he wants it for himself and resents other's possession of and wants to make him suffer through its loss. The degree of blame attached to acts of stealing is held to be determined by two principal factors, the value of the article taken and the moral qualities of the owner. In stealing a very valuable article the degree of blame is obviously greater than in stealing an article of little worth. But where the value of the article is the same the blameworthiness of the action still varies relative to the individual against whom the offense is committed.

As determined by this factor, stealing from a person of high virtuous qualities or a personal benefactor is a more serious transgression than stealing from a person of lesser qualities or from an unrelated person. This factor, in fact, can be even more important than the cash value of the object. Thus if someone steals an almsbowl from a meditative monk, who needs the bowl to collect his food, the moral weight of the act is heavier than that involved in cheating a racketeer out of several thousand dollars, owing to the character of the person affected by the deed. The motivation behind the action and the force of the defilements are also determinative of the degree of moral gravity, hatred being considered more culpable than greed.

ABSTINENCE FROM MISCONDUCT IN REGARD TO SENSE PLEASURES

The third precept reads: Kamesu micchacara veramani sikkhapadam samadiyami, "I undertake the training rule to abstain from misconduct in regard to sense pleasures." The word Kama has the general meaning of sense pleasure or sensual desire, but the commentaries explain it as sexual relations (methunasamacara), an interpretation supported by the suttas. Micchacara means wrong modes of conduct. Thus the precept enjoins abstinence from improper or illicit sexual relations. Misconduct is regard to sense pleasures is formally defined as "the volition with sexual intent occurring through the bodily door, causing transgression with an illicit partner".

The primary question this definition elicits is: who is to qualify as an illicit partner? For men, the text lists twenty types of women who are illicit partners. These can be grouped into three categories: (1) a woman who is under the protection of elders or other authorities charged with her care, e.g., a girl being cared for by parents, by an older brother or sister, by other relatives, or by the family as a whole; (2) a woman who is prohibited by convention, that is, close relatives forbidden under family tradition, nuns and other women vowed to observe celibacy as a spiritual discipline, and those forbidden as partners under the law of the land; and (3) a woman who is married or engaged to another man, even one bound to another man only by a temporary agreement. In the case of women, for those who are married any man other than a husband is an illicit partner. For all women a man forbidden by tradition or under religious rules is prohibited as a partner.

For both men and women any violent, forced, or coercive union, whether by physical compulsion or psychological pressure, can be regarded as a transgression of the precept even when the partner is not otherwise illicit. But a man or woman who is widowed or divorced can freely remarry according to choice. The texts mention four factors which must be present for a breach of the precept to be incurred: (1) an illicit partner, as defined above; (2) the thought or volition of engaging in sexual union with that person; (3) the act of engaging in union; and (4) the acceptance of the union. This last factor is added for the purpose of excluding from violation those who are unwillingly forced into improper sexual relations.

The degree of moral gravity involved in the offense is determined by the force of the lust motivating the action and the qualities of the person against whom the transgression is committed. If the transgression involves someone of high spiritual qualities, the lust is strong, and force is used, the blame is heavier than when the partner has less developed qualities, the lust is weak, and no force is used. The most serious violations are incest and the rape of an arahant (or arahatess). The underlying root is always greed accompanied by delusion.

ABSTINENCE FROM FALSE SPEECH

The fourth precept reads: Musavada veramani sikkhapadam samadiyami, "I undertake the training rule to abstain from false speech." False speech is defined as "the wrong volition with intent to deceive, occurring through the door of either body or speech, arousing the bodily or verbal effort of deceiving another." The transgression must be understood as intentional. The precept is not violated merely by speaking what is false, but by speaking what is false with the intention of representing that as true; thus it is equivalent to lying or deceptive speech. The volition is said to arouse bodily or verbal action. The use of speech to deceive is obvious, but the body too can be used as an instrument of communication - as in writing, hand signals, and gestures - and thus can be used to deceive others.

Four factors enter into the offense of false speech: (1) an untrue state of affairs; (2) the intention of deceiving another;

(3) the effort to express that, either verbally or bodily; and (4) the conveying of a false impression to another. Since intention is required, if one speaks falsely without aiming at deceiving another, as when one speaks what is false believing it to be true, there is no breach of the precept. Actual deception, however, is not needed for the precept to be broken. It is enough if the false impression is communicated to another. Even though he does not believe the false statement, if one expresses what is false to him and he understands what is being said, the transgression of speaking falsehood has been committed.

The motivation for false speech can be any of the three unwholesome roots. These yield three principal kinds of falsehood: (1) false speech motivated by greed, intended to increase one's gains or promote one's status or that of those dear to oneself; (2) false speech motivated by hatred, intended to destroy the welfare of others or to bring them harm and suffering; and (3) false speech of a less serious kind, motivated principally by delusion in association with less noxious degrees of greed or hatred, intended neither to bring special benefits to oneself nor to harm others. Some examples would be lying for the sake of a joke, exaggerating an account to make it more interesting, speaking flattery to gratify others, etc.

The principal determinants of the gravity of the transgression are the recipient of the lie, the object of the lie and the motivation of the lie. The recipient is the person to whom the lie is told. The moral weight of the act is proportional to the character of this person, the greatest blame attaching to falsehoods spoken to one's benefactors or to spiritually developed persons. The moral weight again varies according to the object of the lie, the person the lie affects, being proportional to his spiritual qualities and his relation to oneself in the same way as with the recipient. And thirdly, the gravity of the lie is contingent on its motivation, the most serious cases being those with malicious intent designed to destroy the welfare of others. The worst cases of false speech are lying in a way that defames the Buddha or an arahant, and making false claims to have reached a superior spiritual attainment in order to increase one's own gains and status. In the case of a bhikkhu this latter offense can lead to expulsion from the Sangha.

ABSTINENCE FROM INTOXICATING DRINKS AND DRUGS

The fifth precept reads: Suramerayamajjapamadatthana veramani sikkhapadam samadiyami, "I undertake the training rule to abstain from fermented and distilled intoxicants which are the basis for heedlessness." The word meraya means fermented liquors, sura liquors which have been distilled to increase their strength and flavor. The world majja, meaning an intoxicant, can be related to the rest of the passage either as qualified by surameraya or as additional to them. In the former case the whole phrase means fermented and distilled liquors which are intoxicants, in the latter it means fermented and distilled liquors and other intoxicants. If this second reading is adopted the precept would explicitly include intoxicating drugs used non-medicinally, such as the opiates, hemp, and psychedelics. But even on the first reading the precept implicitly proscribes these drugs by way of its guiding purpose, which is to prevent heedlessness caused by the taking of intoxicating substances.

The taking of intoxicants is defined as the volition leading to the bodily act of ingesting distilled or fermented intoxicants. It can be committed only by one's own person (not by command to others) and only occurs through the bodily door. For the precept to be violated four factors are required: (1) the intoxicant; (2) the intention of taking it; (3) the activity of ingesting it; and (4) the actual ingestion of the intoxicant. The motivating factor of the violation is greed coupled with delusion. No gradations of moral weight are given. In taking medicines containing alcohol or intoxicating drugs for medical reasons no breach of the precept is committed. There is also no violation in taking food containing a negligible amount of alcohol added as a flavoring. This fifth precept differs from the preceding four in that the others directly involve a man's relation to his fellow beings while this precept ostensibly deals solely with a person's relation to himself - to his own body and mind. Thus whereas the first four precepts clearly belong to the moral sphere, a question may arise whether this precept is really ethical in character or merely hygienic.

The answer is that it is ethical, for the reason that what a person does to his body and mind can have a decisive effect on his relations to his fellow men. Taking intoxicants can influence the ways in which a man interacts with others, leading to the violation of all five precepts. Under the influence of intoxicants a man who might otherwise be restrained can lose self-control, become heedless, and engage in killing, stealing, adultery, and lying. Abstinence from intoxicants is prescribed on the grounds that it is essential to the self-protection of the individual and for establishing the well-being of family and society. The precept thus prevents the misfortunes that result from the use of intoxicants: loss of wealth, quarrels and crimes, bodily disease, loss of reputation, shameless conduct, negligence, and madness. The precept, it must be stressed, does not prohibit merely intoxication but the very use of intoxicating substances. Though occasional indulgences may not be immediately harmful in isolation, the seductive and addictive properties of intoxicants are well known. The strongest safeguard against the lure is to avoid them altogether.

Beyond the five precepts Buddhism offers a higher code of moral discipline for the laity consisting of eight precepts (atthasila). This code of eight precepts is not entirely different in content from the fivefold code, but includes the five precepts with one significant revision. The revision comes in the third precept, where abstaining from sexual misconduct is changed to abstaining from incelibacy. The third precept of the eightfold set thus reads: Abrahmacariya veramani sikkhapadam samadiyami, "I undertake the training rule to abstain from incelibacy." To these basic five three further precepts are added:

Vikalabhojana veramani sikkhapadam samadiyami, "I undertake the training rule to abstain from eating beyond the time limit," i.e., from mid-day to the following dawn.

Nacca gita vadita visukhadassana-mala gandha vilepana dharanamandana vibhusanatthana veramani sikkhapadam samamadiyami, "I undertake the training rule to abstain from dancing, singing, instrumental music, unsuitable shows, and from wearing garlands, using scents, and beautifying the body with cosmetics."

Uccasayana mahasayana veramani sikkhapadam samadiyami, "I undertake the training rule to abstain from high and luxurious beds and seats."

There are two ways in which these precepts are observed - permanently and temporarily. Permanent observance, far the less common of the two, is undertaken generally by older people who, having completed their family duties, wish to deepen their spiritual development by devoting the later years of their life to intensified spiritual practice. Even then it is not very widespread. Temporary observance is usually undertaken by lay people either on Uposatha days or on occasions of a meditation retreat. Uposatha days are the new moon and full moon days of the lunar month, which are set aside for special religious observances, a custom absorbed into Buddhism from ancient Indian custom going back even into the pre-Buddhistic period of Indian history. On these days lay people in Buddhist countries often take the eight precepts, especially when they go to spend the Uposatha at a temple or monastery. On these occasions the undertaking of the eight precepts lasts for a day and a night. Then, secondly, on occasions of retreat lay people take the eight precepts for the duration of their retreat, which might last anywhere from several days to several months.

The formulation of two distinct ethical codes follows from the two basic purposes of the Buddhist moral discipline. One is the fundamental ethical purpose of putting a brake on immoral actions, actions which are harmful either directly or indirectly to others. This purpose falls into the province of the fivefold code of precepts, which deals with the restraint of actions that cause pain and suffering to others. In enjoining abstinence from these unwholesome actions, the five precepts also protect the individual from their undesirable repercussions on himself - some immediately visible in this present life, some coming to manifestation only in future lives when the kamma they generate bears its fruit.

The other purpose of the Buddhist training in moral discipline is not so much ethical as spiritual. It is to provide a system of self-discipline which can act as a basis for achieving higher states of realization through the practice of meditation. In serving this purpose the code functions as a kind of ascesis, a way of conduct involving self-denial and renunciation as essential to the ascent to higher levels of consciousness. This ascent, culminating in Nibbana or final liberation from suffering, hinges upon the attenuation and ultimate eradication of craving, which with its multiple branches of desire is the primary force that holds us in bondage. To reduce and overcome craving it is necessary to regulate not only the deleterious types of moral transgressions but also modes of conduct which are not harmful to others but sill give vent to the craving that holds us in subjection.

The Buddhist code of discipline expounded in the eight precepts represents the transition from the first level of moral discipline to the second that is, from Sila as a purely moral undertaking to Sila as a way of ascetic self-training aimed at progress along the path to liberation. The five precepts also fulfill this function to some extent, but they do so only in a limited way, not as fully as the eight precepts. With the eight precepts the ethical code takes a pronounced turn towards the control of desires which are not socially harmful and immoral. This extension of the training focuses upon desires centering on the physical body and its concerns. The change of the third precept to abstinence from incelibacy curbs the sexual urge, regarded in it not as a moral evil but as a powerful expression of craving that has to be held in check to advance to the higher levels of meditation. The three new precepts regulate concern with food, entertainment, self-beautification, and physical comfort. Their observance nurtures the growth of qualities essential to the deeper spiritual life - contentment, fewness of wishes, modesty, austerity, and renunciation. As these qualities mature the defilements are weakened, aiding the effort to reach attainment in serenity and insight.

THE BENEFITS OF SILA

The benefits Sila brings to the one who undertakes it can be divided into three classes: (1) the benefits pertaining to the present life; (2) the benefits pertaining to future lives; and (3) the benefit of the ultimate good. These we will discuss in turn.

Benefits Pertaining to the Present Life

At the most elementary level, the observance of the five precepts protects one from coming into trouble with the law, ensuring immunity from temporal punishment at least with regard to those actions covered by the precepts. Killing, stealing, adultery, bearing false testimony, and irresponsible behavior caused by drunkenness being offenses punishable by law, one who undertakes the five precepts avoids the penalties consequent upon these actions by abstaining from the actions which entail them. Further temporal benefits accrue through the observance of the precepts. Following the precepts helps to establish a good reputation among the wise and virtuous. At a more inward level it leads to a clear conscience.

Repeated violations of the basic principles of ethics, even if they escape detection, still tend to create a disturbed conscience - the pain of guilt, uneasiness, and remorse. But maintaining the precepts results in freedom from remorse, an ease of conscience that can evolve into the "bliss of blamelessness" (anavajjasukha) when our actions and realize them to be wholesome and good. This clarity of conscience fosters another benefit - the ability to die peacefully, without fear or confusion. At the time of death the various actions we have regularly performed in the course of life rise to the surface of the mind, casting up their images like pictures upon a screen. If unwholesome actions were prevalent their weight will predominate and cause fear at the approach of death, leading to a confused and painful end. But if wholesome actions were prevalent in the course of life the opposite will take place: when death comes we will be able to die calmly and peacefully.

Benefits Pertaining to Future Lives

According to the Buddha's teaching the mode of rebirth we take in our next existence is determined by our kamma, the willed actions we have performed in this present existence. The general principle governing the working of the rebirth process is that unwholesome kamma leads to an unfavorable rebirth, wholesome kamma to a favorable rebirth. More specifically, if the kamma built up by breaking the five precepts becomes the determining cause of the mode of rebirth it will conduce to rebirth in one of the four planes of misery - the hells, the realm of tormented spirits, the animal world, or the world of the asuras. If, as a result of some wholesome kamma, a person who regularly breaks the five precepts should take rebirth as a human being, then when his unwholesome kamma matures it will produce pain and suffering in his human state.

The forms this suffering takes correspond to the transgressions. Killing leads to a premature death, stealing to loss of wealth, sexual misconduct to enmity, false speech to being deceived and slandered by others, and the use of intoxicants to loss of intelligence. The observance of the five precepts, on the other hand, brings about the accumulation of wholesome kamma tending to rebirth in the planes of happiness, i.e., in the human or heavenly worlds. This kamma again, coming to maturity in the course of the life, produces favorable results consonant in nature with the precepts and thus abstaining from the taking of life leads to longevity, abstaining from stealing to prosperity, abstaining from sexual misconduct to popularity, abstaining from false speech to a good reputation, and abstaining from intoxicants to mindfulness and wisdom.

The Benefits of the Ultimate Good

The ultimate good is the attainment of Nibbana, deliverance from the round of rebirths, which can be achieved either in the present life or in some future life depending on the maturity of our spiritual faculties. Nibbana is attained by practicing the path leading to deliverance, the noble eightfold path in its three stages of moral discipline, concentration, and wisdom. The most fundamental of these three stages is moral discipline or sila, which begins with the observance of the five precepts. The undertaking of the five precepts can thus be understood to be the first actual step taken along the path to deliverance and the indispensable foundation for the higher attainments in concentration and wisdom. Sila functions as the foundation for the path in two ways. First the observance of Sila promotes a clear conscience, essential to the development of concentration.

If we often act contrary to the precepts our actions tend to give rise to remorse, which will swell up to the surface of the mind when we sit in meditation, creating restlessness and feelings of guilt. But if we act in harmony with the precepts our minds will be imbued with a bliss and clarity of conscience which allows concentration to develop easily. The observance of the precepts conduces to concentration in a second way: it rescues us from the danger of being caught in crossfire of incompatible motives disruptive of the meditative frame of mind. The practice of meditation aimed at serenity and insight requires the stilling of the defilements when we deliberately act in violation of the precepts our actions spring from the unwholesome roots of greed, hatred and delusion. Thus in committing such actions we are arousing the defilements while at the same time, when sitting in meditation, we are striving to overcome them.

The result is inner conflict, disharmony, a split right through the center of our being obstructing the unification of the mind needed for meditative attainment. At the outset we cannot expect to eliminate the subtle forms of the defilements all at once. These can only be tackled later, in the deeper stages of meditation. In the beginning we have to start by stopping the defilements in their coarser modes of occurrence, and this is achieved by restraining them from reaching expression through the channels of body and speech. Such restraint is the essence of sila. We therefore take up the precepts as a form of spiritual training, as a way of locking in the defilements and preventing them from outward eruptions. After they have been shut in and their effusions stopped we can then work on eliminating their roots through the development of concentration and wisdom.

The Undertaking of Sila

The Buddhist tradition recognizes three distinct ways of observing the precepts. One is called immediate abstinence (sampattavirati), which means abstaining from unwholesome actions naturally through an ingrained sense of conscience resulting either from an innately keen ethical disposition or from education and training. The second is called abstinence through undertaking (samadanavirati), which means abstaining as a result of having undertaken rules of training with a determination to follow those rules as guidelines to right action. The third way is called abstinence through eradication (samucchedavirati), which means abstaining from the transgressions covered by the precepts as a result of having cut off the defilements out of which transgressions arise.

For purposes of self-training Buddhism emphasizes the importance of the second type of abstinence. Immediate abstinence is seen as praiseworthy in itself but not sufficient as a basis for training since it presupposes the prior existence of a strong conscience, which is not a reality in the overwhelming majority of men. In order to develop the mental strength to resist the upsurge of the defilements it is essential to undertake the precepts by a deliberate act of will and to form the determination to observe them diligently. There are two ways of formally undertaking the five precepts, the initial and the recurrent, corresponding to the two ways of going for refuge. The initial undertaking takes place immediately after the initial going for refuge.

When the aspirant receives the three refuges from a bhikkhu in a formal ceremony, this will then be followed by the administering of the five precepts, the monk reciting each of the precepts in turn and the lay disciple repeating them after him. If there is no monk available to administer the refuges and precepts, the aspirant can take them upon himself by a strong and fixed mental resolution, preferably doing so before an image of the Buddha. The presence of a monk is not necessary but is generally desired to give a sense of the continuity of the lineage. The undertaking of the precepts is not a one-shot affair to be gone through once and then dropped off into the storage bank of memories. Rather, like the going for refuge, the precepts should be undertaken repeatedly, preferably on a daily basis. This is the recurrent undertaking of the precepts.

Just as the disciple repeats the three refuges each day to strengthen his commitment to the Dhamma, so he should recite the five precepts immediately after the refuges in order to express his determination to embody the Dhamma in his conduct. However, the practice of Sila is not to be confused with the mere recitation of a verbal formula. The recitation of the formula helps reinforce one's will to carry out the training, but beyond all verbal recitations the precepts have to be put into practice in day-to-day life, especially on the occasions when they become relevant. Undertaking the precepts is like buying a ticket for a train: the purchase of the ticket permits us to board the train but does not take us anywhere by itself. Similarly, formally accepting the precepts enables us to embark upon the training, but after the acceptance we have to translate the precepts into action.

Once we have formed the initial determination to cultivate sila, there are certain mental factors which then help to protect our observance of the precepts. One of these is mindfulness (sati). Mindfulness is awareness, constant attention and keen observation. Mindfulness embraces all aspects of our being - our bodily activities, our feelings, our states of mind, and our objects of thought. With sharpened mindfulness we can be aware exactly what we are doing, what feelings and states of mind are impelling us towards particular courses of action, what thoughts form our motivations. Then, by means of this mindfulness, we can avoid the unwholesome and develop the wholesome. Another factor which helps us maintain the precepts is understanding (pañña). The training in moral discipline should not be taken up as a blind dogmatic submission to external rules, but as a fully conscious process guided by intelligence.

The factors of understanding give us that guiding intelligence. To observe the precepts properly we have to understand for ourselves which kinds of actions are wholesome and which are unwholesome. We also have to understand the reason why - why they are wholesome and unwholesome, why the one should be pursued and the other abandoned. The deepening of understanding enables us to see the roots of our actions, i.e., the mental factors from which they spring, and the consequences to which they lead, their long-term effects upon ourselves and others. Understanding expands our vision not only into consequences, but also into alternatives, into the different courses of action offered by any objective situation. Thence it gives us knowledge of the various alternatives open to us and the wisdom to choose some in preference to others.

A third factor that helps in maintaining the precepts is energy (viriya).The training in right conduct is at base a way of training the mind, since it is the mind that directs our actions. But the mind cannot be trained without effort, without the application of energy to steer it into wholesome channels. Energy works together with mindfulness and understanding to bring about the gradual purification of sila. Through mindfulness we gain awareness of our states of mind; through understanding we can ascertain the tendencies of these states, their qualities, roots and consequences; then through energy we strive to abandon the unwholesome and to cultivate the wholesome. The fourth factor conducive to the training in Sila is patience (khanti).

Patience enables us to endure the offensive actions of others without becoming angry or seeking retaliation. Patience also enables us to endure disagreeable circumstances without dissatisfaction and dejection. It curbs our desires and aversions, restraining us from transgressions through greedy pursuits or violent reprisals. Abstinence through eradication (samucchedavirati), the highest form of observing the precepts, comes about automatically with the attainment of the state of an ariyan, one who has reached direct realization of the Dhamma. When the disciple reaches the stage of stream-entry (sotapatti), the first of the ariyan stages, he becomes bound to reach full liberation in a maximum of seven more lives.

He is incapable of reverting from the course of forward progress towards enlightenment. Simultaneously with his attainment of stream-entry the disciple acquires four inalienable qualities, called the four factors of stream-entry (sotapattiyanga). The first three are unshakable faith in the Buddha, the Dhamma, and the Sangha. The fourth is completely purified sila. The noble disciple has cut off the defilements which motivate transgressions of the precepts. Thus he can never deliberately violate the five precepts. His observance of the precepts has become "untorn, unrent, unblotched, unmotiled, liberating, praised by the wise, not clung to, conducive to concentration."

The Breach of Sila

To undertake the precepts is to make a determination to live in harmony with them, not to ensure that one will never break them. Despite our determination it sometimes happens that due to carelessness or the force of our conditioning by the defilements we act contrary to the precepts. The question thus comes up as to what to do in such cases. One thing we should not do if we break a precept is to let ourselves become ridden by guilt and self-contempt. Until we reach the planes of liberation it is to be expected that the defilements can crop up from time to time and motivate unwholesome actions. Feelings of guilt and self-condemnation do nothing to help the matter but only make things worse by piling on an overlay of self-aversion.

A sense of shame and moral scrupulousness are central to maintaining the precepts but they should not be allowed to become entangled in the coils of guilt. When a breach of the precepts takes place there are several methods of making amends. One method used by monks to gain exoneration in regard to infringements on the monastic rules is confession. For certain classes of monastic offenses a monk can gain clearance simply by confessing his transgression to another monk. Perhaps with suitable modifications the same procedure could be applied by the laity, at least with regard to more serious violations. Thus if there are a number of lay people who are earnestly intent on following the path, and one falls into a breach of a precept, he can confess his lapse to a Dhamma friend, or, if one is not available, he can confess it privately before an image of the Buddha. It must be stressed, however, that confession does not aim at gaining absolution. No one is offended by the ethical lapse, nor is there anyone to grant forgiveness.

Also, confession does not abrogate the kamma acquired by the transgression. The kamma has been generated by the deed and will produce its due effect if it gains the opportunity. The basic purpose of confession is to clear the mind of the remorse bearing upon it as a consequence of the breach. Confession especially helps to prevent the concealment of the lapse, a subtle maneuver of the ego used to bolster its pride in its own imagined perfection. Another method of making amends is by retaking the five precepts, reciting each precept in turn either in the presence of a monk or before an image of the Buddha.

This new undertaking of the precepts can be reinforced by a third measure, namely, making a strong determination not to fall into the same transgression again in the future. Having applied these three methods one can then perform more virtuous actions as a way of building up good kamma to counteract the unwholesome kamma acquired through the breach of the precept. Kamma tends to produce its due result and if this tendency is sufficiently strong there is nothing we can do to blot it out. However, kamma does not come to fruition always as a matter of strict necessity.

Kammic tendencies push and tug with one another in complex patterns of relationship. Some tend to reinforce the results of others, some to weaken the results, some to obstruct the results. If we build up wholesome kamma through virtuous actions, this pure kamma can inhibit the unwholesome kamma and prevent it from reaching fruition. There is no guarantee that it will do so, since kamma is a living process, not a mechanical one. But the tendencies in the process can be understood, and since one such tendency is for the wholesome to counteract the unwholesome and hinder their undesired results, a helpful power in overcoming the effects of breaking the precepts is the performance of virtuous actions.

The Similes for Sila

The texts illustrate the qualities of Sila with numerous similes, but as with the three refuges we must again limit ourselves to only a few. Sila is compared to a stream of clear water, because it can wash off the stains of wrong actions which can never be removed by the waters of all other rivers. Sila is like sandalwood, because it can remove the fever of the defilements just as sandalwood (according to ancient Indian belief) can be used to allay bodily fever. Again Sila is like an ornament made of precious jewels because it adorns the person who wears it.

It is like a perfume because it gives off a pleasant scent, the "scent of virtue," which unlike ordinary perfume travels even against the wind. It is like moonbeams because it cools off the heat of passion as the moon cools off the heat of the day. And Sila is like a staircase because it leads upwards by degrees - to higher states of future existence in the fortunate realms, to the higher planes of concentration and wisdom, to the supernormal powers, to the paths and fruits of liberation, and finally to the highest goal, the attainment of Nibbana.

POSITION OF THE LAITY IN EARLY BUDDHISM

In first sermon on the Dharma, he proclaimed the four noble truths.

DHARMA: [LAW, DUTY, TEACHING, AND MENTAL STATE]

Hinayana: the saving truth that was lived and taught by the Buddha

Mahayana: "a more metaphysical significance."

Four noble truths:

1. All existence is suffering (dukhka);
2. All suffering is caused by craving (trishna)
3. All suffering can be ended
4. The way to end suffering is by practicing the noble eightfold path

The path that brings salvation as a "middle way" - between self-indulgence and self-mortification:

Right views will be the torch to light his way.

Right aspirations will be his guide.

Right speech will be his dwelling place on the road.

His gait will be straight, for it is right behavior.

His refreshments will be the right way of earning his livelihood.

Right efforts will be his steps;

Right thoughts his breath;

And right contemplation will give him the peace that follows in his footsteps...

AFTER THE BUDDHA'S DEATH

Establishing the monastic tradition: source:

- Mahaparinabbana Sutta (Sermon of the great decease)
- Sutra Pitaka (basket of discourses) - at the core, sermons or dialogues of the Buddha
- Vinaya Pitaka (basket of monastic rules)

PRIMARY SCHISMS

- Second Council at Visali: 1st half of 4th ct. B.C.E.
- Split between: liberal Mahasanghika (great assembly) and more conservative Sthaviravada (in Pali, Theravada: school of the elders)
- Later, two other groups broke away from the conservatives:

- Vatsiyaputras (or Sammitiyas) who believed in a form of ersonal entity (pudgala)
- Sarvastivadins who believed in the existence of a past and future time.

THE THREE MAIN TRADITIONS

Asoka: ruled 273-232 B.C.E. - his role in the history of Buddhism compared with that of Constantine in Christianity...."What had been, only two centuries before, a small, nonconformist sect was elevated to the status of a potentially universal religion. True to the principles of Buddhism, Asoka practiced tolerance of other religions, including the Brahmans who continued to support Hinduism. Nevertheless, the Buddhists no longer thought of their community simply as a monastic order complemented by a relatively unorganized laity, but rather as a Sangha operating in tandem with a Buddhist state ruled by a Buddhist king."

(After Asoka's death, the empire began to decline. Among other factors, the "proclamation of Buddhist pacifism as a policy....") Hinayana (small boat) - development during the two centuries B.C.E. and two centuries in the C.E.

Concept of the Buddha tendency to divinize the Buddha. "Within the monastic tradition it was asserted that, in addition to his human, physical body, the Buddha possessed a more ultimate Dharma body, or dharmakaya. (Sometimes this was interpreted as a body associated with his practice of the Way, and sometimes as a body associated with the truth he had taught.) The conservative schools kept such speculation in check. In the more liberal traditions, the dharmic body, or body of truth, became more significant, whereas the human, physical body was reduced to the level of mere appearance."

"Among the laity the tendency toward divinization was related to the growing importance of devotional activities." This veneration of the founder hows up initially in the form of great stupas. "By the beginning of the Christian era, images of the Buddha began to appear. Through their enthusiastic participation in the veneration of these stupas and images, the laity came to view the Buddha as a great being who had much in common with the classical HIndu gods such as Brahma and Visnu."

In addition, "development of new and extended accounts of his life." (Devotional cult surrounding Maitreya, a future Buddha residing in the Tusita heaven [fourth in a hierarchy of six heavens constituting the upper regions of the world of desire], awaiting the appropriate time to come into the world and establish his community. In Sarvastivadin strongholds in northwestern India and central Asia, the devout sought to accumulate merit in order to be reborn when Maitreya descended into the human world....society would be perfected, and the eightfold path and nirvana would be accessible to all.

DEVELOPMENT OF THE CONCEPT OF THE DHARMA

Composition of technical doctrinal treatises, their collection:

Abhidarma Pitaka (basket of the higher Dharma) - A third segment of teachings equal in authority to the much older Sutra and Pitakas Vinaya. "...carried forward the early Buddhist effort to analyze all reality into discrete elements which, in this context, were called dharmas. They described the process through which the dharmas that made up the individual beings and the various levels of cosmic reality came together, and they specified the process through which human actions, despite the nonexistence of any kind of self, created their appropriate punishments and rewards. They affirmed the reality of nirvana as a very different 'unconditioned' dharma that was equated with release from the cycle of rebirth. Finally, they analyzed the eightfold path, including its practices of discipline, meditation, and insight. In this way they sought to describe the process thorugh which the causes of the coming together of the conditioned dharmas (that is to say, the causes of existence and suffering) could be uprooted in order to achieve nirvana, the unconditioned."

An equivalent development in teachings directed to the less advanced monks and the laity - e.g., descriptions of various conditions in which a human being could be reborn, including the various hells; the realm of suffering ghosts; the realm of the asuras or fallen deities; the realm of animals, the realm of human beings; and the realm of the gods.

The kinds of deeds that could lead to rebirth were specified. New practices appeared - e.g., "rituals designed to transfer merit from one individual to another, particularly from a living person to a deceased relative who might be languishing in one of the various hells or in the realm of the suffering ghosts." Also, lay-sponsored performance of paritta ceremonies: monks recite particular sutras to produce magical power which would assure their patron's safety, health, and prosperity.

MONASTIC DEVELOPMENT

The efforts of the monks and nuns to legitimate their position in the life of the community led to the collection of teachings on the arya pudgala or noble beings- who had entered one of four stages of the supraworldly path. A few such noble beings, who had obtained the "spotless eye of Dharma" that provided authority in matters of teaching and doctrine, could be placed alongside the Buddha and the Dharma as the third jewel or refuge. These were "a spiritual aristocracy which guaranteed the purity and sacred status of the community as a whole."

Similar legitimating interests apparent in the development of claims "of the existence of an unbroken lineage of 'masters of the Dharma.'...The majority of the later Hinayana schools held that their basic lineage began with the Buddha himself and included Mahaksyapa, the monk who supposedly convened the first council, three early arhants [those who had achieved nirvana] who succeeded him, and Upagupta, the legendary preceptor of Asoka." Continuing splintering - e.g., up to 18 different schools, and widening gap between the conservatives and liberals. "The conservatives emphasized the spiritual superiority of the monks, exalting the perfections of the arhants and other noble beings. The liberals, who question these perfections, were less strict in maintaining the distinction between the monastic and lay traditions." In this way, they literally opened the door of the monastery to innovations from the laity - and thus to the development of the Mahayana [Great Vehicle] tradition.

THE BUDDHA'S APPROACH TO TEACHING THE MORALITIES

The Ten virtues and Ten vices-The cause of human stupidity is in the passions-The Five prohibitions-The Ten prohibitions-Klaproth's praise of Buddhism-But it is atheistic, and therefore this praise should be qualified-Kindness to animals based on the fiction of transmigration-Buddhism teaches compassion for suffering without inculcating obedience to divine law-Story of Shakyamuni-Sin not distinguished from misery-Buddhists teach that the moral sense is innate-They assign a moral nature to animals-The Six paths of the metempsychosis-Hindoo notions of heaven and hell-Countless ages of joy and suffering-Examples-Exemption from punishment gained by meritorious actions-Ten kings of future judgment-Fate or Karma-Buddhism depreciates heaven and the gods-Buddha not God, but a Saviour-Moral influence of the Paradise of the Western heaven-Figurative interpretation of this legend-The contemplative school identifies good and evil-No moral distinctions in the Nirvâna-Buddhism has failed to produce high morality-The Confucianist condemnation of the Buddhists-Mr. P. Hordern's praise of Buddhism in Birmah-The Birmese intellectually inferior to the Chinese-Kindness to animals known to the Chinese before they received Buddhism-Buddha's reasons for not eating flesh.

The books of primitive Buddhism exhibit a higher moral tone than is found in the larger works full of metaphysical abstractions, which succeeded them. The "Book of Forty-two Sections," translated in the first century, and belonging to the former class, speaks of Ten vices and Ten virtues as belonging to mankind. The vices are: three of the body-killing, stealing, and adultery; four of the lips-slandering, reviling, lying, and elegant words (uttered with a vicious intention); three of the mind-jealousy, hatred, and "folly" (ch'ï), the last of which includes not believing in "the Honoured Three" (Buddha, Dharma, Sanga), and holding erroneous opinions. The opposites of these are the Ten virtues.

In the same work Buddha says: "That which causes the stupidity and delusion of man is love and the desires." "Man having many faults, if he does not repent, but allows his heart to be at rest, sins will rush upon him like water to the sea. When vice has thus become more powerful it is still harder than before to abandon it. If a bad man becomes sensible of his faults, abandons them and acts virtuously, his sin will day by day diminish and be destroyed, till he obtains full enlightenment."

In the work Kiau-ch'eng-fa-shu, the three vices of the mind are described as-covetousness, hatred, and folly. The Ten virtues that correspond to the Ten vices are there stated to be-preserving life, almsgiving, a "pure and virtuous life" (fan-hing), peaceful words, yielding words, truthful words, plain unadorned words, abstinence from quarrelling, mercy, and "acting from good causes" (yin-yuen). Hardy, in describing the Buddhism of Ceylon, states the four sins of speech to be-lying, slander, abuse, and unprofitable conversation. The three sins of the mind he states to be-covetousness, malice, and scepticism.

The disciple of Buddha, whether he enters a monastery or wears the prescribed dress and continues in the family, must pledge himself to the five following things :- (1) not to kill; (2) not to steal; (3) not to commit adultery; (4) not to lie; (5) not to drink wine. These are called Wu-kiai, "The five prohibitions." In Hardy's Manual of Buddhism, five evils to be avoided are mentioned-viz., (1) drinking intoxicating liquors; (2) gambling; (3) idleness; (4) improper association; (5) frequenting places of amusement.

In the work called Sheng-t'ien-shïh-kiai-king, "The book of birth in heaven through keeping the ten prohibitions," a Deva informs Buddha that he was born in the "heaven of the Thirty-three Devas" (that of Indra Shakra), as a reward for reverencing the "Three Precious Ones" (Buddha, the Law, and the Priesthood), for not inflicting death, or stealing, or committing adultery, or slandering, or deceiving, or lying, or drinking wine, or eating flesh, or coveting, or holding false opinions.

In the work Kiau-ch'eng fa-shu, the Ten prohibitions are stated to be : -(1) killing; (2) stealing; (3) adultery; (4) lying; (5) selling wine; (6) speaking of others' faults; (7) praising one's-self and defaming others; (8) parsimony joined with scoffing; (9) anger, and refusing to be corrected; (10) reviling the Three Precious Ones. In the comment on the Fan-wang-king, a work of the Great Development School in the Discipline division, by Chï-hiü, the Ten prohibitions are identified with the Ten vices, but in the text the prohibitions are given as in the last quotation.

Other lists of prohibitions might be transcribed amounting to two hundred and fifty, and even higher numbers. For these it will be sufficient to refer to the works already mentioned. Klaproth, having in view these moral precepts, and their effects on the character of nations, speaks of Buddhism as being of all religions next to Christianity in elevating the human race. He says: "The wild nomades of Central Asia have been changed by it into amiable and virtuous men, and its beneficent influence has been felt even in Northern Siberia."

The beneficent influence of this religion would have been much greater had it recognised the love and fear of God as the first of all the virtues. Buddhism, by ascribing the creation, continuance, and destruction of the world to an ever-changing fate, avoided the necessity of admitting a supreme God. This was the side the Buddhists took in their controversies with the Brahmans in India. Atheism is one point in the faith of the Southern Buddhists. By the Chinese Buddhists each world is held to be presided over by an individual Buddha, but they do not hold that one supreme spirit rules over the whole collection of worlds. Klaproth affirms that, according to, the Buddhists and the other Hindoos, "the universe is animated by a single spirit, individualised under innumerable forms, 'by' (par) matter which does not exist except in illusion." This spirit, however, is not God, the universal Creator and Preserver, and separated from the world by His everlasting personality.

Good has resulted doubtless in many instances from the prominent exhibition made by this system of the virtues and vices enumerated. But much more good would have been done if they had rested on a better basis, and been supported by a different view of the future state. The crime of killing rests chiefly on the doctrine of metempsychosis, which ascribes the same immortal soul to animals that it does to man. Faithful Buddhists are told not to kill the least insect, lest in so doing they should cause death to some deceased relative or ancestor whose soul animates the insect. On this account the corresponding virtue is stated to be fang-sheng, "to save life," constantly applied by the Buddhist priests and common people of China to the preservation of the lives of animals.

The monks are vegetarians for the same reasons. They abstain from flesh because they will not share in the slaughter of living beings. They also construct reservoirs of water near the monasteries, in which fish, snakes, tortoises, and small shell-fish, brought by worshippers of Buddha, are placed to preserve them from death. Goats and other land animals are also given over sometimes to the care of the monks, and it is a custom in some monasteries, as at T'ien-t'ung, near Ningpo, to feed a bird with a few grains of rice just before the morning meal has commenced. When the priest appears at the door, the little bird watching in the neighbourhood, and knows how to act on the occasion, flies to receive the gift.

In the Buddhist account of human sins and duties no obligation is included except the duty of lessening the sum of human misery and promoting happiness. These accords with the anecdote already related of Shakyamuni in his youth. His father, remembering the forewarning of a hermit, that the prince his son would wish to abandon the world, erected for him three palaces, where everything fascinating was placed to keep him from such a purpose. The son of a Deva came down to praise the beauty of the gardens and groves. But the prince, then eighteen years old, wished to go out and see the city. The king sent him with a wise minister to attend him. A Deva appeared at one of the city gates transformed into an old man resting on a staff and at another gate a Deva appeared as a sick person in pain and helpless.

At another gate he saw a corpse attacked by ravens-also a Deva. The prince asked in each case the reason of what he saw. The wise counsellor told him these sufferings came from the natural state of the world, and could not be avoided. People must grow old, must suffer from sickness, and must die. The prince was not satisfied, and the next day, seeing a Deva dressed as a monk, he dismounted from his horse and asked him who he was. The reply was, "A Shamen who has left the world." The prince asked him why he had left the world. He said, because he saw men exposed to the evils of birth, old age, sickness, and death; he therefore left the world to seek truth and save living beings. The disguised Deva then ascended into the air and disappeared.

At nineteen, assisted by the Devas, Shakyamuni is said to have gone through the air on horseback two hundred and fifty miles to Baga, a mountain belonging to the Himalayas. Here he lived as a hermit for six years, and became prepared for the office he was to assume. According to the view thus presented of the great object of Buddha's teaching, it is to deliver men from suffering. This is done by persuading them to enter on the monastic or hermit life, and act in obedience to the directions of Buddha.

This system looks on mankind as involved in misery rather than guilt. The Ten vices are rather to be regarded as faults, into which men fall from delusion and ignorance, than positive sins. The common people in China, whose phraseology is extensively infected with Buddhist ideas, see in every attack of sickness, and in other misfortunes, a close connection with "sin" (tsui). They hold that sin is the cause of suffering.

Yet they do not mean by this wilful sin, but some improper act done unconsciously, or in childhood, as treading on an insect, wasting rice-crumbs, or misusing paper that has the native characters upon it. Or they refer the calamity to the sins of a former life. Hence they regard themselves as more to be pitied than blamed for the tsui or "sin" of which their ill fortune gives evidence.

This is an example of the mode in which the better tendencies of the Buddhist system are neutralised by its omissions. Its moral precepts, good as most of them are, would have more power, and the true character of sin be more felt by the people, if the authority of God were recognised as the great reason for acting well-the source of moral obligation. Buddhism shook the faith of the Chinese in Heaven as a personal ruler, and put the Buddhas and Bodhisattwas in the place of that personal ruler. The effect of Buddhism in part was to urge the Chinese mind to see in Heaven only impersonal and material power. Thus the good effect of its moral teaching was neutralised; and then the Chinese had good moral teaching before.

The question that has been raised by European moralists as to whether man has from his natural constitution an inborn moral sense, is decided by the Buddhists, though without holding a controversy on the subject, in the affirmative. They may be said to appeal to a natural conscience, when they teach that all men have within them a good moral nature, and that this principle of good is only prevented from making men virtuous and happy by contact with the world and the delusions of the senses. This is similar to the Confucian doctrine, that all men are born well, and it is only by falling into evil habits subsequently that they become vicious. Most systems of morals, indeed, in words or by implication, admit the existence of conscience, because all men possess it, and cannot be made to understand moral distinctions without it.

The existence of a system of virtues and vices shows the operation of conscience on the maker of it, as the use of that system in moral instruction involves an appeal to conscience in the disciple. The identification of conscience, however, with natural goodness, by the Confucianists and the Buddhists, obscures its true character as the judge between right and wrong. And to tell men that they are naturally good is not only assuming, in compliment to human nature, a fact that should be proved, but it is also likely to induce those who are thus taught to look leniently on their own vices as originating solely in the influences of the outside world. The feebleness of the Buddhist appeal to conscience, as the source of moral obligation, is further increased by its assigning the same originally good nature to each member of the animal creation that it does to man. The motives to well-doing, drawn from a future state of retribution in this system, are derived from the Hindoo popular account of heaven and hell.

The Six life-paths into which living beings can be born are-(1) "Devas" (gods); (2) men; (3) "Asuras" (monsters); (4) "hell" (naraka); (5) hungry ghosts; (6) animals. The first three are assigned to the good, the latter three to the wicked. The moral action is called yin (cause), and its recompense kwo (fruit). All beings, whether virtuous or vicious, continue to be re-born in one of these six states, until saved by the teaching of Buddha. Buddha said: "To leave the three evil states is difficult. When the state of man has been attained, to leave the female sex and be born in the male, is difficult. To have the senses and mind and body all sound is hard. When this is attained, to be born in Central India is hard." He continues to say, that to meet Buddha and be instructed, to be born in the time of a good king, to be born in the family of a Bodhisattwa, and to believe with the heart in the Three Honoured Ones, are all difficult.

Buddha said, in a discourse delivered in the heaven of Indra Shakra, that whatever good man or woman heard the name of Ti-tsang Bodhisattwa, and in consequence performed an act of praise or worship, or repeated that Bodhisattwa's name, or made an offering to him, or drew a picture of him, such a person would certainly be born in the heaven of Indra Shakra. The same Bodhisattwa tells the mother of Buddha, who resides in the paradise just mentioned, that "disobedience to parents, with slaying, and wounding, are punished with an abode in the place of suffering called Wu-kien-ti-yü. Slandering the Three Precious Ones, or wounding the person of Buddha, or dishonouring the sacred books, or breaking the vows, or stealing from a monk, are punished in a similar way. Their punishment will last for ten millions of millions of kalpas. Then their sin being compensated for by sufficient suffering, they will be released.

"If a woman with an ugly countenance and sickly constitution prays to this Bodhisattwa, she will, for a million of kalpas, be born with a beautiful countenance." If any men or women perform music before the image of the same deity, sing, and offer incense, they shall have hundreds and thousands of spirits to protect them day and night, so that no unpleasant sound may enter their ears.

Any one who slanders or ridicules a worshipper of this Bodhisattwa will be transported to the "Avichi naraka" (O-pi ti-yü) till the end of this kalpa. He will then be born a wandering hungry ghost, and, after a thousand kalpas become an animal. After a thousand kalpas more he will again become a man. Such are a few specimens of the doctrine of retribution as taught to the popular mind. It is easy to see that such sensual conceptions of the future existence of man must degrade the common notions of the people on duty and virtue.

The objects for which the common people in China worship in the Buddhist temples are almost all of a very inferior nature. Religious worship, which ought to concern the recovery of man to pure virtue, and the restoration of direct communication with God by the forgiveness of sin, is changed into an instrument for acquiring various kinds of material happiness. The opinion the Buddhists hold on the forgiveness of sin is, that it can be attained by repentance and meritorious actions. A definite amount of gifts and worship will gain the removal of a corresponding amount of sin and its attendant suffering. Thus, a filial daughter, by a certain number of days spent in worshipping a Bodhisattwa, or a Buddha, can obtain the rescue of a mother from hell.

In the popular view of the future state, the Hindoo king of death, "Yama" (Yen-lo) holds a high place as the administrator of the punishments of hell. Nine others are joined with him of Chinese origin. They are called the Ten kings. The wicked at death are conducted to them to receive judgment. The decree by which men are born into the Six states of the metempsychosis is merely that of fate, expressed in the words yin-kwo, "cause and effect," or, employing one factor only, yin-yuen, "causation," or "fate" (karma). "Good actions" are also sometimes called yin-yuen, because they ultimately bring happiness to the doer. The motive to a good life, drawn from heavenly happiness, cannot be considered a strong one, when the Devas and their felicity are systematically depreciated, as they are in Buddhism.

The "Devas" (or popular Hindoo gods; in Chinese, t'ien) are all mortal, and limited in power. The state of man may be so elevated as to approach to that of the paradise of the Devas. Some men attain to nearly the same power as the gods, e.g., Krishna. Southey, in the Curse of Kehama, has made that personage, although a man, a terror to the kings of the Devas, and such a representation is in accordance with Hindoo notions. So in Chinese Buddhist temples, the visitor sees the highest of celestial beings listening humbly to Buddha. It may be said that it is not correct to institute or imply a parallel between Gods as He is in the view of the Christian, and the Hindoo deities. It may be said that a parallel between God and Buddha would be more just. But Buddha is a world-born man, who washes away his sins like others, by penances, offerings, and the teaching of some enlightened instructor.

He is not said to create the universe, or to act as the judge of mankind. He is simply a teacher of the most exalted kind, who, by superior knowledge, passes out of the world of delusion, and gradually attains the Nirvâna. His attitude towards his disciples is simply that of an instructor, not an authoritative superior. The tie by which the disciple is attached to him is that of voluntary not compulsory obedience. In fact, the character ascribed to Buddha is rather that of a Saviour than that of God. The object of his life and teaching is to rescue living beings from their misery. While such is the character of Buddha as he is described in books, he is, as an object of popular worship, like the great Bodhisattwas, simply regarded as a powerful divinity. A brief notice will here be taken of the ethical views of some of the Chinese sects. The Tsing-tu school substitutes a paradise of purely Buddhist invention for that of Hindoo mythology. It makes birth in the Western heaven, the abode of Amitabha Buddha, the reward of virtue.

The description of this paradise consists entirely of things pleasing to the senses. It is popularly regarded as real, but the founder of the Yün-ts'i school in his commentary on the "Amitabha Sutra," explains it as figurative. According to this explanation, the Western heaven means the moral nature, confirmed, pure, and at rest. Amitabha means the mind, clear, and enlightened. The rows of trees mean the mind cultivating the virtues. The music means the harmony of virtues in the mind. The flowers, and particularly the lotus, mean the mind opening to consciousness and intelligence. The beautiful birds mean the mind becoming changed and renovated. It is evident that, on adopting this mode of commenting on the fable of the Western heaven, it cannot any longer be honestly held out as a future state of reward, to attract men to good actions.

The object of this figurative interpretation of the Western paradise of Amitabha was, doubtless, to redeem the Tsing-tu school from the discredit into which it had fallen, by abandoning the Nirvâna in favour of a sensual heaven. The original inventors of the fiction must also have had such a notion of it as that here given, while they did not try to prevent its being accepted as real by the ignorant and uninquiring. In the contemplative school, founded by Bodhidharma, the distinction of vice and virtue is lost. To the mind that is given up to its own abstract meditations, the outer world becomes obliterated. A person who attends simply to his own heart may revile Buddha without sin, for nothing is sin to him. He does not make offerings or pray. All actions are the same to him. This system; however, is not in opposition to ethical distinctions. It only aims to enter a higher sphere. It seeks to attain a sort of Nirvâna even in the present life.

In the books of this school, as in others where the unreality of all sensible phenomena is maintained, virtue and vice occupy an inferior position. These notions only come into existence through the imperfection of the present state. They disappear altogether when an escape from it is effected, by admission into the higher region of pure enlightenment. Virtue and vice, life and death, happiness and misery, the antithetical states originated in the world of delusions to which we belong, are all condemned together as constituting a lower state of existence. All beings should strive to be freed from them, and to rise by Buddha's teaching to that perfection where every such diversity, moral or physical, will be lost in unity. The Nirvâna does not admit any such distinctions as those just mentioned. It is absolute and pure illumination, without anything definite attached to it, whether good or evil, pain or pleasure. Thus there is no place for ethics, except in the lower modes of life.

It is common for intelligent priests in China of the contemplative school to defend their system of idolatry by saying that they do not worship images themselves. They are intended for the ignorant who cannot comprehend the deeper principles of their religion. Religion being purely a matter of the heart, offerings and prostrations are really unnecessary. This exemplifies how what is regarded as a highly virtuous action in the common people, ceases to be so in the case of one who, as he thinks, has made some progress towards the state of Buddha. According to this view the consistent Buddhist will offer worship to no being whatever. He simply aims to raise himself above all the common feelings of human life. We cannot wonder that the Buddhist system of ethics having such deficiencies and such faults as have been pointed out, has failed to produce high morality among its votaries.

The mass of the people have gained from it the notion of a future retribution, but what is the use of this when the promised state beyond death consists merely of clumsy fiction? The metempsychosis, administered by a moral fate, has only provided them with a convenient means for charging their sinfulness and their misfortunes on a former life. What virtue the people have among them is due to the Confucian system. Buddhism has added to it only idolatry, and a false view of the future state, but has not contributed to make the people more virtuous. Klaproth complains of "a worthy and learned English missionary" (Dr. Marshman of Serampore) for saying, "Unhappily for mankind, Buddhism... was now fitted to spread its baneful influence to any extent." These modes of expression are not, however, by any means too strong to describe the effects of this religion in China if we accept the Confucianist view of Buddhism.

No thorough-going disciple of Confucius would think this language too strong if only Buddhism be judged from the standpoint of political and social morality. Surely if the Confucianist cannot see how the monk, who forsakes his family and his duties as a working citizen, is to be excused from heavy condemnation, the Christian also may be permitted to criticise with severity a system which denies the authority of God, identifies the moral nature of men and animals, teaches mankind to look to man instead of to God for redemption, and amuses the imagination with the most monstrous fictions of the unseen world and of the future state. The morality of Buddhism has received very high praise from more recent writers. Professor Max Müller says, "The moral code of Buddhism is one of the most perfect the world has ever known." Mr. P. Hordern, the Director of Public Instruction in Birmah, says, "The poor heathen is guided in his daily life by precepts older and not less noble than the precepts of Christianity. Centuries before the birth of Christ men were taught by the life and doctrine of one of the greatest men who ever lived lessons of the purest morality.

The child was taught to obey his parents and to be tender of all animal life, the man to love his neighbour as himself, to be true and just in all his dealings, and to look beyond the vain shows of the world for true happiness. Every shade of vice was guarded by special precepts. Love in its widest sense of universal charity was declared to be the mother of all the virtues, and even the peculiarly Christian precepts of the forgiveness of injuries and the meek acceptance of insult were already taught in the farthest East. "Throughout Birmah it is a daily thing to see men, women, and children kneeling on the road side, their hands clasped, and their faces turned devoutly to a distant pagoda; while at the weekly festivals, or the full moons, the devotions of the mass of the population are among the most interesting spectacles in the whole East." It is otherwise in China. Though the Buddhists have good precepts they are very much neglected, even in the teaching. Books containing hard metaphysical dogma such as the non-existence of matter form much more the subject of daily reading.

The monks are subject constantly to the Confucianist criticism that they are not filial to parents or useful working members of the commonwealth. A widely-extended monastic system does not approve itself to the Chinese political consciousness any more than it has done to European governments in times of revolution. The charge of laziness and neglect of social duties was made the ground of persecution in former days.

At present, while Confucianism has ceased to persecute Buddhism, it has never withdrawn its indictment against it on the ground of morality. Indeed, all the force of the moral teaching of the Chinese is in Confucianism and not in Buddhism. It is the moral sense of the Chinese themselves that is energetic and influential so far as they are really a moral people. The Buddhist moral code is feebleness itself compared with the Confucianist. This is partly because it is entangled by the coexistence with it of monkery as a life, and of the metempsychosis and metaphysical nihilism as dogma.

Then in regard to the power of Buddhism to elevate a people above the vain shows of the world and render then devotional, the conclusion to be drawn from the effect of this religion in the Chinese is very different from that adopted by Mr. Hordern in regard to Birmah. The Chinese intellect is strong and independent in its judgments, and it does not accept the fictions of Buddhism. The Hindoo mind cannot dominate the Chinese mind, and the contemplative life has no attractions for the countrymen of Confucius. The foreign resident in China does not witness the appearance of devotion which has won the admiration of Mr. Hordern in Birmah. The power shown by Buddhism to win the faith of the Birmese I should rather trace to the superiority of the Hindoo race over the mountain tribes of the Indo-Chinese peninsula.

The Birmese belong, with the Thibetans, to the Bod race, which, having no intellectual development of its own, accepted the Hindoo religion when brought them by the Buddhist teachers. The superiority of Hindoo arts and civilisation helped Buddhism to make this conquest. Bishop Bigandet says: "The Birmese want the capability to understand the Buddhist metaphysics. If the Buddhist moral code in itself has the power to influence a people so far as to render them virtuous and devotional, independently of the element of intellectual superiority, we still lack the evidence of it. "The success of Buddhism is in this respect the reverse of the success of Christianity, which, originating in Judea, subjugated both Greece and Rome without aid from intellectual superiority."

I just add here that the Confucianists do not allow that kindness to animals was first taught them by Buddhism. They find it in their own ancient books. Thus Mencius made the compassion felt by a prince, Tsi Siuen-wang, for a bullock about to be slaughtered, a ground for his exhibiting compassion still more for the people he governed. He had been distressed at the shuddering of the bullock chosen for sacrifice, and ordered it to be changed for a sheep, which was done. Confucianism assumes that pity for animals is natural for the human heart. The mother of Mencius moved her residence from the neighbourhood of a butcher's shop because she would not have her boy, while of tender years, witness daily that which would make him cruel.

Yet it cannot fairly be denied that beneficial effects must follow from the great prominence and publicity assigned to compassion as an attribute of Buddha to be imitated by every devout believer. The salvation of multitudes from suffering is held up as his great achievement, and to this he was prompted by disinterested pity. This the Confucianists would probably admit, while they would never allow that there is any ground to believe in the Buddhist metempsychosis, on which pity for animals is often made to rest for its basis. With Buddhist temples and monks everywhere, the Chinese do not accept the teaching that the souls of men migrate into animals, nor do the monks cordially maintain it. Among the reasons the Buddhists give for sparing the life of all animals, they do not mention the duty of not inflicting unnecessary pain, nor do they say that Buddha has a sovereign power to make laws, and he having made this law it must be obeyed.

Their reasons are of a lower sort, or they are based on dogmatised necessity. This, like other matters, is by the Buddhists treated in a thoroughly utilitarian and selfish way. Only in one point it is not so. They are invariably conscious of "moral fate," the karma, pervading the universe by an inevitable and unconquerable force. Kindness to animals is sure to bring happiness, as cruelty will cause misfortune. The following are the reasons given by Buddha for abstinence from animal food:-

First, In the endless changes of the metempsychosis, persons in the relation to me of any of the six divisions of kindred have become, from time to time, some of the animals used for food. To avoid eating my relations I ought to abstain.

Second, the smell and taste are not clean.

Third, the smell causes fear among the various animals.

Fourth, to eat animal food prevents charms and other magical devices from taking effect.

The writer who invented these reasons and put them in the mouth of Buddha, did not add the certainty of the retribution of the karma, as an additional motive for showing compassion to objects possessed of life, but this is understood and lies underneath all Buddhistic thought.

ADVICE TO THE INDIVIDUAL LAYMAN

Buddhism should not be thought to be a teaching for monks only, as it is sometimes wrongly conceived. In a large number of his discourses, the Buddha has given practical guidance for the lay life and sound advice to cope with life's difficulties. Many of our problems and difficulties for which some people blame circumstances and chance, are, if correctly viewed, the result of ignorance or negligence. They could be well avoided or overcome by knowledge and diligence yet of course, worldly happiness and security are never perfect; they are always a matter of degree, for in the fleeting there is nothing truly firm. The central problem of a lay Buddhist is how to combine personal progress in worldly matters with moral principles. He strives to achieve this by building his life on the foundation of the Fourth Noble Truth, the Noble Eightfold Path, and to shape his activities in accordance with it.

The first step of this Path is Right Understanding; by developing a life style in accordance with it, the other factors of the Path result from it, namely: Right Thoughts, Right Speech, Right Action, Right Livelihood, Right Effort, Right Mindfulness, and Right Concentration. The eight steps of the Path fall into the three divisions of Wisdom (the first two), Morality (the second three), and Mental Culture (the last three). The order of development is, however, Morality (sila), Mental Culture (samadhi), and Wisdom (pañña). The Path outlines the practice of Buddhism, leading to its ultimate goal - Nibbana. As a householder, the Buddhist is particularly concerned with Morality. Right Understanding, however, is the prerequisite. Right Effort is the training of the will, and Right Mindfulness, the all-round helper. Progress to a lay Buddhist means the development of the whole man in society. It is, therefore, an advance on many fronts - the economic, the moral, and the spiritual, the first not as an end in itself but as a means to an end: the full flowing of the human being in the onward-carrying stream of Buddhist ideas and ideals.

A PRACTICAL GUIDE

Right Understanding is the beginning and the end of Buddhism, without which one's vision is dimmed and the way is lost, all effort misguided and misdirected. Right Understanding, in the context of the layman's Dhamma, provides a sound philosophy of life. Right Understanding, the first step of the Path, is seeing life as it really is: the objective understanding of the nature of things as it truly is (yatha bhuta ñana dassana). All things that have arisen, including the so-called being, are nothing but incessant change (anicca), therefore unsatisfactory (dukkha) and productive of suffering. It follows then that what is both impermanent and pain-laden cannot conceal within it anything that is solid, substantial, or unchanging - an eternal soul or an immanent abiding principle (Anatta).

Right Understanding implies further knowledge of the working of kamma - the moral law of cause and effect. We reap what we sow, in proportion to the sowing. Good begets good and evil, evil. Kamma operates objectively, and the results show themselves here or in the hereafter. That is to say, consequences follow causes whether one believes in kamma or not, even as a fall from a height will result in injury or even death, irrespective of one's personal belief or disbelief in the force of gravity.

Kamma is intentional or volitional action; vipaka is the fruit or result, and every action affects character for good or bad. We know that actions consciously performed again and again tend to become unconscious or automatic habits. They, in turn, whether good or bad, become second nature. They more or less shape or mold the character of a person. Likewise, the unconscious or latent tendencies in us, including inborn human instincts, are merely the results of actions done repeatedly in innumerable past lives extending far beyond childhood and the formative years of the present life.

Kamma includes both past and present action. It is neither fate nor predestination. A Buddhist views life in terms of cause and effect, his birth included. Existence (life) was not thrust on him by an unseen Deity to whose will he must blindly bend nor by parents, for the mere fusing of two cells from mother and father does not by itself produce life. It was of his own causing of his own choice: the kammic energy generated from the past birth produced life - made real the potential, in the appropriate sperm and ovum of his human parents at the moment of conception, endowing the new life with initial consciousness (patisandhi viññana), using the mechanism of heredity, duly modified, if necessary. The arising of a being here then means the passing away of another elsewhere.

This changing personality that constitutes "me" - the physical and mental make-up that is "I" - the very environment into which I was born, in which I acted and reacted is more of my own doing, of my own choice, of my own kamma, of one's past actions and thoughts. It is just, it is fair, it is right; what is is the sum of what was; effects exactly balance causes. One gets precisely what one deserves, even as the sum of two plus two is four, never more nor less. Enough of the past that is dead. What remains is the ever-present now, not even the future that's still unborn. The past is dead, yet influences the present, but does not determine it. The past and the present, in turn, influence the future that is yet to be. Only the present is real.

The responsibility of using the present for good or bad lies with each individual and the future, still unborn, is one's to shape. The so-called being which, in fact, is merely a conflux of mind and matter, is, therefore, born of, supported by, and heir to, his kamma. One is driven to produce kamma by tanha or desire which itself is threefold. Where there is tanha, there is ignorance (avijja) - blindness to the real nature of life; and where there is ignorance, there is tanha or craving. They coexist, just as the heat and light of a flame are inseparable. And the beginning of ignorance (avijja) cannot be known.

Because of this lack of understanding of things as they truly are, we, often unmindful of the rights of others, desire for, grasp at, cling to, the wrong sorts of things: the pleasures that money can buy, power over others, fame and name, wishing to go on living forever. We hope that pleasures will be permanent, satisfying and solid, but find them to be passing, unsatisfying, and empty - as hollow as a bamboo when split. The result is frustration and disappointment, disease and an irritating sense of inadequacy and insufficiency. If we don't get all our wishes, we react with hate or take shelter in a world of delusive unreality or phantasy. To remedy this, we must correct our understanding and thinking, and see in our own experiences, so near to us, things as they truly are, and first reduce, and finally remove all shades of craving or desire that are the causes of this restlessness and discontent. This is not easy, but when one does so by treading the noble Eightfold path, one reaches a state of perfection and calm (Nibbana) thereby bringing to an end the pain-laden cycle of birth and death.

As long as there is desire, birth leads to death, and death to birth, even as an exit is also an entrance. Each subsequent individual born is not the same as the preceding one, nor is it entirely different (naca so naca añño) but only a continuity; that is to say, each succeeding birth depends upon, or emerges from, the preceding one. And both, birth and death are but the two sides of the same coin, life. The opposite of life is not death, as some fondly believe, but rest - the rest and peace of Nibbana, in contrast to the restlessness and turmoil that is life. Kamma, as we have seen, is volitional action. It implies making choices or decisions between, broadly speaking, skillful (kusala) and unskillful (akusala) actions. The former are rooted in generosity, loving-kindness, and wisdom leading to happiness and progress, and therefore, to be cultivated again and again in one's life.

The good actions are generosity, morality, meditation, reverence, service, and transference of merit, rejoicing in other's good actions, Hearing the Doctrine, Expounding the Doctrine, and straightening one's views. The unskilled actions are rooted in greed, hate and delusion, leading to pain, grief and decline, and therefore, to be avoided. There are ten such actions: killing, stealing, sexual misconduct, lying, slandering, harsh speech, gossip, covetousness, ill-will and false views. This division of actions is a natural outcome of the Universal Law of Kamma; Kamma is one of the fixed orders of existence. Life is like a ladder. The human being occupies the middle steps.

Above are the celestial worlds of bliss; below, the woeful states of sorrow. With every choice, one moves upward or downward, ascends or descends, for each one is evolved according to one's own actions. Beings are not only owners of kamma but also their heirs. Actions fashion not only one's fortune, how one shall be born, dividing beings into inferior or superior, in health, wealth, wisdom, and the like, but also shapes one's future, where one shall be born, whether in the human, heavenly or animal world. In short, one can progress or regress from the human state. A proper understanding of the Buddhist doctrine of kamma and rebirth can, therefore, improve and elevate the character of a person. Buddhism teaches, above all, moral responsibility - to be mindful of one's actions, because of the inevitability of action being followed by reaction. One therefore strives for one's best to avoid evil and to do good for one's own welfare as well as for the benefit of others.

This conduct leads to peace within and without. It promotes soberness of mind and habit together with self-respect and self-reliance. Finally, this teaching fosters in us a feeling of all-embracing kindness and tolerance toward all living beings and keeps us away from cruelty, hate, and conflict. Man, as a whole, has not made a steady progress toward moral and spiritual perfection. But the individual can pursue the ideal of a perfect man - the Arahant - free from greed, hate, and delusion by treading the Noble Eightfold Path comprising Sublime Conduct, Mental Culture and Intuitive Insight (or wisdom). It is the perfection of human living by perfecting one's understanding and purifying one's mind. It is to know the Truth, do the Truth and become the Truth. Such a one has gone beyond the force of all rebirth-producing kamma, skillful and unskillful. He has attained the highest - Nibbana.

As the Blessed One teaches with incomparable beauty:

Sabba papassa akaranam,

Kusalassa upasampada

Sacittapariyodapanam:

Etam Buddhanusasanam

(To avoid evil,

To do good,

To purify the mind,

This is the advice of all the Buddhas).

This, in brief and simple outline, is the Teaching of the Buddha as it affects the householder's life. It is at once an ideal and a method. As an ideal, it aims at the evolution of a perfect Man - synonymous with the attainment of Nibbana- in this very life itself, by one's own efforts. As a method, it teaches us that the ideal can become real only by the systematic practice and development of the Noble Eightfold Path, at the two levels - that of the monk and that of the layman. Each develops according to his ability and each according to his needs whereby man, using the instrument of mind, by his own endeavor comes to know himself, train himself, and free himself from the thralldom of base desire, the blindness of hate, and the mist of a delusive self, to win the highest of all freedoms - freedom from error and ignorance.

In this Noble Teaching, there is no intellectual error, based as it is on reason and, in keeping with the finding of science, no moral blindness; for its ethics are truly lofty, with a rational basis: namely, evolution in terms of kamma. That Buddhism is eminently practicable is clearly shown by the example of the great Indian Emperor Asoka, when Buddhism became the shaping ideal of the State, and Buddhist ideas and ideals were used to build a just and righteous society, thus ushering in a period of great prosperity: material, moral, and spiritual. It is the only true solution to the manifold problems in the modern world. To this we must now turn.

SOCIAL AND ECONOMIC ASPECTS

Buddha was a rebel. He rebelled against the way of thought, and the way of life, of his age. To the philosophical concept of life as dynamic change (anicca) of no being but becoming (bhava), any thinker but thought, any doer but deed - he added its social equivalent: the doctrine of social fluidity and equality based on nobility of conduct. As the Buddha stated:

> Not by birth is one an outcaste
>
> Not by birth is one a Brahman.
>
> By deeds is one an outcaste,
>
> By deeds is one a Brahman.

And again,

> A birth no Brahman, or non-Brahman makes;
>
> 'Tis life and doing that mold the Brahman true.
>
> Their lives mold farmers, tradesmen, merchants, serfs;
>
> Their lives mold robbers, soldiers, chaplains, kings.

What matters then is not the womb from which one came or the societal class into which one was born but the moral quality of one's actions. As a tree is judged by its fruit, so shall a man be judged by his deeds? In this way, the doors of the Deathless and of the unconditioned freedom beyond, and of social freedom here on earth, were thrown open to all, regardless of caste, color, or class. In his teaching all men unite, lose identity, even as do the waters of the rivers that flow into the sea. No caste, class, or race privileges existed among his lay followers or in the Order of the Sangha that he founded - a fitting complement to the doctrine of Anatta.

For the Buddha, all men are one in that they belong to one species. Social classes and castes are nothing but functional or occupational groupings, neither fixed nor inevitable. They are divisions of society, man-made, subject to change and resulting from social and historical factors. A social doctrine based on the alleged superiority of any caste, class, or race, and advocating keeping it dominant by the use of force, must necessarily lead to the perpetuation of social tensions and conflict, and will never bring about harmony and the fraternity of men. The Buddha's doctrine of equality does not, however, imply that all men are alike physically or mentally. That would be identity. It does mean that each one should be treated equally with human dignity, and given an equal chance to develop the faculties' latent in each, as all are capable of moral and spiritual progress, and of human perfection, in view of the common capacity and capability of humanity. Thus the Buddha's teaching of a classless society requires the progressive refinement of man's nature, as shown by his actions, and the development of his character.

The Buddha was not only the first thinker in known history to teach the doctrine of human equality, but also the first humanist who attempted to abolish slavery, in which term is also included the traffic in, and the sale of, females for commercial purposes. In fact, this is a prohibited trade for his followers. The character of a society depends on the beliefs and practices of its people as well as on its economy. An economic system based on Buddhist ethics and principles, therefore, seems the only alternative. The true nature of man is that he is not only thinking and feeling creature but also a striving creature, with higher aspirations and ideals. If he is aggressive and assertive, he is also cooperative and creative. He is forever making not only things, but himself. And the making of oneself by perfecting the art of living is the noblest of all creative aspirations, yielding the highest happiness and satisfaction in life.

Progress in the material side of life alone is not enough for human happiness, as illustrated by today's "affluent societies." The pursuit of material pleasures in the hope that by multiplying them they will thereby become permanent is a profitless chase, akin to chasing one's shadow: the faster one runs, the faster it eludes. True happiness, contentment, and harmony come from an emancipated mind. Any economic system is therefore, unsatisfactory, if based on a wrong set of values and attitudes, and will fail in the fulfillment of its promises. The only effective remedy for the economic and social ills of the modern world is a more rational and and balanced economic structure based on Buddhist ideas and ideals. In a Buddhist economic system the people deliberately use the state power to maximize welfare, both economic and social, from a given national income.

The methods employed are threefold: economic planning, a suitable fiscal policy, and a comprehensive network of social services assuring to every member of the community, as a right, and as a badge of citizenship and fellowship, the essentials of civilized living, such as minimum standards of economic security, health care, housing, and education, without which a citizen cannot realize his humanity in full. In such a system production, distribution, and values take a different meaning in a new context. Economic activity will be pursued not as an end in itself but a means to an end - the all-round development of man himself. There should be a revision of values. A person's worth, for instance, ought not to be measured in terms of what he has but on what he is. In short, man or the majority of men in society should be helped to see life in perspective. Knowledge and discipline may transform a society into a workshop or a military camp, but it is the cultivation of a proper sense of values that will make it truly civilized.

Perhaps this may be the clue to the paradox of the Western civilization that knows how to go through space and sail across the seas, but not how to live on earth in peace. It is true that such a change of heart and system may, in the present context of the world, take a long time to realize. But what else is the alternative? It is futile to think that reform by revolution will remedy the ills of the world. In the opening stanza of the Dhammapada the Buddha declared the supremacy of mind over matter: "Mind precedes things, dominates them, and creates them" (Mano pubbangama Dhamma mano settha mano maya). However, this must not be interpreted to mean that Buddhism is against social and economic reform. It is far from it. Buddhism stands for a society of equals, in which justice and ethical principles shall supplant privilege and chaos. But reform must take place by peaceful persuasion and education without resorting to violence; worthy aims must be realized by worthy means even as democracy must be maintained by the methods of democracy.

Buddhism concedes that the economic environment influences character, but denies that it determines it. A person can use his free will, within limits, and act according to his conscience irrespective of the social structure to which he belongs. It all depends on mind and its development. Society does not stand still. Like any other conditioned phenomenon, it changes constantly and Buddhism teaches us that we cannot change society as something different from its members. Social progress is their progress, social regress their regress. If the individual perfects his life, thinks and acts clearly, lives in accordance with the Dhamma and the moral law of kamma, to that extent will there be social order and discipline. Initial improvements from within will result in corresponding changes without. Social order and discipline follow, not preceded, the state of mind of the individuals comprising that society. Society reflects the character of its people; the better the people, the better the society. Every society is a projection or extension of the collective personality of its members.

But humanity in the mass can be influenced for good by the example of a few really noble and selfless men with vision and wisdom, with ideas and ideals to live for and to die for. They provide the guiding star round which others, too timid to lead but strong enough to follow, cluster around and become willing followers. It is these few who set the standards for the many at the bottom, and their impact and influence on the way of life and thought of the human race can be tremendous. The messages they bring carries with it the indelible stamp of truth and are, therefore, never obsolete. Most outstanding among the great teachers is the Buddha Gotama. It is through his Teachings that all the Buddhist nations, including Sri Lanka, were molded and into the fabric of national life were woven the strands of his Teaching.

It is then the duty of every genuine Buddhist to help to make known, far and wide, the Teaching of the Buddha in all its many aspects, and thereby make possible tomorrow the seemingly impossible of today - a new and just socio-economic order based on Buddhist ethics, principles, and practices. Such a society will be both democratic and socialistic, with liberty, equality, fraternity, and economic security for all, not as ends in themselves but as means to an end - the full development of man into a well-rounded, happy human being in the setting of the Teaching of Gotama the Buddha, Guide Incomparable to a troubled world.

BUDDHISM AND DAILY LIFE

A follower of the Buddha learns to view life realistically, which enables him to adjust to everything that comes his way. Buddhism tells him the meaning and purpose of existence and his place in the scheme of things. It suggests the lines of conduct, supported by cogent reasons, by which he should live his daily life. It clarifies what his attitude should be to specific matters like self, job, sex, and society. Thus it assists him in the business of living, for to lead a full life four fundamental adjustments have to be made. He must be happily adjusted to himself and the world, his occupation, his family, and his fellow beings.

Himself and the World

A Buddhist tries to see things as they really are. He remembers the instability of everything and understands the inherent danger in expecting to find permanence in existence. In this way, he strives to insulate himself from potential disappointments. So, a discerning lay Buddhist is not unduly elated or upset by the eight worldly conditions of gain and loss, honor and dishonor, praise and blame, pleasure and pain. He does not expect too much from others, nor from life, and recognizes that it is only human to have one's share of life's ups and downs.

He looks at life's events in terms of cause and effect, however unpleasant or painful they may be. An understanding layman accepts dukkha as the results of his own kamma - probably a past unskillful (akusala) action ripening in the present.

He sees the connection between craving and suffering and therefore tries to reduce both the intensity and variety. As the Dhammapada states:

From craving springs grief, from craving springs fear,

For him who is wholly free from craving, there is no grief - whence fear? - Dhammapada 215

Therefore, he is mindful of a scale of values - knowing clearly what is really important to him as a Buddhist layman, what is desirable but not so important, and what is trivial. He tries to eliminate the non-essential and learns to be content with the essential. Such a person soon discovers that to need less is to live better and happier. It is a mark of maturity. It is progress on the path to inner freedom. One should wisely seek and carefully choose in one's actions and strive to maintain a Buddhist standard of conduct, whatever disappointments life may bring. And when disappointments come, one tries to look at them with some degree of detachment, standing, as it were, apart from them. In this way, a person gains a feeling of inner security and frees himself from fears, anxieties, and many other heavy burdens. This attitude to life and the world brings courage and confidence.

How does a lay Buddhist view himself? In the Buddha Dhamma, the human being is an impersonal combination of ever-changing mind and matter. In the flux is found no unchanging soul or eternal principle. The self or soul is then a piece of fiction invented by the human mind. To believe in such an absurdity is to create another source of unhappiness. One should therefore see oneself as one truly is - a conflux of mind and matter neither energized by tanha or craving, containing immense possibilities for both good and evil, neither overestimating nor underestimating one's capacities nor capabilities. One must also take care to recognize one's limitations and not pretend that they do not exist. It is simply a matter of accepting what one is, and deciding to make the most of one. With this determination, one's position in this world will be decided by one's efforts. And everyone has a place, however humble it may be, and a contribution to make as well.

Seeing that no two are alike, physically or psychologically, in the light of kamma, a wise person should, therefore, avoid comparing himself with others. Such profitless comparison can only lead to unnecessary sorrow and suffering. If he thinks that he is better than others, he may become proud and conceited and develop a superiority feeling - of an inflated "I." If the person thinks he is worse than others, he is liable to develop an inferiority feeling - of a deflated "I," and to withdraw from the realities and responsibilities of life. If he considers that he is equal to others, there is likelihood of stagnation and disinclination to further effort and progress. So, instead of keeping pace with, or outdoing others, socially, financially, and in other ways, the understanding layman proceeds to do something more useful. He decides to take stock of himself, to know himself, his true nature in all aspects, as a first step to improving it: the secular (such as his physical, mental, emotional qualities), the moral, and the spiritual, through careful self-examination and observation, by past performance, and by the candid comments of sincere friends.

Seeing himself as a whole, he plans for life as a whole in the context of the Noble Eightfold Path. Such a plan when drawn up will include all important events of a normal layman's life including occupation, marriage, and old age. Lay happiness and security lies then in finding out exactly what one can do and in actually doing it. A plan like this brings order into an otherwise aimless and meaningless life, prevents drift and indicates the right direction and drive. A thoughtful lay Buddhist will not simply do what others do. He can resist the pull of the crowd when necessary. He is ever mindful both of ends pursued and the means employed. He does not merely go through life aimlessly; he knows clearly where he wants to go, with a purpose and a plan based on reality. To be born as a human being is hard, but made easier in a Buddha Era - that is, an age when his teachings are still remembered and practiced. The reasons why a lay Buddhist should consciously direct his life for purposeful living with a right end, by right endeavor, to a right plan; this is the quintessence of Buddha's teachings.

Earning a Living

Men work to satisfy the primary or basic urges of hunger, thirst, and sex, as well a host of secondary wants and desires created by a commercial civilization such as ours. The Buddha's teaching is a teaching of diligence and right effort or exertion. The opposite of diligence is negligence - aimless drift, sloth, and laziness which are hindrances to both material and moral progress. It is the active man who lives purposefully, who blesses the world with wealth and wisdom. So work is essential for happy living. Life without work would be an eternal holiday, which is the hell of boredom.

A large part of our waking life is spent earning a living. So it is easy to appreciate why we should be at least moderately happy in our job. But choosing a suitable career, like choosing a marriage partner, is one of the most important yet one of the most difficult tasks in life. The economic aspect of a community profoundly affects its other aspects. The Buddha says that society, as with all conditioned phenomena, has no finality of form and therefore changes with the passage of time. The mainsprings of social change are ideology and economics - for men are driven to action by beliefs and desires. Some systems emphasize the latter; the Buddha the former for an economic structure can only influence but never determine man's thought. Man must live and the means of his livelihood are matters of his greatest concern.

A hungry man is an angry man. And a man poisoned by discontent is hardly in a fit frame of mind to develop his moral and spiritual life. The spirit may be willing but the flesh may prove to be weak. Unemployment and economic insecurity lead to tension, irritability, and loss of self-respect without which a healthy mental life is impossible. And one of the essential needs of a man is to feel he is wanted in the world. Of human rights the right of work should, therefore, be assured to all, as a pre-requisite for the good life. It is the duty of the state to uphold justice, and provide for the material and spiritual welfare of its subjects. While Buddhism recognizes that bread is essential for existence, it also stresses that man does not live by bread alone.

This is not all. How he earns and why he does it are equally relevant. He should not gain a living by methods detrimental to the welfare of living beings - anakula ca kammanta, "a peaceful occupation," as the Discourse on Blessings (Maha-mangala Sutta) has it. So the Buddha forbade five kinds of trade to a lay Buddhist, and refraining from them constitutes Right Livelihood, the seventh step of the Path. They are: trading in arms, human beings, flesh (including the breeding of animals for slaughter), intoxicants and harmful drugs, and poisons. These trades add to the already existing suffering in the world.

Economic activity should also be regarded as a means to an end - the end being the full development of man. Work should serve men, not enslave him. He should not be so preoccupied with the business (or, busy-ness, to be more accurate) of earning a living that he has no time to live. While income and wealth through righteous means will bring satisfaction and lay happiness, the mere accumulation of riches for their own sake will only lead to unbridled acquisitiveness and self-indulgence resulting later in physical and mental suffering. The enjoyment of wealth implies not merely its use for one's own happiness but also the giving for the welfare of others as well. The Buddha further says that the progress, prosperity, and happiness of a lay person depends on hard and steady effort - rather discouraging, no doubt, to many people who want something for nothing.

Efficiency in work, be it high or humble, makes a useful contribution to the production of socially desirable goods and services. It gives one's work meaning and interest, besides enabling one to support oneself and one's family in comfort. Conservation and improvement of one's resources and talents, acquired or inherited, with balanced living, living within one's income, ensuring freedom from debt is a sure indicator of right seeing or understanding.

Lastly, a blameless moral and spiritual life should be the aim of right livelihood. Life is one and indivisible, and the working life a part of the whole. The man who is unhappy at work is unhappy at home, too. Unhappiness spreads. Likewise, business life is part of life. The Dhamma of the Blessed One should therefore pervade and permeate one's entire life for only wealth rooted in righteous endeavor can yield true happiness.

Bringing up a Family

In the Maha Mangala Sutta the Buddha teaches us that:

Mother and father well supporting,

Wife and children duly cherishing,

Types of work unconflicting,

This, the Highest Blessing. - Samyutta Nikaya, 2.4

The essentials of happy family life are then a partnership of two parents with common aims, attitudes, and ideals who love, respect, and trust each other; who love and understand their children, on whom they, in turn, can depend for the same treatment and sound guidance grounded on true values, living by Right Livelihood, and supporting aged parents. In Buddhism, however, marriage is not a compulsory institution for all lay followers. It is optional. This brings us to the important question of sex. The sex instinct is a powerful impersonal impulse or force in us all to ensure the preservation of the race. Nature, to make sure of its objective, made the reproductive act of sexual union highly pleasurable so that it is inevitably sought by the individual for its own sake. There is no special mating season for humans, and males and females may find that they are physically attracted at any time.

Sex is an essential part of life. In some form or other it affects us every day, and often ends in choosing a partner for life. It can make or mar a householder's life. What is the Buddhist attitude to sex? For a lay person, there is nothing sinful or shameful in sex, nor does it carry lifelong burdens of guilt. Sexual desires, in its personal aspect, are just like another form of craving and, as craving, leads to suffering. Sexual desire, too, must be controlled and finally totally eradicated. This happiness arises only at the third stage of Sainthood, that of Anagami. When a lay Buddhist becomes an Anagami, he leads a celibate life.

But sexual behavior, in its social context, demands mindfulness of the fact that at least one other person's happiness is at stake and, possibly, that of another - a potential child. And children born of premarital relations, when deprived and unwanted, often develop into juvenile delinquents. Besides, pre-marital sex may carry with it the risks of venereal infection. A compassionate Buddhist, mindful of his own and others' welfare, acts wisely and responsibly in sexual matters. Misconduct for a layman means sexual union with the wives of others or those under protection of father, mother, sister, brother, or guardian, including one's employees. Adolescence is a period of stress and strain. It is at this time that the sex instinct becomes active, and sensible parents should guide and help their children to adjust to the changes. This sexual energy could be diverted not merely to outdoor games and sports, but also to creative activities like hand work, gardening, and other constructive activities.

It is not easy for an unmarried adult to practice sexual self-restraint till such time as he is able to marry. No doubt he lives in a sex-drenched commercial civilization where sex is seen, heard, sensed, and thought of most the time. But the ideal of sex only within marriage is something worth aiming at. The Buddhist's ultimate objective is, after all, to be a Perfect Man - not a perfect beast. And a start has to be made some day, somewhere - and now is the best time for it. At all times in a man's life, it is mind that dominates man's actions. It is mind that makes one what one is. There is no doubt about this. Truly, it is an encouraging fact - one tends to become what one wants to be. And, if one wishes to be chaste, one can be. One's life will then move irresistibly in the direction of its fulfillment.

Much can be done by sublimating the instinct by diverting the energy in the sex impulse into other activities. Developing an occupational interest or hobbies or sports can divert the mind and provide suitable outlets. Moderation in eating is helpful. But what is most important is the guarding of thoughts regarding all sexual matters. One must also avoid situations and stimuli likely to excite sexual desires. When sensual desires do arise, the following methods may be tried:

i. Mindfully note the presence of such thoughts without delay; when they tend to arise, merely notice them without allowing yourself to be carried away by these thoughts.

ii. Simply neglect such thoughts, turning your mind either to beneficial thoughts or to an activity that absorbs you.

iii. Reflect on the possible end results.

Steps should also be taken to foster and maintain all that is wholesome, as for instance, wise friendship, and keeping oneself usefully occupied at all times. If one has succeeded in meditative practice, the happiness derived from it will be a powerful counter-force against sexual desires. This mindfulness is the only way to achieve self-mastery. It is a hard fight requiring patient and persistent practice; nevertheless, it is a fight worth waging and a goal worth winning.

Social Relationships

A lay Buddhist lives in society. He must adjust himself to other people to get on smoothly with them. Human relationships - the education of the emotions - are the fourth R in education and play an important part in everyday life. So instead of keeping pace with, or outdoing others socially, financially, and in other ways, the understanding layman proceeds to do something more useful. Happiness and security then lie in finding out exactly what one can do, and doing it well. The lay person, who practices morality (sila) by reason of his virtue, gives peace of mind to those around him. He controls his deeds and words by following the third, fourth, and fifth steps of the noble Eightfold Path, namely Right Speech, Right Action and Right Livelihood or by observing the Five Precepts (Pañca Sila).

Such regulated behavior flows from proper understanding of the Buddhist doctrine of kamma, that a man is what he is because of action and the result of action. If one is genuinely trying to tread the path, one's daily life should reflect it. So, the Buddhist avoids killing living beings, stealing, sexual misconduct, drugs, intoxicants, and harmful lying, tale-bearing, harsh words, and idle talk. The Buddha's attitude toward stupefying drugs and intoxicants is clear and simple: complete abstinence from both. And why? The immediate aim of a Buddhist layman is happiness and security, here and now - in the present existence, while his distant objective is the lasting peace and security of Nibbana and, therewith, freedom from repeated births and deaths, with their attendant frustrations, disappointments, and the pain of temporal life.

Now, the one and only tool he has at his disposal to achieve both of these goals is the weapon of the mind, which, under the wise guidance of the Master's teaching, he gradually learns to use with skill, without ill to himself or others. And one of the best ways of impairing the efficiency of this precious mental instrument - to make it dull and blunt, is to partake of intoxicating drinks and drugs. Even when taken in moderation they have a pernicious influence on the mind and on the body, as well as on the character and the moral qualities. Under their baneful effects, mind becomes confused, and the drinker finds it difficult to distinguish between right and wrong, good and bad, the true and false. Such a person, then, wrongs himself, wrongs those who live with him, and wrongs society at large.

On the other hand, he who faithfully follows the Buddha's advice and abstains completely from the use of all intoxicants and harmful drugs, is always sober in mind, and is therefore able to exercise physical, mental, and moral control. Such a one has always a clear mind and can easily understand what is going on within, and also without, one's mind. But what of a Buddhist who, as a rule, refrains from alcoholic drinks and drugs, but occasionally finds himself placed in a delicate situation such as when offered an intoxicating drink at a party given by his superior or at an important occasion? Should he accept or refuse?

At least two possible courses are open to him: he could politely decline excusing himself on medical grounds (which are justifiable), and ask instead for a non-alcoholic drink, mindfully noting what is taking place, and impress on his mind that even a single deviation from the ideal of total abstinence is to open the way, even temporarily, to heedlessness, recklessness, and mental confusion.

Alcohol does impair the ability to think clearly, to decide wisely, and to perform any work of an exacting nature. If a Buddhist layman, while aiming at absolute perfection occasionally lapses, and is content with approximations, he is free to do so - but at his own grave peril. Positively, the Buddhist layman is kind and compassionate to all, honest and upright, pure and chaste, sober and heedful in mind. He speaks only that which is true, in accordance with facts, sweet, peaceable, and helpful. Morality is a fence that protects us from the poisons of the outer world. It is, therefore, a pre-requisite for higher spiritual aspirations and through it character shines. The development of personality on such lines results in charm, tact, and tolerance - essential qualities to adjust oneself to society, and to get on well with other people.

In the Sigalovada Sutta, the Buddha explained to young Sigala the reciprocal relationship that should exist among the members of society. They are worth mentioning in brief; parents have to look after their children, and guide and educate them; children have to respect their parents, perform their duties and maintain family traditions; teachers must train and instruct pupils in the proper way; and pupils in turn must be diligent and dutiful; a husband should be kind, loyal, and respectful of his wife, supply her needs and give her due place in the home, and she in return should be faithful, understanding, efficient, industrious, and economical in the performance of her duties; friends should be generous, sincere, kindly, and helpful to one another, and a sheltering tree in time of need; employers must be considerate to their employees, give adequate wages, ensure satisfactory conditions of work and service and they, in return must work honestly, efficiently and be loyal to their masters; the laity should support and sustain the monks and other holy men who, in turn, should discourage them to do evil, encourage them to do good, expound the teaching and show the way to happiness.

Buddhist morality is grounded on both thought and feeling. A Buddhist monk does social service when he himself, while not engaging in the worldly life, so teaches the Dhamma that he makes the lay followers better Buddhists, and thereby induces them to take to social work, which is an ideal practical form of the Four Sublime States, Loving Kindness, Compassion, Sympathetic Joy, and Equanimity, besides their practice of these at the meditational levels. They should be the four cornerstones of genuine lay Buddhist life.

The Four Sublime States form the foundation of individual and social peace, and combine in them the realism of human nature and the idealism of youth to work for the social betterment, out of natural sympathy and concern for fellow-beings. But social work to be of real value should spring from genuine love, sympathy, and understanding for fellow-men, guided by knowledge and training. It is the living expression of Buddhist brotherhood. The cultivation of the neglect of these duties is a matter for each one of us, but their promotion will undoubtedly foster healthier inter-personal relationships, decrease social tension and irritability, and appreciably increase social good, stability, and harmony.

MENTAL HEALTH

Life is full of stress and strain, but we have to live in conditions as they are and make the best of them. Successful adjustment to life in the light of Buddha's teachings will, however, ensure the all-round progress of the lay Buddhist, maximizing happiness and minimizing pain. The Buddha names four kinds of lay happiness: the happiness of possession as health, wealth, longevity, wife, and children; the enjoyment of such possessions; freedom from debt; and a blameless moral and spiritual life. Yet even the happiest person cannot say when and in what form misfortune may strike him. Against suffering, the externals of life will be of little or no avail. Real happiness and security are then to be sought in one's own mind, to be built up by constant effort, mindfulness, and concentration.

So the wise layman while being in this world will try to be less and less of it. He will train his mind to look at life mindfully with detachment, and soon discover that modern civilization is, by and large, a commercial one, for the benefit of a powerful minority at the expense of the unthinking majority, based on the intensification and multiplication of artificial wants, often by arousing and stimulating the undesirable and lower elements of human nature, and that the increasing satisfaction of these wants leads not to peace and stillness of mind, but only to chronic discontent, restlessness, dissatisfaction, and conflict. He therefore decides to practice voluntary simplicity and finds a new freedom; the less he wants, the happier and freer he is.

Thinking man realizes that there are but four essential needs for the body - pure food, clothing, shelter, and medicine. Corresponding to these, there are four for the mind - right knowledge, virtue, constant guarding of the sense doors, and meditation. Bhavana, or meditation, is the systematic training and culture of the mind with Nibbanaas its goal. The emotions are controlled, the will is disciplined, and the instinctive energies are diverted from their natural ends - led along the Four Great Efforts (the sixth step of the path) - to the sublimated ideal of a perfect Man (the Arahant) or Nibbana. If there is an urgent felt need, the ideal has the power of drawing out all one's instinctive impulses so that they are sublimated and harmonized, giving satisfaction to the individual, and therefore benefiting the community as well.

Closely connected with our instincts are the emotions. By emotion is meant a feeling which moves us strongly. We get stirred up, as it were. Examples of emotion are fear, anger, and strong sexual passion. When emotion floods the mind, reason retreats or disappears, and we often do things for which we repent later. So some emotional control is necessary, for, without it, character cannot be developed, and moral and spiritual progress is impossible. Fear is a common emotion that darkens our lives. It is anticipation of deprivations. One tries to live in two periods of time at once - the present and the future. To know how fear arises enables us to take the right steps for its removal. It results from wrong seeing, not understanding things as they really are. Uncertainty and change are the keynotes of life. To each one of us there is only one thing that is truly "ours," is "us": our character, as shown by our actions.

As for the rest, nothing belongs to us. We can visualize everything else being taken away, save this. But this, one's character, nobody and nothing else can deprive one of. Why then go to pieces when all other things that is liable to break, do break? Why fret about the fragility of the frail? Besides, are we so careful of not taking other people's things, as we are of preserving ours? Our past actions of depriving others may only end in others now depriving us. It is only fair and just. This attitude of detachment to life's storms is the only sound philosophy that can bring one a true security and a true serenity. Or again, there is no such thing as justifiable anger in Buddhism, for if one is in the right, one should not be angry, and if one is in the wrong, one cannot afford to be angry. Therefore, under any circumstances one should not become angry.

A good way to secure emotional control is to practice noticing mindfully and promptly an incipient hindrance (or any other mental state of mind); then, of its own, it tends to fade away. If done as often as possible, it will be very effective. The five hindrances are undue attachment to sensual desire; ill-will; laziness and inertia; agitation and worry; and doubt. The last here refers to indecision or un-steadiness in the particular thing that is being done. One must know exactly one's own mind - not be a Hamlet, unable to decide, because one is always mistrusting one's own judgment. Daily practice is the way to progress. Even a little practice every day, brings a person a little nearer to his object, day by day.

6

The Layman's Duties to his Associates

From the point of view of Dhamma, there are two categories of persons: Those who adhere to Dhamma, that is to say those who rely on Buddha's teaching; and those who do not adhere to Dhamma. Among those that do not adhere to Dhamma, whether we deal with followers of a religion or not, whether we deal with followers of a school of thought or not, one finds all the persons who adopt one or several beliefs among the group of those that exist apart from Dhamma. As an example, the simple fact to think that nothing does remain whatsoever after death is a kind of belief in the same way as any other is.

In this group, we find monks and nuns, who totally dedicate themselves to the practice suggested by their respective doctrines so as to reach the goal that these one assert. We find hermits, who isolate themselves in remote places to observe an ascetic mode of existence. They do it so as to reach the purpose that is supposed to get training proposed by their own faith. Those do not belong to any religious school. We find "priests" and "priestesses", who are relatively involved into the suggested or imposed practice by the teachings in connection with their faith, and who organise or direct the practice of the laymen. Finally, we find laymen, who, according to the individual cases, adhere to a religion, to a school of thought (philosophy, sect, etc.) or only to their own ideas. In the first two cases, they do it by devoting themselves to religious or ritual practices, ceremonies, recitations, prayers, considerations,philosophic debates, or by being self-contented with beliefs in ideas expounded by a monk, a guru, a philosopher, a book or any another support.

In the last case (layman adhering to his own ideas), he shapes his own way to be followed, according to the faiths, or he believes that what does occur after the death is the same thing for all, whatever are the actions being performed prior to it (Examples: Rebirths do occur in a totally unpredictable way; everybody is reborn in a realm of paradise or blissful celestial world (or demoniac); everybody reaches the stage of the divinity; before and after life, only nothingness does prevail, as soon as one dies, nothing whatsoever does remain; etc.) This type of belief is one of the most widespread; it explains why so many persons live so selfishly by enjoying pleasant things, which they get access to, to the full, by radically running away from all that which seems to be unpleasant, devoid of pleasure or boring. Among those who adhere to Dhamma, there are bhikkhus, whom we often call the "Buddhist monks". They fully devote all their time to the practice, to the realisation, to the study and to the Dhamma teachings.

There were bhikkhunís, "Buddhist nuns", who did exactly the same thing, but their community disappeared since the 10th century, at the same time as sikkhamánas, who were women of intermediate status between sámašerís and bhikkhunís, also did. They were in period of training, intending to become bhikkhunís. There are sámašeras, whom we call "novices" or the "little monks". They learn monastic life, they dress in the monks' robe, but their discipline is sharply more flexible than those of the bhikkhu. To become bhikkhu, they have to wait to reach twenty years of age. There were sámašerís, feminine version of sámašera, whose presence vanished since the end of the feminine monastic community. There are those whom we call the "nuns", who are women who opt for a monastic or semi-monastic existence. They do have a little particular status, halfway between the one of the bhikkhu and the one of the laity. Besides certain rules, they have to observe eight rules. Their life is dedicated to the Dhamma, even though they perform many activities specific to the laity.

Finally, among the people who adhere to the Dhamma, all those who are not bhikkhus, or sámašeras, or nuns are laity. We can divide lay people into three categories:

- There are some laity who, although approving Buddha's word, only dedicate their life a little, or not at all, to the practice of the Dhamma. They like to claim that they are Buddhists, but do little else than run after pleasures and engage in business activities; if they observe one or two precepts, it is only because it is easy for them; they don't want to dedicate any effort to the rest. Even though they claim to be inclined to meditation, they convince themselves that they never have any time to practice it.
- There are also lay people who try to dedicate more time and effort to follow a way suitable to the development of knowledge (of reality). They more or less observe the five precepts (sometimes the eight), they like everything that concerns the Dhamma aesthetically (monuments, statues, ceremonies), they readily spend time reciting texts dealing with Buddha's teaching, watching the quality of their actions, regularly making donations, attending meditation sessions, and sometimes, taking ordination for a short period.
- Finally, there is laity who, within their possibilities, tries their best to progress quickly and effectively on the path to the cessation of suffering. These ones very regularly train in being generous, in being vigilant and in applying full mindfulness. Their observance of the five precepts, if not eight, is scrupulous. Some of them even intend to lead a monastic life permanently.

Although they all point to a sole aim, the objectives of Buddha's teaching are very diverse. They consist, among others, in:

- Inducing the first category of laity to improve their way of life so as to become laity of the second category.

- Encouraging the laity of the second category to maintain the positive aspects of their way of life and inciting them to improve on this so as to become laity of the third category.
- Encouraging the laity of the third category to maintain the positive aspects of their way of life and suggesting them the experience of complete renunciation (monastic life).

KAMMA AND THE PÁRAMÍTAS

In a prison cell lived four men. The first was ignorant and lazy, the second was ignorant and hard working, the third was skilful and lazy, and the fourth was skilful and hard working. Each had the possibility to work and earn a little money. The lazy ignoramus had a thoroughly miserable existence; he did nothing at all during the day, was terribly bored and never obtained anything more than the bare minimum for his subsistence. The hard-working ignoramus enjoyed a more comfortable life, because his work allowed him extra food and small treats such as a bottle of wine or magazines.

The skilful lazy person did not have a very pleasant existence. As he did not put any effort in his work, he did not earn the money needed to buy things that would have allowed him to enjoy a better quality of life. However, knowing how to think, he suffered less than the lazy ignoramus, because he knew how to manage his condition better. Thus, he succeeded more easily in being satisfied with little. However, his incorrigible laziness eventually prevented him from thinking properly. The skilful worker was competent in his work. Knowing how to think properly, he knew how to manage his money wisely. He learnt to content himself with little to save most of the money he earned. He had nothing good to drink or eat, or pleasant readings to offer him. Nevertheless, after a while, having endured the necessary time, he was able to pay off the bail to get out of prison.

To make the analogy of this story, we can say that:

The prison represents the continual dissatisfaction of

existence (dukkha), with its "ups and downs", the cycle of rebirths (samsará).

1. Ignorance represents ignorance.
2. Skill represents wisdom.
3. Laziness represents the lack of motivation to cultivate wholesome actions.
4. Work represents effort (the effort to develop and maintain what is beneficial, the effort to practice properly).
5. The money represents the consequence of positive actions, merit (kusala).
6. The release represents liberation (from any form of dissatisfaction).

To develop merit, it is necessary to perform positive actions, to make efforts of generosity, honesty and concentration. Nevertheless, if this is done with ignorance, merit will be badly used and, so to speak, "wasted". Thus, it remains profitless. For this merit to be beneficial, it must be cultivated with wisdom, that is, positive actions should be performed with the intention to take care of and develop the Dhamma (for one's own progress and that of others). Comment:

More than positive actions, the more profitable actions are simply abstinences from destructive or worthless actions. This explains why it is essential to understand clearly the actions that we perform and know how we have to carry them out if we wish them to be really profitable. The prison story also shows us that wisdom is useless without effort, which is indispensable for the development of wisdom. Thus, only the development of páramítas does allow us to progress on the path to liberation, at whatever level one may be.

If someone benefits from all the elements which allow him (her) to make of his (her) existence a training in the Dhamma (birth as human being, in a favourable environment, in a place and time when the teaching of a Buddha (sásana) is accessible, understanding the value of such a training, urge to embark in it, lack of serious obstacles such as a poor health, etc.), this means that he (she) has already developed numerous páramítas in the past. If, besides these conditions, someone devotes himself (herself) with ease to "meditation" (training into satipatthána), it means that he (she) has developed even more páramítas. If a person opts for the life of renunciation by joining, in a most natural way, the monastic community (sangha), it means that even more páramítas have been developed. Finally, when our páramítas reach complete maturity, we cannot but experience Nibbána, the cessation of all suffering.

THE TEN PÁRAMÍTAS

Buddha gave us a list of the ten páramítas:

1. Dána páramíta: Abandonment of possessions (animals or non-living objects) by making donations.
2. Síla páramíta: Control of actions and speech to avoid unwholesome actions.
3. Nekkhamma páramíta: Renunciation of the lay life in favour of the solitary life (bhikkhu, hermit).
4. Pañña páramíta: Development of knowledge and understanding through study and analytical reflection. To teach knowledge to others. To use one's wisdom for a maximum of benefits.
5. Viriya páramíta: Effort to work as much as possible for the good of others, even at the risk of one's life.
6. Khantí páramíta: Establishment of an always perfect tolerance, irrespective of the actions and words of others towards oneself.
7. Saccá páramíta: Truthfulness (to say only what is right).
8. Adhitthána páramíta: Decision to devote oneself to beneficial actions and to remain steadfast on it.
9. Mettá páramíta: Maintaining a state of mind turned to the happiness of others, to practise love for all beings without exception.
10. Upekkhá páramíta: Rejection of hatred and worship. Not to follow any particular idea. Maintaining the mind in equanimity.

TOWARDS WHOM TO DEVELOP LOVE

If we wish to progress on the path, it is essential to develop mettá. The love in question is an unlimited love that encompasses all beings, whatever they are. As we can read in the mettá sutta (discourse on loving kindness), it consists of developing mettá towards all beings, humans as well as animals, those we know as well as those we do not know, those we see as well as those we do not see, those that are pleasant as well as those that are hostile, those that are close as well as those that are far, those that are small as well as those that are big, etc. Naturally, one does not need a lot of effort to practice mettá, benevolence and tolerance, towards those who are dear to him (her).

However, when the question arises as to apply it towards those who cause us trouble, those who act badly towards us, those who commit only hateful and unwholesome actions, it becomes more difficult. It is precisely this difficulty that gives us the opportunity to progress on the path of wisdom. It is exactly the same with meditation: When everything is well, when everything is comfortable, when there is no pain, no itch, when it is not too warm or too cold and when silence is total, we feel well, assured, but we shall have no opportunity to progress correctly.

As with anything in the Dhamma, we could begin to develop mettá, benevolence and tolerance, gradually. For this, it is simply sufficient to get used to cultivate, from time to time, a state of benevolence towards one or several beings, to strive to send mettá mentally to someone who behaves badly towards us, to tolerate as far as possible an action that displeases us, whether committed voluntarily or not. Or still, we suppress those prejudices that we could easily have when seeing someone having a bizarre attitude, and pay attention for a few moments, to notice possibly that this person is anguished, ill-at-ease, and apparently leading a painful existence.

At that time, it will be natural to develop feelings of compassion and benevolence towards this person. If he (she) is sensitive and if he meets our glance, he (she) will see immediately that we show him sincere affection; he (she) will be able to feel less rejected and benefit from a positive mood. If there is a chance, we could even engage in a conversation with him (her), talking about simple things which may eventually be linked with him (her), and which could be a precious help to him (her). For a generalised practice of mettá and benevolence, we begin for example with our close relations, the members of our family and our friends, then we gradually expand, including at first our neighbours, our work colleagues, our companions in study, sports or any group.

We then add all the beings that we meet. For example, when on a bus, we can occasionally spend a short while to develop thoughts of benevolence towards all those who are in the vehicle. We continue by including all the beings in the village, district or city, without forgetting the mosquitoes that sting us!

PRAYERS

To develop the páramítas, many of us who do not feel able to follow a training into concentration, such as the application of attention to physical and mental perceptions, could more or less regularly devote time to the practice of mettá and benevolence by means of prayer. To do this, we recite a sutta dealing with mettá, benevolence and compassion. While reciting them, we close the eyes and concentrate on the words we pronounce. Such a sutta recited in a group, can provide support not only to develop mettá, benevolence or compassion more easily and more enduringly, but also some concentration that will be greatly beneficial for the cultivation of the páramítas. Naturally, for this to be effective, these prayers must be recited with an understanding of what is said, or at least with an idea of what the texts in question say (otherwise the value is lesser), and to concentrate on this, avoiding to let the mind wander somewhere else. It is important to do this wholeheartedly.

If we want this practice to bear fruit, it is necessary also to try to preserve the same state of mind at the beginning and after the prayers. Similarly, one must try to remain tranquil for at least a few moments before the prayers, in order to have the mind well attuned. Ideally one should keep this state of mind at all times, so that the time of prayer is only a focusing permitting to maintain an almost permanent state of benevolence. Buddha showed to us how to reach the definitive cessation of any form of dissatisfaction. Before reaching it, the path is long, it requires for each of us to perfect at all levels, beginning from the base, otherwise how could we build anything on impure bases? Let us feel reassured, the Buddha does not forget anybody; he explains, giving invaluable details, how every person has to act if he/she wishes to benefit from an existence that is as profitable as possible for oneself and for others, regardless of the social milieu and position in society.

He explains, among other things, how to manage a business or how a king (or a head of state) should act towards his people, and all, quite naturally, with the aim of establishing an ideal for all in terms of human relations and mutual respect, and, consequently, to offer everyone a framework suitable for training in the Dhamma. Thus, the duties of one to others according to the Buddha for wishing to lead his life in the most noble and the most profitable way is of the Dhamma. Comment: Cultural customs are very different from one country to another and from one time to the other. It is necessary in certain cases, to know how to adapt in consequence.

The Duties of a Child to his (her) Parents

1. To nourish them when they are not longer able to provide for their own needs because of their age. 2. To take care of their administrative procedures. 3. To continue the good practices of the family like honesty, generosity, etc. 4. To be worthy to receive their material and spiritual heritage and 5. To perform ceremonies after their death.

The Duties of a Parent to his (her) Children

1. To accustom them from very small to a good moral conduct.

2. To teach them good social manners (respect for others).
3. To transmit them knowledge and a harmless profession.
4. To marry them to a partner of good moral conduct who is suitable for them.
5. To bequeath them their inheritance when the time comes.

THE DUTIES OF THE PUPIL TO HIS (HER) TEACHER

1. To get up in sign of respect and go to receive him (her) when he (she) arrives.
2. To render him (her) a service if necessary.
3. To be eager to listen to his (her) advice.
4. If living with him (her), to help him (her) with the daily chores.
5. To try hard to learn what one does not yet know and not to forget what one has already learnt.

The Duties of the Teacher to his (her) Pupil

1. To instruct him (her) well in matters concerning social life, customs and manners, as well as in the spiritual field.
2. To make sure that he (she) retains well what one teaches by making him repeats several times in the day.
3. To teach everything one knows without concealing anything.
4. To introduce him (her) to one's friends and associates so that he (she) can obtain a job.
5. To guarantee his (her) material and spiritual safety (recitation of protective texts).

The Duties of the Husband to his Wife

1. To be respectful to her and not to address her with vulgar words.
2. Not to disdain her.
3. To be faithful.
4. To give her the housekeeping money and allow her free management of it.
5. To buy her beautiful clothes and jewellery.

The Duties of the Wife to her Husband

1. To be prudent and to dedicate herself entirely to the care of the household.
2. Know how to receive his friends and members of his family.
3. To be faithful.
4. To administer suitably the property and finances.
5. To be skilled in all household duties (cookery, sewing, ironing, etc.)

The Duties of a Young Man to his Friends

1. To be generous and open-hearted.
2. To speak politely.
3. To be ready to render service.
4. To avoid putting himself above others and to give the same chances to everybody.
5. To be honest.

The Duties of Friends to Young Men

1. To protect their health when they are unconscious (drunk, doped).
2. To protect their possessions when they are unconscious (drunk, doped).
3. To protect them from imminent dangers.
4. Not to abandon them when they have troubles.
5. To take care with benevolence of their children (giving them employment or other services).

The Duties of an Employee to his (her) Employer

1. To get up before him (her).
2. To go to bed after him (her).
3. To take only what is given.
4. To take one's duties seriously.
5. Not to speak badly of him (her), to speak well of him (her).

The Duties of an Employer to his (her) Employees

1. To give them work according with their capacity.
2. To give them food and a salary.
3. To take care of them in case of illness.
4. To share with them the good food or drink when available.
5. To grant them proper leave.

The Duties of a Lay Person to a Monk

1. To perform actions motivated by loving kindness.
2. To say words motivated by loving kindness.
3. To have thoughts of loving kindness.
4. To invite him to visit one's house if necessary and to invite him to report his needs.
5. To provide him with the four requisites: lodging, clothing, food and medicines, within the limitations of one's means.

The Duties of a Monk to a Lay Person

1. To teach in order to avoid what is unwholesome (cause of suffering for oneself and others).
2. To encourage him (her) in what is wholesome (source of happiness) like generosity, virtue and meditation.
3. To generate loving kindness towards him (her).
4. To teach what he does not know.
5. To repeat what he already knows.
6. To show the way to a more comfortable rebirth (deva world) or towards nibbána.

7

The Layman's Relation to the State

In order to determine the cultural and political implications of Buddhism in the modern world we must first define Buddhism itself, and ascertain the general nature of its relation to culture and to politics. A glimpse of the cultural achievements of Buddhism during its twenty-five centuries of history, and of its political status and influence in the same period will be helpful in understanding the cultural implications of Buddhism today, not only in the East but also in the West, besides grasping its current political implications for Asia and the world at large.

THE NATURE OF BUDDHISM

Buddhism, or more accurately, the Dharma, may best be defined simply as the means to enlightenment. The Buddha himself compares it to a raft. Just as a raft, after being fashioned out of grass, sticks, branches and leaves, serves to cross over great stretches of water and is then abandoned, so the Dharma, by means of which we ferry over the waters of birth and death to the other shore, nirvana, is not something to be taken with us but something to be left behind. In short, it is not an end in itself, but only a means to an end. In modern parlance, its function is purely instrumental and therefore its value only relative. This of course does not mean that it can be dispensed with. When we have arrived safely on the other shore, the raft may indeed be abandoned; but so long as we remain on this shore, or are still paddling across the stream, it is indispensable.

The pragmatic nature of the Dharma is emphasized in the words addressed by the Blessed One to his foster-mother and aunt, Mahapajapati Gautami, who had asked him to give her precept, hearing which she might dwell "alone, solitary, ardent and resolved." The, Buddha replies, "Of whatsoever teachings, Gotami, thou canst assure thyself thus: 'These doctrines conduce to dispassion, not to passions : to detachment, not to bandage : to decrease of (worldly) gains, not to increase of them : to frugality, not to covetousness : to content, and not discontent : to solitude, not company: to energy, not sluggishness: to delight in good, not delight in evil': of such teachings thou mayest with certainty affirm, Gotami, 'This is the Dharma. This is the Vinaya. This is the Master's Massage. It is for this reason that the Mahayanists were not only able to say, with Ashoka, "Whatever the Blessed One has said is well said", but also "Whatever is well said is the word of the Buddha [Adhyasayasamcudana Sutra, Siksa Samuccaya of Santideva, tr. by Cecil Bendall and W.H. D. Rouse].

The means to enlightenment comprise three groups of practices. Ananda, questioned about the Master's teaching some time after the mahaparinirvana, tells his interrogator, a young Brahmana, that the Blessed One taught sila, samadhi, prajna and gives an explanation of each of these terms in turn. According to the Mahaparinibbana sutta, these three groups had, in fact, formed the substance of the farewell discourse delivered by the Buddha at the various places through which he passed in the course of his last journey. Sila, or ethics, traditionally consists of the five precepts incumbent upon all Buddhists, both monks and laymen, as well as the 227 or 250 binding upon Hinayana and Mahayana monks respectively, and various special precepts observed by the Bodhisattvas.

In samadhi, or meditation, are included mindfulness, and self-possession (satisampajanna), contentment (santutthita) the overcoming of the five hindrances (pancanivarana), the attainment of the four (or eight) stages of super-consciousness (jhana) by means of one or more of the forty classical supports of concentration (kammatthana), and the development of various psychic powers (iddhi). Prajna (Pali: Panna), generally rendered as wisdom, includes all the doctrines of Buddhism, that is to say, teachings relating to the conditioned co-production (pratityasamutpada) of phenomena, the three characteristics (trilaksana) of mundane existence, the four noble truths (aryasatya), universal emptiness (sarvadharmanairaimya), the three kinds of reality (svabhava), mind only (citta-matrata), and the three bodies of the Buddha (trikaya).

Through each of these three stages in turn must the disciple pass in order to attain Nirvana? While some of the practices enumerated under Sila and samadhi are found in other traditions, the doctrines which constitute the conceptual formulations of prajna are peculiar to Buddhism.

BUDDHISM AND CULTURE

Culture, which is derived from a Latin word meaning 'tilling,' can be looked at from three principal points of view, First of all, it is the act of developing the moral, intellectual and aesthetic nature of man through education and discipline. Secondly, it is that familiarity with and taste in the fine arts, humanities and broad aspects of science that enlightened and refined state or temper of mind, which such education and discipline tend to induce. Thirdly, it is those activities and objects which are the effect in the artist, and the cause in the rasika, or savourer of a work of art, of the enlightenment and refinement referred to. Thus, culture comprises the act of cultivation, or education (literally a 'bringing out'), the thing cultivated, in this case a mental state, and the fruits of such cultivation; in short, works of science and of art. Buddhism is obviously connected with culture in all three senses.

But what is the nature of the connection between the two? Is it merely a historical and accidental relation having nothing to do with the essential nature of either Buddhism or of culture, or does it spring from some deep and hidden affinity? Buddhism, as we have seen, is the means to enlightenment, and as such threefold, consisting of sila, samadhi and prajna. In order to have an inner, as distinct from a merely outer, connection with Buddhism, culture must be able to function as a means to enlightenment. In other words, it must be possible for us to subsume it under the category of ethics, or of meditation, or of wisdom. Can this be done?

According to the Theravada tradition, it can. Speaking of bhavana, or mental culture, Dr. C. L. A. de Silva, a distinguished exponent of this school, writes, 'The volitions arising in the processes of thought during the time of learning the Dhamma Vinaya (the doctrine) or any arts, sciences and so on, too, are included under the heading of mental culture or bhavana. Though the connotation of bhavana is on the whole more active than samadhi, the two terms are in the present context more or less synonymous. Culture may be subsumed under samadhi, the second of the path to nirvana, because, like the more direct and specialized methods pertaining to the practice of meditation, the arts and sciences also contribute to the purification refinement and elevation of consciousness.

This fact has been recognized, in practice, even if not in theory, by all schools of Buddhism. But since the fine arts, by reason of their greater emotional appeal, are able to heighten consciousness to a far greater extent than the sciences, it is with painting, music and poetry, rather than with mathematics and chemistry, that Buddhism is most intimately related. This connection is twofold. Art may be either sacred or profane. In the first case, art is deliberately used, in conjunction with other methods, as a means of rising to a higher plane of consciousness.

The Buddha image springs to the mind as the best known example of this type of art. By fixing his mind on such an image, instead of on something that is not a work of art, the devotee is enabled to purify and refine his consciousness not only by the act of concentration itself but also by the aesthetic appeal of the image. Buddhist art, in which painting, sculpture, music and poetry, are all integrated into the spiritual tradition, and utilized, not merely as media of religious propaganda, but as objects of concentration and meditation, is one of the most effective means of heightening the consciousness ever devised by man. Profane art, or art which has no formal connection with the Dharma, though capable of producing an effect of the same kind is rarely able to produce it to the same degree.

Not being reinforced and stabilized by the methodical practice of concentration, and having, as sometimes happens, no firm foundation in the moral life, whatever heightening of consciousness it is able to produce is of momentary duration only. For this reason art, though it may greatly assist and powerfully reinforce the practice of meditation, the second stage of the Path, can never be a substitute for it. Much less can art be a substitute for religion. The Dharma as a means to enlightenment comprises, as we have already seen, not only sila and samadhi, ethics and meditation, but prajna or wisdom.

Even if it could be shown that art alone is capable of inducing the dhyanas, or states of super-consciousness, that it was capable of producing prajna there is this difference that the former, however high it may soar, is still mundane, whereas the latter is transcendental. Hence the Dharma, since it is not only ethics and meditation but also wisdom does not merely include culture but transcends it. However, Buddhism is traditionally associated not only with the sacred but also with the profane variety of art. By this we mean that besides making direct use of art for meditative purposes it also recognizes the purifying and refining power of "a thing of beauty", and therefore not only tolerates but also encourages the independent cultivation of the arts. Thus we have not only the images of Buddhas, and Bodhisattvas but statues of yaksas, yaksinis and apsaras, who, though belonging to the mythology of Buddhism, have nothing to do with its doctrine.

Asvaghosa composes an epic poem on the life of the Buddha; but Wang Wei sings of mountains, mists, and streams. Broadly speaking, the Mahayana, the liberal and progressive wing of Buddhism, was concerned more with the integration into the doctrine, as a supplementary means to enlightenment, of as many arts and sciences as possible. Thus, its art is on the whole sacred art. The Flinayana, which was somewhat conservative, pursued the cultivation of the arts and sciences parallel to the study and practice of the doctrine. Hence, its works of art are on the whole profane. To these generalizations there are, of course, many exceptions. The Mahayana has produced a great deal of profane art, while the Hinayana has produced a great deal of sacred art.

BUDDHISM AND POLITICS

The relation between Buddhism and politics is not quite as simple as that between Buddhism and culture. For, being concerned with the individual rather than with the group, culture is related to Buddhism as personal religion, but not to Buddhism as institutional religion. Moreover, Buddhism comprises, from the institutional point of view, two groups, one large and one small, the first being the community of lay believers, both male and female, the second the noble Order of monks. These two groups need not have the same kind of relation to politics. In order to understand clearly the relation between Buddhism, both personal and institutional, on the one hand, and politics in the various senses of the term, on the other, it would be necessary to investigate the relations between (a) the Buddhist doctrine and political theories, (b) Buddhism and the State, (c) the laity and the government, (d) the Sangha and the government, (e) the individual monk and the government, (f) the layman and practical politics, and (g) the monk and practical politics.

a. As far as our knowledge goes, the Buddha confined his attention strictly to questions of religious discipline, and refrained from making any pronouncement upon the relative merits of rival political theories and system. During his lifetime, as is well known to historians, two types of government prevailed in north-eastern India, the monarchical and the republican; but the Buddha did not praise or condemn either. His statement that so long as the Vajjians, a confederacy of republican tribes, would "assemble repeatedly and in large numbers, just so long their prosperity might be looked for and not their decay" [D. II. 73] cannot be regarded as favouring republicanism, any more than if he had said that King Ajatasatru could, if he was clever enough, break the confederacy, his statement could have been interpreted as approving autocracy. He merely stated the facts of the case without passing any ethical judgement.

On one point, however, the Buddha, and after him the entire Buddhist tradition was quite explicit: the government must uphold the moral and spiritual law. Being the means to enlightenment, Buddhism naturally demands that the State should recognize the fact that the true goal of life is not to eat, drink and reproduce the species, but to attain nirvana, and that, therefore, it has the duty of providing for its citizens a political and social organization within which both monks and the laity can live in accordance with the Dharina. Between Buddhism, on the one hand, and any political theory which recognizes, either implicitly or explicitly, the supremacy of the moral and spiritual law and makes provision for its individual and collective application, on the other, there can be no disagreement.

From the Buddha's social egalitarianism, as well as from his deliberate decentralization of authority in the Sangha, it may be inferred that a form of government, in theory democratic, in effect aristocratic (for an intelligent electorate would naturally elect the best man), would be most in accordance with his Teaching. Buddhism has no objection to either a socialistic or to a capitalist state provided it makes provision not only for the material but also for the moral and spiritual well-being of its subjects.

b. The nature of the relation between Buddhism and the State will vary in accordance with two factors, one being, of course, the nature of the State itself, the other the relative strength of the Buddhist population. In a predominantly non-Buddhist State, Buddhism would expect to enjoy the same rights as other religious minorities. That is to say, it would demand complete freedom to practise and propagate its tenets. Whether persecuted or tolerated, however, Buddhist citizens would always remain loyal to the State to which they belonged.

In a predominantly Buddhist State, Buddhism would naturally expect official recognition as the State religion. Under democracy, the State is the people, and the government is only the agency through which the will of the people is carried out. If in their individual capacity the citizens support Buddhism it is only logical that they should do so in their collective capacity too and also, Buddhism being divided not into sects but schools. Its recognition as the State religion is attended by no difficulty. In Ceylon, Burma, Siam, Cambodia and Laos only the Theravada exists. In Mahayana lands, such as China and Japan, the laity generally respects and supports all schools, and the State would do the same. Buddhist schools are tolerant, in fact, not only of each other, but also of non-Buddhist traditions.

c. Not much need be said about the relation between the individual Buddhist citizen and the government, because Buddhism has no means of enforcing among its adherents uniformity of action in the affairs of secular life. It is true that Buddhism does not only inculcate certain principles but-also indicates the main lines of their application; the details of the application are left to be worked out by the individual Buddhist, each for himself. Buddhism exhorts, it does not command. It tells us, for example, that to take life is morally wrong; but it leaves us free to determine for ourselves whether the acceptance of this teaching obliges us to be a vegetarian or a conscientious objector. A Buddhist, however, should take an active interest in whatever concerns the material, moral and spiritual well-being of his fellow-citizens. In short, it should be his endeavour to live his social and political life in accordance with the Dharma.

d. The relation of the Government to the Sangha is the same as that of the individual lay Buddhist to the individual bhiksu: it is the Sangha-dayaka, the patron and supporter of the Sangha. Just as it is the duty of the individual devotee to build temples, and monasteries, publish religious books and periodicals, so it is the duty of the government of a Buddhist State to finance similar undertakings which, either because of the greatness of the cost involved or the complexity of the organization required to carry them out, are beyond the capacity of private citizens. In the same way, the relation of the Sangha to the Government corresponds to the relation between the bhiksu and the layman.

Just as the monk, in his capacity of -guide, philosopher and friend-, indicates to the lay, devotee the path of righteousness, so it is the right and duty of the Sangha, in the person of its seniormost members, to advise the government not only on the propagation of the Dharma but also on its application to the soical and political life of the nation. The Sangha must also be able to draw attention to and freely criticize deviations from the Dharma on the part of the government, the people, and the political leaders. Objection should not be levelled against such a connection between the Sangha and the Government on the ground that monks should not meddle in politics. Unless the Dharma is applied to the national life, it will gradually lose its hold over domestic life. Being concerned with the preservation of the Dharma, the Sangha is inevitably concerned with its application also, whether to politics or any other sphere of life.

And in any case, there would be no question of the Sablia's becoming involved in the rought and tumble of practical politics. Needless to say, it is unthinkable that the advice of the Sangha should ever tend to the promotion of anything but peace and prosperity both at home and abroad. For whether it spoke to a king or to an emperor, to a President or to a Party Chairman, the Sangha would have but one message: Never in this world does hatred cease by hatred: it ceases only by love.

e. The individual monk should have no relation with the government as government except through the Sangha, or with the consent of the Sangha. Unless there happens to be a separate portfolio for religious affairs, or a special rovision for ecclesiastical councillors, as there is in Siam, he should not accept any off-ice in the government, and even in such cases as these he should not accept any remuneration. A monk cannot be required to undertake any form of national service; neither is he liable to conscription. In a Buddhist State these rights would be recognized automatically. Monks suspected of committing offences against the civil and criminal law should, in a Buddhist State, first of all be tried by an ecclesiastical tribunal and if found guilty they should be disrobed and handed over to the civil court for further trial and punishment.

f. Since the Buddhist layman is connected with the government, he is obviously obliged to take part in practical politics, and all that can usefully be said in this connection is that here, too, he should act in accordance with the Dharma.

g. The monk, however, is under no such obligation. On the contrary, by virtue of the rules which, at the time of his ordination, he undertakes faithfully to observe, he is obliged to refrain from participation in practical politics. "Onepath leads to wordly gains, quite another path leads to Nibbana. Let not the bhikkhu, the follower of the Buddha, yearn for honour, but let him, on the contrary, develop dispassion." In order to conform to this advice, the monk should not join, or support, or even vote for, any political organisation. Neither should he participate in meetings or any other public functions of a political or quasi-political nature. For those members of the Sangha who feel, as some of Burma and Ceylon have felt in recent times, that their duties as citizens have a stronger claim on them than their obligations as monks, the only honourable course is to leave the Sangha. Enlightenment and elections cannot be won together.

THE CULTURAL AND POLITICAL HERITAGE OF BUDDHISM

Since the heritage of Buddhism constitutes, in one way or another, the theme of practically everything that is discussed in these pages, all that need be done here is to indicate such broad trends and basic principles a relate to (a) culture, civilization and education, and (b) war and peace. Since culture generally, and in particular the fine arts, can be subsumed under the heading of samadhi or meditation, they may be included within the means to enlightenment. Culture is part of Buddhism. It is not an ornament on its apparel but one of the limbs of its body. Where Buddhism is, there is culture. Whither in the world Buddhism goes, thither goes culture too.

This is, indeed, one of the most obvious lessons of the spread of Buddhism throughout Asia, and it is repeated here only because its significance for the modern world in general and for modem India in particular, is not always sufficiently appreciated. Ceylon, Burma, Siam, Cambodia, Laos, Japan, Tibet Mongolia, Nepal, Sikkim, Bhutan and Ladakh received with Buddhism not only their religion but practically the whole of their civilization and culture. How much the introduction of Buddhism meant to the people of Japan, for example, has been clearly stated by Dr. D. T. Suzuki. Speaking of the eagerness with which they took up the study of the Dharma in the Nara period, he remarks, "Buddhism was to them a new philosophy, a new culture, and an inexhaustible mine of artistic impulses."

Again, speaking of the reasons which led the government of that period to build temples and monasteries, maintain monks and nuns, and erect a gigantic bronze image of Buddha Vairocana, he reminds one of the fact that "In those days the Buddhist temples were schools, hospitals, dispensaries, orphanages, refuges, for old age; and the monks were schoolmasters, nurses, doctors, engineers, keepers of free lodges, cultivators of land, explorers of the wilderness, etc. When the community was still in a primitive stage of evolution the Buddhists were leaders in every sense, and the government naturally encouraged their activities."

The monks were also poets, painters, sculptors, carvers and metallurgists. Suzuki's statement, together with our own rider, is true not only of Japan but of all the other countries that have been mentioned. Is it not more than a coincidence that Milarepa, the greatest poet of Tibet, should also have been at the same time her most famous yogin, and that Siri Rahula, who occupies in Simhalese literature a corresponding position, should have been the Sangharaja of Ceylon? China alone, of all the nations of Asia, had developed a civilization and culture of her own prior to the advent of Buddhism; but even China is indebted to Buddhism, if not for her culture, at least for its finest flowering. Buddhism was, in fact, a spring wind blowing from one end of the garden of Asia to the other and causing to bloom not only the lotous of India, but the rose of Persia, the temple flower of Ceylon, the zebina of Tibet, the chrysanthemum of China and the cherry of Japan.

Asian culture is, as a whole, Buddhist culture. Therefore, as Suzuki says at the conclusion of the article already quoted, "If the East is one, 1 and there is something that differentiates it from the West, the differentiation must be sought in the thought that is embodied in Buddhism. For it is in Buddhist thought and in no other that India, China, and Japan, representing the East, could be united as one. Each nationality has its own characteristic modes of adapting the thought to its environmental needs, but when the East as a unity is made to confront the West, Buddhism supplies the bond."

The Full significance of this declaration will emerge later. Here it would suffice to emphasize the fact that if the history of Buddhism in Asia has any lesson for the world today, it is that, in their long trek from the burning marl of the Gangetic valley to the gem-encrusted rocks of Ceylon in the South, the wind-swept uplands of Central Asia in the North, and the sun-confronting islands of Japan in the East, Buddhism, culture, civilization and education were inseparable friends and companions. Hardly less striking is the almost invariable association of Buddhism with peace. The exceptions were not only extremely rare but of merely local importance. King Aniruddha of Burma made war upon the neighbouring kingdom of Thaton in order to seize a copy of the Tripitaka which the king of Thaton refused to have copied. This was, of course, not the most Buddhistic way of obtaining the precious documents. The monks of mediaeval Japan, who lived in huge fortress monasteries, raised and fought in their own armies, and for seven hundred years, until the destruction of their strongholds, Hieizan and Negoro, by the Nobunaga and Hideyoshi in the sixteenth century, were a menace to the secular arm. Even the most industrious research has been unable to dig out from the two thousand five hundred years of Buddhist history, during which time it spread over more than a quarter of the land surface of the globe, as many as ten incidents of this kind. Not a single page of Buddhist history has ever been lurid with the light of inquisitorial fires, or darkened with the smoke of heretic or heathen cities ablaze or red with the blood of the guiltless victims of religious hatred.

Like the Bodhisattva Manjusri, Buddhism wields only one sword, the Sword or Wisdom, and recognizes only one enemy - ignorance. This is the testimony of history, and is not to be gainsaid. But even admitting the close association of Buddhism with peace in Asia it may be questioned whether Buddhism was really the cause and peace the effect. Perhaps their association was fortuitous. Buddhism has a bloodless and Christianity a bloody record, it might be argued, not so much because of any difference between their teachings but because one was propagated among the warlike tribes of Western Europe and the other among the peaceable nations of Asia. The contention is unfounded. Tibet, before the introduction of Buddhism, was the greatest military power in Asia. The early history of Burma, Siam, and Cambodia shows that the people of those countries were originally of an extremely warlike, even aggressive, disposition.

The Mongol hordes at one time overran not only the whole of Central Asia, but also India, China, Persia and Afghanistan, and thundered even at the gates of Europe. China exhibited at various periods of her history considerable military activity. The martial spirit of Japan is far from being subdued after nearly fifteen centuries of Buddhism. With the possible exceptions of India and China, the nations of Asia were originally no less pugnacious and predatory than those of Europe. Their subsequent peacefulness was due very largely to the influence of the pacific teachings of Buddhism. But one can hardly expect to be able to pacify turbulent and warlike nations by preaching to them a God of Battles. It may therefore be concluded that the association between Buddhism and peace is not fortuitous but inevitable. Buddhism has been in the past, is at present, and will continue to be in the future, a factor contributing to the establishment of universal peace.

BUDDHISM AND CULTURE TODAY

After four or five hundred years of comparative stagnation, the present century is witnessing a resurgence of Buddhism in many parts of Asia. In Japan this resurgence began as long ago as 1868, when the disestablishment of Buddhism at the commencement of the Meiji Era and the mild for in of persecution which for some years overtook the religion and its adherents acted as a stimulus.

A few years later Buddhism again raised its head in Ceylon, where the activities of Meggetuwatte, Gunananda, H. Sumangala and Col. H. S. Olcott precipitated a landslide in the direction of the national religion, Buddhist revival in India began as an organized movement in 1891, when Anagarika Dharmapala founded the Maha Bodhi Society. In China, the Buddhist awakening began with the work of His Eminence T'ai-Hsu, while the resurgence of the Dharma in Burma is associated with the name of another great scholar-saint, Ledi Sayadaw.

Now, culture being subsumed under samadhi as part of the means to enlightenment as has been seen already, the most important of the cultural implications of Buddhism today, is, naturally, the fact that its resurgence and revival in Asia is sowing the seeds of an efflorescence of culture. Shoots are springing up in many places, and even a few scattered blossoms can be seen. Brief mention must therefore be made of the stimulus which Buddhism has given to culture in certain Buddhist countries of Asia and in India, the original home of the Buddha's teachings. Since from the East Buddhism has now spread to the West, some note must be taken of its cultural implications for that part of the world also. Of all the Buddhist countries of Asia, it is in Ceylon and Burma perhaps, the Buddhism is now most triumphantly resurgent.

The achievements of Ceylon, considering that it is a tiny island with little more than five million Buddhist inhabitants, have indeed been remarkable. It gave birth to two great international Buddhist organizations, the Maha Bodhi Society and the World Fellowship of Buddhists. With the possible exception of Japan, Ceylon, out of her scanty resources, has sent abroad for more dharmadutas, or messengers of the Dharma, than any other Buddhist land. Her contributions to culture have been no less significant and far-reaching. Scholars like Coomaraswamy, Malalasekera and Buddhadatta; painters like Manjurri Thera and George Keyt, and writers and poets like Siri Nissanka, Dhanapala and Tambimuttu are known and respected far beyond the confines of their native land.

Within the country itself, the indigenous arts and crafts, customs and traditions are being revived. Link by link the chains of various alien and anti-Buddhist cultures, in which the Simhalese people had for centuries been fettered, are being snapped. With the attainment of self-government within the Commonwealth of Nations, Simhalese had begun to rival English in importance, and though modern Simhalese literature has not yet produced any figure of more than local significance, there is every possibility of its doing so before long. Similar trends can be observed in Burma; her political independence has led not only to a sudden and striking resurgence of Buddhism but also to a revival of Burmese Buddhist culture. No international figure has, however, yet emerged, nor any religious or cultural achievements of more than national interest and value.

If in Siam, Cambodia and Laos the resurgence of Buddhism and the revival of Buddhist culture are less noticeable, it is largely because, being less subject to foreign influence, neither Buddhism nor its associated arts, crafts, customs and institutions ever declined to the extent that they did elsewhere. A certain benumbing lethargy did, however, creep over these lands, and even though they may not have needed a revival, in the sense of bringing back to life something that was dead, they did need a more vigorous circulation of the blood. That such a quickening of the pulse did eventually take place in the present century is demonstrated by the publication, in forty-five volumes, of the entire Pali Canon in Siamese script. This magnificent edition, known as the Royal Siamese Tripitaka, is still the only complete and uniform edition of the Theravada Canon to have been printed in Asia.

In Japan, which has been subject to the influence of modern industrial civilization to a far greater extent than any other Asian country, the resurgence of Buddhism has led not so much to a revival of Buddhist culture, which here too, was never dead, as to an attempt to preserve and consolidate it amidst the essentially alien and hostile environment of modem life. Though that attempt seems to be succeeding on the whole, it is so great a drain on the spiritual vitality of Japanese Buddhism that there can be little energy to spare for fresh cultural achievements. Yet it is Japanese, Dr. D.T. Suzuki, who through his writings and lectures exercises on European and American thought and cultures a deeper and wider influence than any other Buddhist. In China, Tibet, Nepal and other parts of the Buddhist world, politics have temporarily assumed paramount importance, so that little can be said on the present cultural implications of Buddhism in those countries.

However, the recent action of the People's Republic of China in presenting to Burma two grains of the Buddha's relic bones, one set of the Chinese Tripitaka, two suits of robes used by the Han and Tibetan monks, one alms bowl and one cane staff, is perhaps not without significance. The revival of Buddhism which has been going on in India for the last sixty years, but particularly during the past decade, is one of the strangest and most striking events in the history of religions. Nowhere else in the world does one find a parallel case of a religion being revived centuries after its disappearance, not by the command of a despot, not as the result of foreign conquest, but simply because it is the will of the people.

Yet this is what is happening in India today. Less than a century ago Buddhism was unheard of in the land of its birth: if remembered at all, it was as an objectionable but fortunately extinct heterodoxy which had for a brief space troubled the placid waters of Brahminism. Today it is a household word. Over the chair of the President of the Republic of India, in the House of the People, the message dharmachakara-pravarttanaya, 'to turn the Wheel of the Dharma' flashes forth in electric light to the assembled representatives. At the very centre of the national flag as it floats over ten thousand public buildings, the same historic symbol reminds the nation not only of the sublime doctrine of the Buddha but also of the dharmavijaya or Conquest by Righteousness of Ashoka. Similarly, the lion-capital of Ashoka representing the fearless proclamation in the Dharma to the four quarters of space has been adopted as the official seal of the Republic.

It is hardly necessary to insist that the revival of Buddhism is inseparably linked with a renaissance of culture. Such a renaissance has, of course, been going on in India for some time and the revival of Buddhism, despite its importance, is by no means the only contributing factor. Indeed, from another point of view the revival of Buddhism is itself part of the great movement for the regeneration of the religious, cultural, economic and political life of the nation that has been agitating the whole sub-continent for more than a hundred years. Nevertheless, it would be a mistake to think that the revival of Buddhism in India is, for this reason, linked with the renaissance of culture only to the extent that it contributes to the renaissance of Indian, in the sense of non-Buddhist, culture. It is also linked with the renaissance of a culture specifically and distinctively Buddhist.

This Buddhist culture, as far as its manifestations in India are concerned, is an integral part of Indian culture. India has recognized the importance of studies in Pali, Sanskrit, Tibetan and Chinese for a full understanding of Buddhism and the subject has been discussed elsewhere. These naturally have had their effect on writers in the modern Indian languages, which either translated Buddhist works from the original or were inspired to write independent, books that reflect Buddhist thought. Rabindranath Tagore's magnificent invocations to the Buddha, his drama, Natir Puja (The Dancing Girl's Worship), and his narrative poem, Abitisar, are fine examples of the free handling of Buddhist themes.

Other writers whose work has been deeply influenced by Buddhism include Yashpal, one of the greatest masters of the modem Hindi short story and novel, Gurubaksh Singh, whose Asia da Chanana, a prose translation of Sir Edwin Amold's The Light of Asia, is regarded as a classic in modern Punjabi literature, and Kumaran Assan, one of the three greatest Malayalarn poets of the twentieth century. But like hundreds of less well-known poeis, dramatists and novelists, they are all Hindus who have been deeply moved by the sublimity of the Buddhist ideal and the beauty of its cultural manifestations. Only two or three Indian Buddhists have succeeded in carving niches for themselves in the temple of literary fame. Dharmananda Kosambi's numerous writings on Buddhist subjects-described elsewhere'-have secured him a name in Marathi literature, while the writings of Rahul Sankrityayan and Anand Kausalyayan are outstanding contributors to Hindi belles-lettres.

Hardly less stimulating has been the effect of Buddhist revival on the visual arts. Inspired by the frescoes of Ajanta, then newly discovered, and guided by the great art critic, E.B. Havell, the Bengal school of painting developed a style which, for the first time in centuries, handled Indian themes in a traditionally Indian manner. Both Abanindranath Tagore, and Nandalal Bose, the two great masters of this school, exhibited a marked fondness for subjects drawn, not only from the life of the Buddha but also from Buddhist history and legend. Contemporary Indian art is, in many cases, only superficially Indian. The best known painters, one or two of whom enjoy international fame, derive their technique, style and inspiration almost exclusively from the latest European and American models.

Those who remain faithful to the indigenous tradition and whose work is inspired by an awareness of spiritual values, regardless of their very high standard of achievement, seem unable to obtain anything like the recognition and appreciation they merit. Among these neglected artists are many whose work reflects deep Buddhist influence. There is, however, no professedly Buddhist painter of outstanding eminence. Once again the influence of Buddhism, deeply and subtly felt penetrates far beyond the formal boundaries of Buddhism. Though the Dharma is resurgent in Ceylon and Burma, and undergoing revival in India, the latest Buddhist renaissance has a long way to go before it reaches its peak. One swallow does not make a summer, and the cultural manifestations of Buddhist resurgence and revival, though at times strikingly beautiful, in comparison with the efflorescence of past ages do not yet amount to much more than two leaves and a bud. Even more so is this the case in Europe and America.

Though Buddhism seems to have struck firm roots in Western soil, the roots have not had time to go very deep, and the cultural flowering which has so far taken place, perhaps prematurely, though beautiful, is inconspicuous. As in India, it relates chiefly to literature and the visual arts. Here too we must distinguish between non-Buddhist writers and artists whose work exhibits traces of Buddhist influence and the creations of those who, being professed Buddhists, derive their main inspiration from Buddhism. From the historical point of view, perhaps the most striking feature of the Buddhist movement in the West is its absolute spontaneity. For reasons largely academic, about a century ago -oriental religion and culture in general, and Buddhism in particular, started attracting the attention of Western scholars.

Sanskrit, Pall, Chinese, and Tibetan became subjects of study at the universities. This led first to the publication and then to the translation of a number of Buddhist texts. Though Csoma de Koros (1784-1849) was undoubtedly the inaugurator of Buddhist studies in the West, it is to the great French scholar, Eugene Burnotif, which the credit for having placed them upon a scientific basis belongs. Thereafter a number of distinguished savants devoted themselves to the study of Buddhism. Prominent among them were Max Muller, who besides editing the two well-known series, The Sacred Books of the East (in which a number of Buddhist works were included) and The Sacred Books of the Buddhists, himself edited and translated some important Buddhist scriptures, and T.W. Rhys Davids, who in addition to publishing texts, translations and what are still standard works on Buddhism, founded the Pali Text Society, which since its inception has published considerably more than one hundred volumes of texts and translations, as well as the famous dictionary.

Hard on the heels of the scholars is the popularizers. Sir Edwin Arnold's The Light of Asia (1879), easily the most widely known English book on Buddhism and the stories and other writings of Paul Carus are the literary landmarks of this period. At the turn of the century Buddhism had begun to attract the attention not merely of philologists and historians but of men and women looking for a religion and a way of life more satisfying than Christianity. Schopenhauer, as early as the second decade of the nineteenth century, had declared himself a Buddhist, and his Die Welt als Wille und Vorstellung had for more than half a century been popularizing a version of Buddhism all over Europe. But though of far-reaching influence, his was an isolated case and it was only towards the end of the century that Buddhism began to strike root in the West. Buddhist groups sprang up in a number of European capitals and in many parts of the United States.

The Theosophical Society, especially during the lifetime of its founders, also helped in the dissemination of Buddhism. At present the Dharma may be said to be firmly established in England, Germany, France, and the United States. Though the number of adherents is still small, their sphere of influence is steadily expanding. Since the end of World War II, not a year has gone by without the publication of important books on Buddhism in at least one European language, and there is an increasing tendency for such books to be the work of practising Buddhists. References to Buddhism (not always intelligent) are becoming more and more frequent in modem literature and in the daily press. Rainer Maria Rilke, the greatest German poet since Heine, has written a beautiful sonnet on the Buddha and John Masefield, the present Poet Laureate of England, a creditable narrative poem. T.S. Eliot's The Waste Land (1922) contains a striking reference to the Buddha's Fire Sermon [line 308] while the imagery of a short passage in Edith Sitwell's "the Coat of Fire" is derived from The Tibetan Book of the Dead.

W.B. Yeats' Hermits upon Mount Meru of Everest and Caverned in night under the drifted snow are probably Buddhist hermits. Many of the poems rendered from the Chinese by Arthur Waley are Buddhist in theme or sentiment, and two or three of these have been included in anthologies of modem verse as English poems in their own right. The voluminous writings of Aldous Huxley, Bertrand Russell and Carl Gustayjung, all of whom enjoy world-wide reputation, carry important and, on the whole, appreciative references to Buddhism. Jung's interest in Buddhism is, in fact, well known, while Russell has gone so far as to declare that if he were compelled to choose between the religions of the world he would choose Buddhism. None of the poets and writers so far mentioned is Buddhists, however, and a Buddhist has yet to make a name for himself in modern European and American literature.

In the field of the visual arts the converse is true. While Buddhism seems to have had no influence at all upon modern Western painting and sculpture, the Buddhist movement in the West has already produced Buddhist artists of outstanding brilliance, Nicholas Roerich, who achieved international fame with his decor for Diaghilief s ballet version of Stravinsky's Le Sacre du Printemps, subsequently produced, mainly under the inspiration of Tibetan Buddhism, of which he had direct knowledge, series after series of canvases marked by powerful composition, brilliant colouring and profound symbolism, and all not only bathed in "the light that never was on sea or land- but pervaded by a mighty rushing wind of inspiration which would have been demoniacal had it not been so divine.

Earl H. Brewster, though in his later years he lost touch with Buddhism, produced his best work under its influence.

Only his own retiring disposition prevented his sculptures and paintings of the -Buddha from being more widely known. Like Roerich, Lama A. Govinda, who is not only an artist but a writer, scholar? Thinker and mystic of no ordinary calibre, derives his main inspiration from Tibetan Buddhism. He is, in fact, a member of a Tibetan religious order, and his art is perhaps even more deeply and purely Buddhist than that of either Roerich or Brewster. Not without significance is the fact that all three artists eventually made their home in India. Roerich and Brewster spent their last years here, while Govinda still works in the shadow of the Himalayas. All three, again, have shown.S that in its westward no less than in its eastward movement Buddhist art can retain the spiritual elevation, the sheer sublimity, which has ever been its, most striking and characteristic feature. The influence of Buddhism on Western music has been negligible. Mention should; however, be made of Berg's "Musicfor Wesak."

BUDDHISM AND POLITICS TODAY

Though mere numbers have little cultural significance, they do count politically, so that the political, unlike the cultural, implications of Buddhism in the modem world are necessarily confined to Asia in which continent alone it counts its adherents by the million. From what has been said above, it should already be clear that in the present, no less than in the past, Buddhism implies peace. But this peace is not a condition of unstable political equilibrium but rather a state of mind purified from all feelings of antagonism and thoroughly permeated by that impersonal and universal love which the Buddhists call maitri.

Buddhism works from within outwards. Its hierarchy enjoys no international diplomatic status, and chooses to act not by means of behind-the-scenes political wire-pulling but by the open parctice and propagation of the pacific teachings of the Buddha. On the political plane, Buddhism does not take sides. Love, in the sense of maitri, is the most powerful force in the world; but it is a neutral force. Whether one's love be directed towards concrete persons and things, or whether it be directed towards abstract conceptions and ideals, if it causes one to feel hatred towards some other object, of a different kind, it is of a limited extent, and therefore, not true love but only a species of attachment. Similarly, if peace, which is a form of love, is not universal it is not peace at all.

The conclusion of a private peace between two or more nations to the exclusion of the remainder is in reality impossible. Should such a peace in anyway threaten the security of any other state, even its observance would be on no, higher a moral plane than the honesty that is popularly supposed to exist among thieves. India having accepted Ashoka's great ideal of dharmavijaya or Conquest by Righteousness, it was inevitable that this very Buddhist maitri, or love and goodwill towards all, should form the ultimate spiritual basis of her policy of dynamic neutrality in world affairs. It is the raison d'etre of the fact that, while working unremittingly for world peace, the Government of India consistently refuses to align itself with any power bloc. Such an attitude has naturally drawn her closer to the Buddhist countries of South-East Asia, whose respective policies are naturally inspired by one and the same ideal. But by its very nature, such a relationship does not and cannot imply hostility or even indifference towards any other country or group of countries.

In fact, it is not one political group among other groups, with its own exclusive preferences and limited loyalties, but rather a slowly expanding centre radiating to the world the impersonal, universal and neutral power of maitri. It is in this light that one must view the Government of India's attempts to renew her ancient ties with the countries of Asia. It is because Buddhism alone can provide the necessary basis for these attempts that its political implications for Asia, and through Asia for the whole world, are so enormous and so important.

THE FUTURE

Prophesying is a proverbially hazardous game; but it may be confidently asserted that if we had the power of dipping into the future "as far as human eye can see," we should behold there Buddhism softly pacing through the centuries hand in hand with culture and peace. So far as the immediate future is concerned, there is little doubt that the tempo of Buddhist resurgence and revival throughout Asia, as well as that of it is propagation all over the non Buddhist world, will be accelerated with the passing of every remaining decade of the present century.

The culture manifestations of Buddhism will bloom more and more profusely while the grey-green olive of peace, lovingly tended by the ever-stronger growing hands of the Dharma, will put forth their black, shining fruits for the healing of the nations in ever greater abundance. If the cultural and political implications of Buddhism in the modern world succeed in working themselves out along the present lines of their development, our two leaves and a bud will soon grow into a whole forest of flowers.

8

The Ultimate Goal

STATEMENT OF THE AIM

When you hear something about Buddhism in the daily news you usually think of it having a background of huge idols and yellow-robed monks, with a thick atmosphere of incense fumes. You never feel that there is anything in it for you, except, maybe, an exotic spectacle. But is that all there is in Buddhism? Do the news photographers take pictures of the real Buddhism? Do the glossy magazines show you the fundamentals, or only the externals? Let us see, then, what Buddhism really is, Buddhism as it was originally expounded and as it still exists underneath the external trappings and trimmings.

Although generally regarded as a religion, Buddhism is basically a method of cultivating the mind. It is true that, with its monastic tradition and its emphasis on ethical factors, it possesses many of the surface characteristics that Westerners associate with religion. However, it is not theistic, since it affirms that the universe is governed by impersonal laws and not by any creator-god; it has no use for prayer, for the Buddha was a teacher and not a god; and it regards devotion not as a religious obligation but as a means of expressing gratitude to its founder and as a means of self-development. Thus it is not a religion at all from these points of view.

Again, Buddhism knows faith only in the sense of confidence in the way recommended by the Buddha. A

Buddhist is not expected to have faith or to believe in anything merely because the Buddha said it, or because it is written in the ancient books, or because it has been handed down by tradition, or because others believe it. He may, of course, agree with himself to take the Buddha-doctrine as a working hypothesis and to have confidence in it; but he is not expected to accept anything unless his reason accepts it. This does not mean that everything can be demonstrated rationally, for many points lie beyond the scope of the intellect and can be cognized only by the development of higher faculties. But the fact remains that there is no need for blind acceptance of anything in the Buddha-doctrine.

Buddhism is a way of life based on the training of the mind. Its one ultimate aim is to show the way to complete liberation from suffering by the attainment of the Unconditioned, a state beyond the range of the normal untrained mind. Its immediate aim is to strike at the roots of suffering in everyday life. All human activity is directed, either immediately or remotely, towards the attainment of happiness in some form or other; or, to express the same thing in negative terms, all human activity is directed towards liberation from some kind of unsatisfactoriness or dissatisfaction. Dissatisfaction, then, can be regarded as the starting point in human activity, with happiness as its ultimate goal. Dissatisfaction, the starting point in human activity, is also the starting point in Buddhism; and this point is expressed in the formula of the Four Basic Statements, which set out the fact of dissatisfaction, its cause, its cure, and the method of its cure.

DISSATISFACTION IS INESCAPABLE IN EN-SELF-ED LIFE

In its original meaning, the word which is here rendered as "dissatisfaction" and which is often translated as "suffering" embraces the meanings not only of pain, sorrow, and displeasure, but also of everything that is unsatisfactory, ranging from acute physical pain and severe mental anguish to slight tiredness, boredom, or mild disappointment. Sometimes the term is rendered as "dissatisfaction" or "unsatisfactoriness"; in some contexts these are perhaps more accurate, while at other times the word "suffering" is more expressive. For this reason we shall use both "suffering" and "dissatisfaction" or "unsatisfactoriness" according to context.

In some translations of the original texts it is stated that birth is suffering, sickness is suffering, old age is suffering, and pleasure is suffering. In English, this last statement fails to make sense; but if we restate it as "pleasure is unsatisfactory" it becomes more readily understandable, for all pleasure is impermanent and is eventually succeeded by its opposite, and from this point of view at least it is unsatisfactory. Now the Buddha-doctrine teaches that dissatisfaction or suffering is inescapable in en-self-ed life; and the term "en-self-ed life" needs some explanation. In brief, the doctrine teaches that the self, considered as a fixed, unchanging eternal soul, has no reality. The central core of every being is not an unchanging soul but a life-current, an ever-changing stream of energy which is never the same for two consecutive seconds.

The self, considered as an eternal soul, therefore, is a delusion, and when regarded from the ultimate standpoint it has no reality; and it is only within this delusion of selfhood that ultimate suffering can exist. When the self-delusion is finally transcended and the final enlightenment is attained, the ultimate state which lies beyond the relative universe is reached. In this ultimate state, the Unconditioned, suffering is extinguished; but while any element of selfhood remains, even though it is a delusion, suffering remains potentially within it. We must understand, then, that the First Basic Statement does not mean that suffering is inescapable; it means that sufferings is inescapable in enselfed life, or while the delusion of selfhood remains.

We can now move on to the Second Basic Statement, which says: The Origin of Dissatisfaction is Craving

If you fall on a slippery floor and suffer from bruises, you say that the cause of your suffering is the slippery floor. In an immediate sense you are right, of course, and to say that the cause of your bruises is craving fails to make sense. But the

Second Statement does not refer to individual cases or to immediate causes. It means that the integrating force that holds together the life-current is self-centered craving; for this life-current - this self-delusion - contains in itself the conditions for suffering, while the slippery floor is merely an occasion for suffering. It is obviously impossible, by the nature of the world we live in, to cure suffering by the removal of all the occasions for suffering; whereas it is possible in Buddhism to strike at its prime or fundamental cause.

Therefore the Third Basic Statement states: Liberation May Be Achieved by Destroying Craving

It is self-centered craving that holds together the forces which comprise the life-current, the stream of existence which we call the self; and it is only with self-delusion that unsatisfactoriness or suffering can exist. By the destruction of that which holds together the delusion of the self, the root cause of suffering is also destroyed. The ultimate aim of Buddhist practice, then, is to annihilate the self. This is where a great deal of misunderstanding arises, and naturally so; but once it is realized that to annihilate the self is to annihilate a delusion, this misunderstanding disappears. When the delusion is removed, the reality appears; so that to destroy delusion is to reveal the reality. The reality cannot be discovered while the delusion of self continues to obscure it.

Now what is this reality which appears when the delusion is removed? The ultimate reality is the Unconditioned, called also the Unborn, the Unoriginated, the Uncreated, and the Uncompounded. We can, inadequately and not very accurately, describe it as a positive state of being. It is characterized by supreme bliss and complete freedom from suffering and is so utterly different from ordinary existence that no real description of it can be given. The Unconditioned can be indicated - up to a point - only by stating what it is not; for it is beyond words and beyond thought. Hence, in the Buddhist texts, the Unconditioned is often explained as the final elimination from one's own mind, of greed, hatred and delusion. This, of course, also implies the perfection of the opposite positive qualities of selflessness, loving-kindness, and wisdom. The attainment of the Unconditioned is the ultimate aim of all Buddhist practice, and is the same as complete liberation from dissatisfaction or suffering. This brings us to the last of the Four Basic Statements:

The Way of Liberation is the Noble Eightfold Path

The eight factors of the path are these:

1. Right understanding, knowledge of the true nature of existence.
2. Right thought, thought free from sensuality, ill-will and cruelty.
3. Right speech, speech without falsity, gossip, harshness, and idle babble.
4. Right action or the avoidance of killing, stealing and adultery.
5. Right livelihood, an occupation that harms no conscious living being.
6. Right effort or the effort to destroy the defilements of the mind and to cultivate wholesome qualities.
7. Right mindfulness, the perfection of the normal faculty of attention.
8. Right concentration, the cultivation of a collected, focused mind through meditation.

In the Noble Eightfold Path there is nothing of an essentially religious nature; it is more a sort of moral psychology. But in the East as well as in the West people as a whole demand external show of some sort, and - on the outside at least - the non-essentials have assumed more importance than the essentials. While some external features in the practice of Buddhism must of necessity vary according to environment, the essential and constant characteristics of that practice are summed up in the following outline of the Noble Eightfold Path, the Middle Way between harmful extremes, as taught by the Buddha.

Although it is convenient to speak of the various aspects of the eightfold path as eight steps, they are not to be regarded as separate steps, taken one after another. On the contrary, each one must be practiced along with the others, and it might perhaps be better to think of them as if they were eight parallel lanes within the one road rather than eight successive steps. The first step of this path, right understanding, is primarily a matter of seeing things as they really are - or at least trying to do so without self-deceit or evasion. In another sense, right understanding commences as an intellectual appreciation of the nature of existence, and as such it can be regarded as the beginning of the path; but, when the path has been followed to the end, this merely intellectual appreciation is supplanted by a direct and penetrating discernment of the principles of the teaching first accepted intellectually.

While right understanding can be regarded as the complete understanding of the Buddha doctrine, it is based on the recognition of three dominating characteristics of the relative universe, of the universe of time, form and matter. These three characteristics can briefly be set out in this way:

1. Impermanence: All things in the relative universe are unceasingly changing.
2. Dissatisfaction: Some degree of suffering or dissatisfaction is inherent in en-selfed life, or in life within the limitations of the relative universe and personal experience.
3. Egolessness: No being - no human being or any other sort of being - possesses a fixed, unchanging, eternal soul or self. Instead, every being consists of an ever-changing current of forces, an ever-changing flux of material and mental phenomena, like a river which is always moving and is never still for a single second.

The self, then, is not a static entity but an ever-changing flux. This dynamic concept of existence is typical of deeper Buddhist thought; there is nothing static in life, and since it is ever-flowing you must learn to flow with it. Another aspect of right understanding is the recognition that the universe runs its course on the basis of a strict sequence of cause and effect, or of action and reaction, a sequence just as invariable and just as exact in the mental or moral realm as in the physical. In accordance with this law of moral action and reaction all morally good or wholesome will actions eventually bring to the doer happiness at some time, while unwholesome or morally bad will-actions bring suffering to the doer.

The effects of wholesome and unwholesome will-actions - that is to say, the happiness and suffering that result from them - do not generally follow immediately; there is often a considerable time-lag, for the resultant happiness and suffering can arise only when appropriate conditions are present. The results may not appear within the present lifetime. Thus at death there is normally a balance of "merit" which has not yet brought about its experience of happiness; and at the same time there is also a balance of "demerit" which has not yet given rise to the suffering which is to be its inevitable result.

After death, the body disintegrates, of course, but the life-current continues, not in the form of an unchanging soul, but in the form of an ever-changing stream of energy. Immediately after death a new being commences life to carry on this life current; but the new being is not necessarily a human being, and the instantaneous rebirth may take place on another plane of existence. But in any case, the new being is a direct sequel to the being that has just died. Thus the new being becomes an uninterrupted continuation of the old being, and the life-current is unbroken. The new being inherits the balance of merit built up by the old being, and this balance of merit will inevitably bring happiness at some future time. At the same time, the new being inherits the old being's balance of demerit, which will bring suffering at some time in the future.

In effect, in the sense of continuity, the new being is the same as the old being. In just the same way - that is, in the sense of continuity only - an old man is the same as the young man he once was, the young man is the same as the boy he once was, and the boy is the same as the baby he once was. But the identity of the old man with the young man, and with the boy, and with the baby, is due only to continuity; there is no other identity. Everything in the universe changes from day to day and from moment to moment, so that every being at this moment is a slightly different being from that of the moment before; the only identity is due to continuity. In the same way, the being that is reborn is different from the previous one that died; but the identity due to continuity remains as before.

These teachings are basic to the Buddha-doctrine - the illusory nature of the self, the law of action and reaction in the moral sphere, and the rebirth of the life-forces - but there is no need for anyone to accept anything that does not appeal to his reason. Acceptance of any particular teaching is unimportant; what is important is the continual effort to see things as they really are, without self-deceit or evasion.

So much for a brief outline of the doctrine under the heading of right understanding. The second step, right thought or aim, is a matter of freeing the intellectual faculties from adverse emotional factors, such as sensuality, ill-will, and cruelty, which render wise and unbiased decisions impossible. Right speech, right action, and right livelihood together make up the moral section of the path, their function being to keep the defilements of the mind under control and to prevent them from reaching adverse expression. These defilements, however, cannot be completely eradicated by morality alone, and the other steps of the path must be applied to cleanse the mind completely of its defilements.

Now in the next step - right effort - we enter the sphere of practical psychology, for right effort in this context means effort of will. In other words, the sixth step of the path is self-discipline, the training of the will in order to prevent and overcome those states of mind that retard development, and to arouse and cultivate those that bring about mental progress. The seventh step of the path is also one of practical psychology; this is the step called right mindfulness, and it consists of the fullest possible development of the ordinary faculty of attention. It is largely by the development of attention - expanded and intensified awareness - that the mind can eventually become capable of discerning things as they really are.

The primary function of the seventh step, right mindfulness, is to develop an increasing awareness of the unreality of the self. However, it functions also by continually improving the normal faculty of attention, thus equipping the mind better to meet the problems and stresses of the workaday world. In the Buddha-way, mindfulness consists of developing the faculty of attention so as to produce a constant awareness of all thoughts that arise, all words that are spoken, and all actions that are done, with a view to keeping them free from self-interest, from emotional bias, and from self-delusion. Right mindfulness has many applications in the sphere of everyday activities. For example, it can be employed to bring about a sharpened awareness, a clear comprehension, of the motives of these activities, and this clear comprehension of motive is extremely important.

In right concentration, the last of the eight steps, the cultivation of higher mind-states - up to the meditative absorptions - is undertaken, and these higher mind-states serve to unify, purify, and strengthen the mind for the achievement of liberating insight. In this ultimate achievement the delusion of selfhood, with its craving and suffering, is transcended and extinguished. This penetrating insight is the ultimate goal of all Buddhist practices, and with it comes a direct insight into the true nature of life, culminating in realization of the Unconditioned.

While the Unconditioned is the extinction of self, it is nevertheless not mere non-existence or annihilation, for the extinction of self is nothing but the extinction of a delusion. Every description of the Unconditioned must fail, for it lies not only beyond words but beyond even thought; and the only way to know it is to follow the Noble Eightfold Path to its end. This, then, is the original Buddhism; this is the Buddhism of the Noble Eightfold Path, of the path that leads from the bondage of self to liberating insight into reality.

NIRVANA

In sramanic thought, Nirvana is the state of being free from both suffering and the cycle of rebirth. It is an important concept in Buddhism and Jainism. "Nibbâna" is a Pâli word that means "blowing out" - that is, blowing out the fires of greed, hatred, and delusion. Buddha described nirvana as the perfect peace of the state of mind that is free from craving, anger and other afflictive states (kilesa). The subject is at peace with the world, has compassion for all and gives up obsessions and fixations. This peace is achieved when the existing volitional formations are pacified, and the conditions for the production of new ones are eradicated. In Nibbana the root causes of craving and aversion has been extinguished such that one is no longer subject to human suffering (dukkha) or further states of rebirths in samsara.

The Pali Canon also contains other perspectives on nirvana; for one, it is linked to the seeing-through of the empty nature of phenomena. It is also presented as a radical reordering of consciousness and unleashing of awareness. Scholar Herbert Guenther states that with nirvana "the ideal personality, the true human being" becomes reality. The Buddha in the Dhammapada says of nirvana that it is "the highest happiness". This happiness is an enduring, transcendental happiness integral to the calmness attained through enlightenment or bodhi, rather than the happiness derived from impermanent things. The knowledge accompanying nirvana is expressed through the word bodhi.

The Buddha explains nirvana as "the unconditioned" (asankhata) mind, a mind that has come to a point of perfect lucidity and clarity due to the cessation of the production of volitional formations. This is described by the Buddha as "deathlessness" (Pali: amata or amaravati) and as the highest spiritual attainment, the natural result that accrues to one who lives a life of virtuous conduct and practice in accordance with the Noble Eightfold Path. Such a life engenders increasing control over the generation of karma (Skt; Pali, kamma).

It produces wholesome karma with positive results and finally allows the cessation of the origination of karma altogether with the attainment of Nibbana. Otherwise, beings forever wander through the impermanent and suffering-generating realms of desire, form, and formlessness, collectively termed samsara. Each liberated individual produces no new karma, but preserves a particular individual personality which is the result of the traces of his or her karmic heritage. The very fact that there is a psycho-physical substrate during the remainder of an arahant's lifetime shows the continuing effect of karma. While nirvana is "unconditioned", it is not "uncaused" or "independent."

The stance of the early scriptures is that attaining Nibbanain either the current or some future birth depends on effort, and is not pre-determined. Furthermore, salvation according to the Pali Nikayas is not the recognition of a pre-existing or eternal perfection, but is the attainment of something that is hitherto unattained. This is also the orthodox Yogacara position, and that of Buddhaghosa. Nirvana is a compound of the prefix ni[r]- (ni, nis, nih) which means "out, away from, without", and the root vâ[na] (Pali. vâti) which can be translated as "blowing" as in "blowing of the wind", and also as "smelling, etc".

The Abhidharma-mahavibhâsa-sâstra, a Sarvastivâdin commentary, gives the complete context of the possible meanings from its Sanskrit roots:

- Vâna, implying the path of rebirth, + nir, meaning leaving off' or "being away from the path of rebirth."
- Vâna, meaning 'stench', + nir, meaning "freedom": "freedom from the stench of distressing karma."
- Vâna, meaning "dense forests", + nir, meaning "to get rid of" = "to be permanently rid of the dense forest of the five aggregates" (panca skandha), or the "three roots of greed, hate and delusion" (raga, dvesa, avidya) or "three characteristics of existence" (impermanence, anitya; unsatisfactoriness, dukkha, soullessness, anàtman).
- Vâna, meaning "weaving", + nir, meaning "knot" = "freedom from the knot of the distressful thread of karma."

Nirvana in sutra is never conceived of as a place (such as one might conceive heaven), but rather the antinomy of samsara which itself is synonymous with ignorance (avidyâ, Pâli avijjâ). This said:

"'the liberated mind (citta) that no longer clings' means Nibbâna" (Majjhima Nikaya 2-Att. 4.68).

Nirvâna is meant specifically - as pertains gnosis - that which ends the identity of the mind (citta) with empirical phenomena. Doctrinally Nibbâna is said of the mind which "no longer is coming (bhava) and going (vibhava)", but which has attained a status in perpetuity, whereby "liberation (vimutta) can be said".

It carries further connotations of stilling, cooling, and peace. The realizing of nirvana is compared to the ending of avidyâ (ignorance) which perpetuates the will (cetana) into effecting the incarnation of mind into biological or other form passing on forever through life after life (samsara). Samsara is caused principally by craving and ignorance. A person can attain nirvana without dying. When a person who has realized nirvana dies, his death is referred as parinirvana (Pali: parinibbana), his fully passing away, as his life was his last link to the cycle of death and rebirth (samsara), and he will not be reborn again.

Buddhism holds that the ultimate goal and end of samsaric existence (of ever "becoming" and "dying" and never truly being) is realization of nirvana; what happens to a person after his parinirvana cannot be explained, as it is outside of all conceivable experience. Through a series of questions, Sariputta brings a monk to admit that he cannot pin down the Tathagata as a truth or reality even in the present life, so to speculate regarding the ontological status of an arahant after death is not proper.

Individuals up to the level of non-returning may experience nirvana as an object of mental consciousness. Certain contemplations while Nibbana is an object of samadhi lead, if developed, to the level of non-returning or the gnosis of the arahant. At that point of contemplation, which is reached through a progression of insight, if the meditator realizes that even that state is constructed and therefore impermanent, the fetters are destroyed, arahantship is attained, and Nibbana is realized.

LUMINOUS CONSCIOUSNESS

Although an enlightened individual's consciousness is a karmic result, it is not limited by usual samsaric constraints. The Buddha discusses in the context of nirvana a kind of consciousness described as:

Consciousness without feature, without end, luminous all around.

This "consciousness without surface" differs from the kinds of consciousness associated to the six sense media, which have a "surface" that they fall upon and arise in response to. In a liberated individual it is directly known, without intermediary, free from any dependence on conditions at all. In one interpretation, the "luminous consciousness" is identical with nirvana. Others disagree, finding it to be not nirvana itself, but instead to be a kind of consciousness accessible only to arahants. A passage in the Majjhima Nikaya likens it to empty space.

For liberated ones the luminous, unsupported consciousness associated with Nibbana is directly known without mediation of the mental consciousness factor in dependent co-arising, and is the transcending of all objects of mental consciousness. It differs radically from the concept in the pre-Buddhist Upanishads and the Bhagavad Gita of Self-realization, described as accessing the individual's inmost consciousness, in that it is not considered an aspect, even the deepest aspect, of the individual's personality, and is not to be confused in any way with a "Self". Furthermore, it transcends the sphere of infinite consciousness, the sixth of the Buddhist Jhanas, which is in itself not the ending of the conceit of "I". Nagarjuna alluded to a passage regarding this level of consciousness in the Digha Nikaya in two different works. He wrote:

The Sage has declared that earth, water, fire, and wind, long, short, fine and coarse, good, and so on are extinguished in consciousness... Here long and short, fine and coarse, good and bad, here name and form all stop.

A related idea, which finds support in the Pali Canon and the contemporary Theravada practice tradition despite its absence in the Theravada commentaries and Abhidhamma, is that the mind of the arahant is itself Nibbana. There is a clear reference in the Anguttara Nikaya to a "luminous mind" present within all people, be they corrupt or pure, whether or not it itself is pure or impure. The Canon does not support the identification of the "luminous mind" with nirvanic consciousness, though it plays a role in the realization of nirvana. Upon the destruction of the fetters, according to one scholar, "the shining nibbanic consciousness flashes out" of it, "being without object or support, so transcending all limitations."

NIRVANA AND SAMSARA

In Mahâyâna Buddhism, nirvana and samsara are said to be not-different in the sense that there is no metaphysical barrier between the two. An individual can attain nirvana by following the Buddhist path. If they were ultimately different this would be impossible. Thus, the duality between nirvana and samsara is only accurate on the conventional level. Another way to arrive at this conclusion is through the analysis that all phenomena are empty of an essential identity, and therefore suffering is never inherent in any situation. Thus liberation from suffering and its causes is not a metaphysical shift of any kind. For better explication of this thinking see two-truth doctrine.The Theravâda school makes the antithesis of samsara and Nibbâna the starting point of the entire quest for deliverance.

Even more, it treats this antithesis as determinative of the final goal, which is precisely the transcendence of samsara and the attainment of liberation in Nibbâna. Where Theravada differs significantly from the Mahâyâna schools, which also start with the duality of samsara and nirvana, is in not regarding this polarity as a mere preparatory lesson tailored for those with blunt faculties, to be eventually superseded by some higher realization of non-duality. From the standpoint of the Pâli Suttas, even for the Buddha and the Arahants suffering and its cessation, samsara and Nibbâna, remain distinct. Both schools agree that Shakyamuni Buddha was in samsâra while having attained Nirvana, in so far as he was seen by all while simultaneously free from samsara.

PATHS TO NIRVANA IN THE PALI CANON

In the Visuddhimagga, Ch. I, v. 6, Buddhaghosa identify various options within the Pali canon for pursuing a path to nirvana, including:

1. By insight (vipassana) alone
2. By jhana and understanding
3. By deeds, vision and righteousness
4. By virtue, consciousness and understanding
5. By virtue, understanding, concentration and effort
6. By the four foundations of mindfulness

Depending on one's analysis, each of these options could be seen as a reframing of the Buddha's Threefold Training of virtue, mental development and wisdom.

SOME MAHAYANA PERSPECTIVES ON NIRVANA

The idea of Nirvana as purified, non-dualistic 'superior mind' can be found in some Mahayana/Tantric texts. The Samputa, for instance, states:

'Undefiled by lust and emotional impurities, unclouded by any dualistic perceptions, this superior mind is indeed the supreme nirvana.'

Some Mahayana traditions see the Buddha in almost docetic terms, viewing his visible manifestations as projections from within the state of Nirvana. According to Professor Etienne Lamotte, Buddhas are always and at all times in Nirvana, and their corporeal displays of themselves and their Buddhic careers are ultimately illusory. Lamotte writes of the Buddhas: 'they are born, reach enlightenment, set turning the Wheel of Dharma, and enter Nirvana. However, all this is only illusion: the appearance of a Buddha is the absence of arising, duration and destruction; their Nirvana is the fact that they are always and at all times in Nirvana.'

Some Mahayana sutras go further and attempt to characterize the nature of Nirvana itself. The Mahayana Mahaparinirvana Sutra, which has as one of its main topics precisely the realm or dhatu of Nirvana, has the Buddha speak of four essential elements which make up Nirvana. One of these is 'Self' (atmạn), which is construed as the enduring Self of the Buddha. Writing on this Mahayana understanding of Nirvana, William Edward Soothill and Lewis Hodous state:

'The Nirvana Sutra claims for nirvana the ancient ideas of permanence, bliss, personality, purity in the transcendental realm. Mahayana declares that Hinayana, by denying personality in the transcendental realm, denies the existence of the Buddha. In Mahayana, final nirvana is transcendental, and is also used as a term for the Absolute.'

At the time this scripture was written, there was already a long tradition of positive language about nirvana and the Buddha. While in early Buddhist thought nirvana is characterized by permanence, bliss, and purity, it is viewed as being the stopping of the breeding-ground for the "I am" attitude, and is beyond all possibility of the Self delusion. The Mahaparinirvana Sutra, a long and highly composite Mahayana scripture, refers to the Buddha using the term "Self" in order to win over non-Buddhist ascetics. From this, it continues: "The Buddha-nature is in fact not the self. For the sake of [guiding] sentient beings, I describe it as the self."

The Ratnagotravibhaga, a related text, points out that the teaching of the tathagatagarbha is intended to win sentient beings over to abandoning "affection for one's self" - one of the five defects caused by non-Buddhist teaching. Youru Wang notes similar language in the Lankavatara Sutra, and then writes: "Noticing this context is important. It will help us to avoid jumping to the conclusion that tathagatagarbha thought is simply another case of metaphysical imagination." However, some have objected to this reading regarding the Mahaparinirvana Sutra in particular, and claim that the Buddha then caps his comments in this passage with an affirmation of the reality of the Self, declaring that he is in fact that Self:

'Due to various causes and conditions, I have also taught that that which is the self is devoid of self, for though there is truly the self, I have taught that there is no self, and yet there is no falsehood in that. The Buddha-dhatu is devoid of self. When the Tathagata teaches that there is no self, it is because of the Eternal. The Tathagata is the Self, and his teaching that there is no self is because he has attained mastery/sovereignty [aisvarya].'

In the Nirvana Sutra, the Buddha states that he will now teach previously undisclosed doctrines (including on Nirvana) and that his earlier teaching on non-Self was one of expediency only. Dr. Kosho Yamamoto writes:

'He says that the non-Self which he once taught is none but of expediency ... He says that he is now ready to speak about the undisclosed teachings. Men abide in upside-down thoughts. So he will now speak of the affirmative attributes of Nirvana, which are none other than the Eternal, Bliss, the Self and the Pure.'

According to some scholars, the language used in the Tathagatagarbha genre of sutras can be seen as an attempt to state orthodox Buddhist teachings of dependent origination using positive language instead, to prevent people from being turned away from Buddhism by a false impression of nihilism. For example, in some of these sutras the perfection of the wisdom of not-self is stated to be the true self; the ultimate goal of the path is then characterized using a range of positive language that had been used in Indian philosophy previously by essentialist philosophers, but which was now transmuted into a new Buddhist vocabulary to describe a being who has successfully completed the Buddhist path.

Dr. Yamamoto points out that this 'affirmative' characterization of Nirvana pertains to a higher form of Nirvana – that of 'Great Nirvana'. The ordinary Nirvana which is normally spoken about might be likened to eating only a little food after a period of hunger: the bliss and peace that ensue are commensurate with that. Yamamoto goes on to state:

'But such a nirvana cannot be called "Great Nirvana". And it [i.e. the Buddha's new revelation regarding Nirvana] goes on to dwell on the "Great Self", "Great Bliss", and "Great Purity", all of which, along with the Eternal, constitute the four attributes of Great Nirvana.'

According to some scholars, the "Self" discussed in and related sutras do not represent a substantial Self. Rather, it is a positive language expression of emptiness and represents the potentiality to realize Buddhahood through Buddhist practices. In this view, the intention of the teaching of 'tathagatagarbha'/Buddha nature is soteriological rather than theoretical. However, this interpretation is contentious. Not all scholars share it.

Writing on the diverse understandings of tathagatagarbha doctrine as found in the Nirvana Sutra and similar scriptures, Dr. Jamie Hubbard comments on how some scholars see a tendency towards absolutism and monism in this Tathagata-garbha [a tendency which Japanese scholar Matsumoto castigates as non-Buddhist]. Dr. Hubbard comments:

'Matsumoto [calls] attention to the similarity between the extremely positive language and causal structure of enlightenment found in the tathagatagarbha literature and that of the substantial monism found in the atman/Brahman tradition. Matsumoto, of course, is not the only one to have noted this resemblance. Takasaki Jikido, for example, the preeminent scholar of the tathagatagarbha tradition, sees monism in the doctrine of the tathagatagarbha and the Mahayana in general ... Obermiller wedded this notion of a monistic Absolute to the tathagatagarbha literature in his translation and comments to the Ratnagotra, which he aptly subtitled "A Manual of Buddhist Monism" ... Lamotte and Frauwallner have seen the tathagatagarbha doctrine as diametrically opposed to the Madhyamika and representing something akin to the monism of the atman/Brahman strain, while yet others such as Nagao, Seyfort Ruegg, and Johnston (the editor of the Ratnagotra) simply voice their doubts and state that it seems similar to post-Vedic forms of monism.

Yet another camp, represented by Yamaguchi Susumu and his student Ogawa Ichijo, is able to understand tathagatagarbha thought without recourse to Vedic notions by putting it squarely within the Buddhist tradition of conditioned causality and emptiness, which, of course, explicitly rejects monism of any sort. Obviously, the question of the monist or absolutist nature of the tathagatagarbha and Buddha-nature traditions is complex.

Dr. Hubbard summarises his research on tathagatagarbha doctrines with the words:

'the teaching of the tathagatagarbha has always been debatable, for it is fundamentally an affirmative approach to truth and wisdom, offering descriptions of reality not in negative terms of what it is lacking or empty of (apophatic description, typical of the Pefection of Wisdom corpus and the Madhyhamika school) but rather in positive terms of what it is (cataphatic description, more typical of the devotional, tantric, Mahaparinirvana and Lotus Sutra traditions, and, it should be noted, the monistic terms of the orthodox Brahmanic systems)'.

According to Paul Williams, the similarity to the monism of atman/Brahman thought is explained when the Nirvana sutra presents its Self teachings as an attempt to win over non-Buddhist ascetics:

It is tempting to speak of Hindu influence on Buddhism at this point, but simply to talk of influences is almost always too easy... Having said that, of course the Mahaparinirvana-Sutra itself admits Hindu influence in a sense when it refers to the Buddha using the term 'Self' in order to win over non-Buddhist ascetics. Nevertheless, it would be wrong to think in particular of the transcendental Self-Brahman of Advaita Vedanta as necessarily influencing Buddhism at this point. It is by no means clear that the Self which is really no-Self of the Mahaparinirvana-Sutra is at all comparably to the Advaita Brahman, and anyway these Tathagatagarbha sutras are earlier than Gaudapada (seventh century), the founder of the Hindu Advaita School...

The sutra also states that the Buddha-nature is really no-Self, but is said to be a Self in a manner of speaking. In another section of the same sutra, it is stated that there are three ways for a person to "have" something; to have it in the past, to have it in the present, and to have it in the future. It states that what it means by "all beings have Buddha-nature" is that all beings will in the future become Buddhas.

NIRVANA AS MOKSHA

Uttaradhyana Sutra provides an account of Gautama explaining the meaning of nirvana to Kesi a disciple of Parsva.

"There is a safe place in view of all, but difficult of approach, where there is no old age nor death, no pain nor disease. It is what is called Nirvâna or freedom from pain, or perfection, which is in view of all; it is the safe, happy, and quiet place which the great sages reach. That is the eternal place, in view of all, but difficult of approach. Those sages who reach it are free from sorrows; they have put an end to the stream of existence.

FREEING OF MIND, FREEING OF INSIGHT

While mindfulness can be practiced quite well without Buddhism, Buddhism cannot be practiced without mindfulness. In its Buddhist context, mindfulness meditation has three overarching purposes: knowing the mind; training the mind; and freeing the mind.

KNOWING THE MIND

It is easy to spend an hour, a day, or even a lifetime so caught up with thoughts, concerns, and activities as to preclude understanding deeply what makes us operate the way we do. People can easily be clueless as to what motivates them, the nature of their reactions and feelings, and even, at times, what they are thinking about. The first step in mindfulness practice is to notice and take stock of who we are. What is going on in the body, in the mind, in our emotional life? What underlying dispositions are operating? This part of mindfulness practice is a simple process of discovery; it is not judging something as good or bad. Meditative discovery is supported by stillness. Whatever our degree of stillness, it acts as a backdrop to highlight what is going on.

It doesn't take much stillness to notice a racing, agitated mind. Discovery means becoming familiar with what a racing mind is like instead of being critical of it. What is the mind itself like, and what is its effect on the body? What emotions are present? What thoughts and beliefs? The knowing aspect of mindfulness is deliberate and conscious. When you know something this way, not only do you know it, but also a presence of mind grows in which you clearly know that you know. It is like being one of two calm people in an unruly crowd.

Neither of you gets caught up in the crowd's agitation, and a spark of recognition, maybe even a smile, passes between you as you share knowing that both of you are not caught. When the focus is on knowing, we make no attempt to try to change anything. For people who are always trying to make something happen, just observing the mind can be a radical change and a relief.

TRAINING THE MIND

The mind is not static. It is a process or, more accurately, a series of interacting processes. As such, the mind is malleable and pliable: it can be trained and shaped in new ways. An important part of Buddhist practice is taking responsibility for the dispositions and activities of our own mind so that it can operate in ways that are beneficial. When we don't take responsibility for our own mind, external forces will do the shaping: media, advertisements, companions, and other parts of society.

A good starting point is to train the mind in kindness and compassion. Even a little mindfulness will sometimes prove the cliche, "Self-knowledge is seldom good news." Mindfulness may reveal mental conflict with us, others, or the inconstant nature of life. Such conflict can take the form of aversion, confusion, anger, despair, ambition, or discouragement. Meeting conflict with further conflict will only add to our suffering. Instead, we can begin exploring how to be kinder, more forgiving and spacious with ourselves. Sometimes how one makes effort in meditation can be counterproductive. Striving too hard, trying to escape something, clinging to views and ideals, meditating as penance or obligation, and measuring every little bit of progress are some of the things that interfere with meditation.

An antidote to this struggle is training the mind to be more at ease with how things are. Rather than trying to organize the conditions of the world, we can cultivate an ability to be relaxed with whatever is happening. Once the mind experiences some ease in meditation, it is easier to train it in other ways. We can develop concentration or mental stability. We can foster the growth of generosity, ethical virtue, courage, discernment, and the capacity to release clinging. Often a Buddhist practitioner will choose one particular quality to cultivate for a period of time.

FREEING THE MIND

Central to Buddhist practice is training the capacity to let go of clinging. Sooner or later, the first aspect of Buddhist meditation, knowing the mind, will reveal how and where clinging is present. Some of the more painful forms of grasping are clinging to such things as pleasure, desire, self-image and judgments, opinions and ideals, people, and possessions. All clinging limits the mind's freedom and peace. The good news of Buddhism is that we can release clinging. We can free the mind. Or, if you prefer, you can call it "freeing the heart." The ultimate aim of Buddhist practice is to liberate the heart so there are no barriers, shackles, or constrictions to our heart's freedom. Usually freeing the heart begins in small steps, each bringing a corresponding peace. Freed completely, the heart is completely at peace. Complete freedom is not easily attained. It requires knowledge and training.

Knowing, training, and freeing the mind develop together. The more we know ourselves, the easier it is both to train ourselves and to know what needs to be released. The more our minds are trained, the easier it is to know ourselves and the more strength and wisdom we have to let go. And the more we let go, the fewer the obstructions to understanding ourselves and the easier it will be to train the mind. Few people care for their own minds as they do their own bodies, their clothes, or their possessions. Care of the body is a daily task. The mind too needs regular care, exercise, and training. With freedom from suffering as the goal, knowing, training, and freeing are the three Buddhist ways of caring for the mind.

ORIGIN OF ATTAINMENT

Theravada Buddhism focused primarily on meditation and concentration, the eighth of the Eightfold Noble Path; as a result, it centered on a monastic life and an extreme expenditure of time in meditating. This left little room for the bulk of humanity to join in, so a new schism erupted within the ranks of Buddhism in the first century AD, one that would attempt to reformulate the teachings of Buddha to accomodate a greater number of people. They called their new Buddhism, the "Greater Vehicle" (literally, "The Greater Ox-Cart") or Mahayana, since it could accomodate more people and more believers from all walks of life. They distinguished themselves from mainstream Theravada Buddhism by contemptuously referring to Theravada as Hinayana, or "The Lesser Vehicle."

The Mahayanists, however, did not see themselves as creating a new start for Buddhism, rather they claimed to be recovering the original teachings of Buddha, in much the same way that the Protestant reformers of sixteenth century Europe claimed that they were not creating a new Christianity but recovering the original form. The Mahayanists claimed that their canon of scriptures represented the final teachings of Buddha; they accounted for the non-presence of these teachings in over five hundred years by claiming that these were secret teachings entrusted only to the most faithful followers.

Whatever the origins of Mahayan doctrines, they represent a significant departure in the philosophy. Like the

Protestant Reformation, the overall goal of Mahayana was to extend religious authority to a greater number of people rather than concentrating it in the hands of a few. The Mahayanists managed to turn Buddhism into a more esoteric religion by developing a theory of gradations of Buddhahood. At the top was Buddhahood itself which was preceded by a series of lives, the bodhisattvas. This idea of the Bodhisattva was one of the most important innovations of Mahayana Buddhism. The Boddhisattva, or "being of wisdom," was originally invented to explain the nature of Buddha's earlier lives.

Before Buddha entered his final life as Siddhartha Gautama, he had spent many lives working towards Buddhahood. In these previous lives he was a Bodhisattva, a kind of "Buddha-in-waiting," that performed acts of incredible generosity, joy, and compassion towards his fellow human beings. An entire group of literature grew up around these previous lives of Buddha, called the Jataka or "Birth Stories." While we do not know much about the earliest forms of Buddhism, there is some evidence that the earliest followers believed that there was only the one Buddha and that no more would follow. Soon, however, a doctrine of the Maitreya, or "Future Buddha," began to assert itself. In this, Buddhists believed that a second Buddha would come and purify the world; they also believed that the first Buddha prophesied this future Buddha. If a future Buddha was coming, that meant that the second Buddha is already on earth passing through life after life. So someone on earth was the Maitreya.

It could be the person serving you food. It could be a child playing in the street. It could be you. What if there was more than one Maitreya? Five? Ten? A billion? That certainly raises the odds that you or someone you know is a future Buddha. The goal of Theravada Buddhism is practically unattainable. In order to make Buddhism a more esoteric religion, the Mahayanists invented two grades of Buddhist attainment below becoming a Buddha. While the Buddha was the highest goal, one could become a Pratyeka-buddha, that is, one who has awakened to the truth but keeps it secret. Below the Pratyeka-buddha is the arhant, or "worthy," who has learned the truth from others and has realized it as truth. Mahayana Buddhism establishes the arhant as the goal for all believers.

The believer hears the truth, comes to realize it as truth, and then passes into Nirvana. This doctrine of arhanthood is the basis for calling Mahayan the "Greater Vehicle," for it is meant to include everyone. Finally, the Mahayanists completed the conversion of Buddhism from a philosophy to religion. Therevada Buddhism holds that Buddha was a historical person who, on his death, ceased to exist. There were, however, strong tendencies for Buddhists to worship Buddha as a god of some sort; these tendencies probably began as early as Buddha's lifetime. The Mahayanists developed a theology of Buddha called the doctrine of "The Three Bodies," or Trikaya.

The Buddha was not a human being, as he was in Theravada Buddhism, but the manifestation of a universal, spiritual being. This being had three bodies. When it occupied the earth in the form of Siddhartha Gautama, it took on the Body of Magical Transformation (nirmanakaya). This Body of Magical Transformation was an emanation of the Body of Bliss (sambhogakaya), which occupies the heavens in the form of a ruling and governing god of the universe. There are many forms of the Body of Bliss, but the one that rules over our world is Amithaba who lives in a paradise in the western heavens called Sukhavati, or "Land of Pure Bliss." Finally, the Body of Bliss is an emanation of the Body of Essence (dharmakaya), which is the principle underlying the whole of the universe.

This Body of Essence, the principle and rule of the universe, became synonymous with Nirvana. It was a kind of universal soul, and Nirvana became the transcendent joining with this universal soul. The doctrine of pratîtyasamutpâda, often translated as "dependent arising," is a cardinal doctrine within Buddhist Philosophy. Common to all schools of Buddhism, it states that phenomena arise together in a mutually interdependent web of cause and effect. It is variously rendered into English as "dependent origination", "conditioned genesis", "dependent co-arising", "interdep-endent arising", or "contingency".

DEPENDENT ORIGINATION

The enlightenment (or bodhi, a word that means "to awaken") of the Buddha was simultaneously his liberation from suffering (dukkha) and his insight into the nature of the Universe - particularly the nature of the lives of sentient beings (principally humans and animals). What the Buddha awakened to was the truth of dependent origination.

This is the understanding that any phenomenon exists only because of the existence of other phenomena in an incredibly complex web of cause and effect covering time past, time present and time future. This concept of a web is symbolized by Indra's net, a multidimensional spider's web on which lies an infinite amount of dew drops or jewels, and in these are reflected the reflections of all the other drops of dew ad infinitum.

Stated in another way, everything depends on everything else. A human being's existence in any given moment is dependent on the condition of everything else in the world at that moment, but in an equally significant way, the condition of everything in the world in that moment depends conversely on the character and condition of that human being. Everything in the Universe is interconnected through the web of cause and effect such that the whole and the parts are mutually interdependent. The character and condition of entities at any given time are intimately connected with the character and condition of all other entities that superficially may appear to be unconnected or unrelated.

Because all things are thus conditioned and transient (anicca), they have no real independent identity (anatta) and thus do not truly exist, though to ordinary minds this appears to be the case. All phenomena are therefore fundamentally insubstantial and empty (sunya). Wise human beings, those who "see things as they are" (yatha-bhuta-ñana-dassana), renounce attachment and clinging, transform the energy of desire into awareness and understanding, and eventually transcend the conditioned realm of form becoming Buddhas or Arhats.

The general formulation has two well-known applications, one to the Buddhist conception of suffering, and the other to that of rebirth.

THE FOUR NOBLE TRUTHS

The application of pratîtyasamutpâda to suffering is known as the Four Noble Truths:

1. Dukkha: There is suffering. Suffering is an intrinsic part of life also experienced as dissatisfaction, discontent, unhappiness, impermanence.
2. Samudaya: There is a cause of suffering, which is attachment or desire (tanha).
3. Nirodha: There is a way out of suffering, which is to eliminate attachment and desire.
4. Magga: The path that leads out of suffering is called the Noble Eightfold Path.

TWELVE NIDANAS

The application of pratîtyasamutpâda to the process of rebirth is known as the Twelve Nidanas or the Twelve Links of Conditioned Existence. The nikayas themselves do not give a systematic explanation of the nidana series. As an expository device, the commentarial tradition presented the factors as a linear sequence spanning over three lives; this does not mean that the "past", "present", and "future" factors are mutually exclusive, and in fact as many suttas show, they are not. The twelve nidanas categorized in this way are:

Former Life:

- Ignorance
- Volitional formations (activities which produce karma)

Current Life:

- Consciousness
- Mind and body (personality or identity)
- The six sense bases (five physical senses and the mind)
- Contact (between objects and the senses)

- Feeling (registering the contact)
- Craving (for continued contact)
- clinging
- Becoming (similar to volitional formations)

Future Life:

- Birth
- Old age and death

This twelve-factor formula is the most familiar presentation, though a number of early suttas introduce less-known variants which make it clear that the sequence of factors should not be regarded as a linear causal process in which each preceding factor gives rise to its successor through a simple reaction. The relationship among factors is always complex, involving several woven strands of conditionality. For example, whenever there is ignorance, craving and clinging invariably follow, and craving and clinging themselves indicate ignorance.

With respect to the destinies of human beings and animals, dependent origination has a more specific meaning, as it describes the process by which such sentient beings incarnate into any given realm and pursue their various worldly projects and activities with all concomitant suffering. Among these sufferings are aging and death. Aging and death are experienced by us because birth and youth have been experienced. Without birth there is no death. One conditions the other in a mutually dependent relationship. Our becoming in the world, the process of what we call "life", is conditioned by the attachment and clinging to ideas and projects.

This attachment and clinging in turn cannot exist without craving as its condition. The Buddha understood that craving comes into being because there is sensation in the body which we experience as pleasant, unpleasant or neutral. When we crave something, it is the sensation induced by contact with the desired object that we crave rather than the object itself. Sensation is caused by contact with such objects of the senses. The contact or impression made upon the senses (manifesting as sensation) is itself dependent upon the six sense organs which themselves are dependent upon the psychophysical entity that a human being is. The whole process is summarized by the Buddha as follows:

The thrust of the formula is such that when certain conditions are present, they give rise to subsequent conditions, which in turn give rise to other conditions and the cyclical nature of life in samsara can be seen. This is graphically illustrated in the Bhavacakra (wheel of life).

Contemporary teachers often teach that it can also be seen as a daily cycle occurring from moment to moment throughout each day. There is scriptural support for this as an explanation in the Abhidharmakosa of Vasubandhu, insofar as Vasubandu states that on occasion "the twelve parts are realized in one and the same moment":

For example, in the case of avidyâ, the first condition, it is necessary to refer to the three marks of existence for a full understanding of its relation to pratityasamutpada. It is also necessary to understand the Three Fires and how they fit into the scheme. The Three Fires sit at the very center of the schemata in the Bhavacakra and drive the whole edifice. In Himalayan iconographic representations of the Bhavacakra such as within Tibetan Buddhism, the Three Fires are known as the Three Poisons which are often represented as the Gankyil. The Gankyil is also often represented as the hub of the Dharmacakra. Nirvana is often conceived of as stopping this cycle. By removing the causes for craving, craving ceases. So, with the ceasing of birth, death ceases. With the ceasing of becoming, birth ceases, and so on, until with the ceasing of ignorance no karma is produced, and the whole process of death and rebirth ceases.

MADHYAMAKA AND PRATITYASAMUTPADA

Though the formulations above appear might seem to imply that pratityasamutpada is a straightforward causal model, in the hands of the Madhyamaka School, pratityasamutpada is used to demonstrate the very lack of inherent causality, in a manner that appears somewhat similar to the ideas of David Hume. The conclusion of the Madhyamikas is that causation, like being, must be regarded as a merely conventional truth (samvrti), and that to take it as really (or essentially) existing would be both a logical error and a perceptual one, arising from ignorance and a lack of spiritual insight.

According to the analysis of Nâgârjuna, the most prominent Madhyamika, true causality depends upon the intrinsic existence of the elements of the causal process (causes and effects), which would violate the principle of anatman, but pratîtyasamutpâda does not imply that the apparent participants in arising are essentially real. Because of the interdependence of causes and effects (because a cause depends on its effect to be a cause, as effect depends on cause to be an effect), it is quite meaningless to talk about them as existing separately. However, the strict identity of cause and effect is also refuted, since if the effect were the cause, the process of origination could not have occurred. Thus both monistic and dualistic accounts of causation are rejected.

Therefore Nâgârjuna explains that the úûnyatâ (or emptiness) of causality is demonstrated by the interdependence of cause and effect, and likewise that the interdependence (pratîtyasamutpâda) of causality itself is demonstrated by its anatta. In his Entry to the Middle Way, Candrakirti asserts, "If a cause produces its requisite effect, then, on that very account, it is a cause. If no effect is produced, then, in the absence of that, the cause does not exist."

PRATITYASAMUTPADA IN DZOGCHEN

In Dzogchen tradition the interdependent origination is considered illusory:

[One says], "all these (configurations of events and meanings) come about and disappear according to dependent origination." But, like a burnt seed, since a nonexistent (result) does not come about from a nonexistent (cause), cause and effect do not exist.

What appears as a world of apparently external phenomena is the play of energy of sentient beings. There is nothing external or separate from the individual. Everything that manifests in the individual's field of experience is a continuum. This is the Great Perfection that is discovered in the Dzogchen practice. "Being obsessed with entities, one's experiencing itself [sems, citta], which discriminates each cause and effect, appears as if it were cause and condition."

DEPENDENT ARISING OF ENLIGHTENMENT

The early discourses present nirvana as "unconditioned by dispositions", but it is never considered to be independent, or uncaused. Pratityasamutpada is most commonly used to explain how suffering arises depending on certain conditions, the implication being that if one or more of the conditions are removed (if the "chain" is broken), suffering will cease. There is also a text, the Upanisa Sutta in the Samyutta Nikaya, in which a discussion of the conditions not for suffering but for enlightenment is given. This application of the principle of dependent arising is referred to in Theravada exegetical literature as "transcendental dependent arising". The chain in this case is:

1. Suffering (dukkha)
2. Faith (saddhâ)
3. Joy (pâmojja, pâmujja)
4. Rapture (pîti)
5. Tranquillity (passaddhi)
6. Happiness (sukha)
7. Concentration (samâdhi)
8. Knowledge and vision of things as they are (yathâbhûta-ñâna-dassana)
9. Disenchantment with worldly life (nibbidâ)
10. Dispassion (virâga)
11. Freedom, release, emancipation, deliverance (vimutti)
12. Knowledge of destruction of the cankers (âsava-khaye-ñâna)

INTERBEING AND DEEP ECOLOGY

Nobel Peace Prize nominee Thich Nhat Hanh, a follower of the Vietnamese Zen tradition, has coined the term 'interbeing' as a synonym of pratityasamutpada. This phrase expresses the reality of mutual interdependence in human relationship both in the sense of relating one to another and in the wider sense of humanity's relationship to the natural world as a whole. The Sramanic religious traditions of India (Theravada Buddhism and Jainism) have been characterised by an unusual sensitivity to living beings. Monks of both traditions are strictly forbidden from harming any life forms, including even the smallest insects and vegetation.

One of the basic ideas behind the Buddha's teaching of mutual interdependence is that ultimately there is no demarcation between what appears to be an individual creature and its environment. Harming the environment (the nexus of living beings of which one forms but a part) is thus, in a nontrivial sense, harming oneself. This philosophical position lies at the heart of modern-day deep ecology and some representatives of this movement (e.g. Joanna Macy) have shown that Buddhist philosophy provides a rational basis for deep ecological thinking.

Bibliography

Akira, Hirakawa, The Formation of the Panca-Sila in Early Buddhism, *World Fellowship of Buddhists Review* 32 (3): 8–23, 1995.

Barua, Dipak Kumar, *Viharas in Ancient India: A Survey of Buddhist Monasteries,* Calcutta: Indian Publications, 1969.

Cousins, L. S., Ethical Standards in World Religions: III. Buddhism, *The Exository Times* Vol. LXXXV, pp. 100–104, 1974.

Cousins, L. S., Good or Skilful? Kusala in Canon and Commentary, *Journal of Buddhist Ethics* 3:136–64, 1996.

Dharmasiri, G., *Fundamentals of Buddhist Ethics,* Antioch, CA.: Golden Leaves Publ. Co., 1989.

Frauwallner, E., *The Earliest Vinaya and the Beginnings of Buddhist Literature,* Rome: Istituto Italiano per il Medio ed Estremo Oriente, 1956.

Fu, C. W., and S. A. Wawrytko, eds., *Buddhist Ethics and Modern Society: an International Symposium,* New York: Greenwood Press, 1991.

Guenther, Herbert V., *Philosophy and Psychology in the Abhidharma,* Berkeley, Calif.: Shambhala, 1976.

Harvey, P., *An Introduction to Buddhism: Teachings, History and Practices,* Cambridge: Cambridge University Press, chap. 9, 1990.

Harvey, P., *An Introduction to Buddhist Ethics: Foundations, Values and Issues,* Cambridge: Cambridge University Press, 2000.

Harvey, P., *An Introduction to Buddhist Ethics: Foundations, Values and Issues*, Cambridge: Cambridge University Press, pp. 11-31, 2000.

Hinderey, R., *Comparative Ethics in Hindu and Buddhist Traditions*, Delhi: Motilal Banarsidass, 1978.

Jacobson, Nolan Pliny, *Buddhism, the Religion of Analysis.* London: Feffer & Simons, 1974.

Jayatilleke, K. N., *Ethics in Buddhist Perspective: Wheel Booklet no,*175/176. Kandy, Sri Lanka: Buddhist Publication Society, 1972.

Keown, D. (ed), *Contemporary Buddhist Ethics*, London: Curzon Press, 2000.

Keown, D., *The Nature of Buddhist Ethics*, London: Macmillan, 1992.

Keown, D., *Buddhism and Bioethics*, London: Macmillan; New York: St. Martin's Press, chap. 1, 1995.

Little, D. and S. B. Twiss., *Comparative Religious Ethics: A New Method,* New York: Harper and Row, 1978.

Mahasi Sayadaw, *Sallekha Sutta: A Discourse on the Refinement of Character*, Hinsdale, Il.: Buddhadharma Meditation Center, 1981.

McDermott, J. P., *Development in the Early Buddhist Concept of Kamma/Karma*, New Delhi: Munshiram Manoharlal, 1984.

Misra, G. S. P., *Development of Buddhist Ethics*, New Delhi: Munshiram Manoharlal, 1984.

Nhat Hanh, Thich, et al., *For a Future to be Possible: Commentaries on the Five Wonderful Precepts*, Berkeley, CA.: Parallax Press, 1993.

Nyanaponika, *The Roots of Good and Evil: Wheel booklet no,* 251/253. Kandy, Sri Lanka: Buddhist Publication Society, 1978.

Pardue, Peter, *Buddhism: A Brief Account.* New York: Macmillan, Social history, 1971.

Prebish, C. S., ed., *Buddhist Ethics: A Cross-cultural Approach*, Kendall/Hunt, 1992.

Whitehill, James, "Buddhism and the Virtues" in Keown, D. (ed) *Contemporary Buddhist Ethics*, London: Curzon Press, 17-36, 2000.

Saddhatissa, H., *Buddhist Ethics: Essence of Buddhism*, London: George Allen and Unwin, 1970.

Saddhatissa, H., *The Buddha's Way*, New York: Brazillier, Reprint, London: Allen and Unwin, 1985.

Varma, Vishvanath Prasad, *Early Buddhism and Its Origins.* Delhi: Munshiram Monaharlal, 1973.

Index

U